WITHDRAWN

P9-CBM-108

IN JERUSALEM

IN JERUSALEM

THREE GENERATIONS
OF AN ISRAELI FAMILY
AND A PALESTINIAN FAMILY

LIS HARRIS

BEACON PRESS

BOSTON

BEACON PRESS
Boston, Massachusetts
www.beacon.org

Beacon Press books
are published under the auspices of
the Unitarian Universalist Association of Congregations.

22 21 20 19   8 7 6 5 4 3 2 1

This book is printed on acid-free paper that meets the uncoated paper
ANSI/NISO specifications for permanence as revised in 1992.

Text design by Nancy Koerner at Wilsted & Taylor

Endpaper photos © Thomas Struth

Taha Muhammad Ali, excerpt from "Twigs" from *So What: New & Selected Poems
1971–2005*, trans. Peter Cole, Yahya Hijazi, and Gabriel Levin. Copyright © 2006 by
Taha Muhammad Ali. Translation copyright © 2000, 2006 by Peter Cole, Yahya Hijazi,
and Gabriel Levin. Reprinted with the permission of The Permissions Company, Inc.,
on behalf of Copper Canyon Press, www.coppercanyonpress.org.

Some names and other identifying characteristics of people mentioned
in this work have been changed to protect their identities.

Library of Congress Cataloging-in-Publication Data

Names: Harris, Lis, author.
Title: In Jerusalem : three generations of an Israeli family and a
    Palestinian family / Lis Harris.
Description: Boston : Beacon Press, [2019] | Includes bibliographical
    references and index. |
Identifiers: LCCN 2019003810 (print) | LCCN 2019009337 (ebook) | ISBN
    9780807029961 (ebook) | ISBN 9780807029688 (hardback)
Subjects: LCSH: Jews—Jerusalem—Biography. | Palestinian
    Arabs—Jerusalem—Biography. | Pinczower family. | Ezrahi family. |
    Abuleil family. | Arab-Israeli conflict. | Jerusalem—Social conditions. |
    West Bank—Social conditions. | BISAC: HISTORY / Middle East / Israel.
Classification: LCC DS126.6.A2 (ebook) | LCC DS126.6.A2 H37 2019 (print) |
    DDC 956.94/42050922—dc23
LC record available at https://lccn.loc.gov/2019003810

To Martin

CONTENTS

THE FAMILIES

RUTH HACOHEN'S FAMILY: THE PINCZOWERS AND EZRAHIS

Eliezar Pinczower	Ruth's father
Esther Pinczower	Ruth's mother, née Fraenkel
Ruth HaCohen	a professor of musicology
Yaron Ezrahi	Ruth's husband, a political analyst
Ariel Ezrahi	Ruth's stepson, a lawyer
Christina Ezrahi	Ariel's wife, a writer and dance scholar
Edna Pinchover	Rami's wife, principal of pediatrics, Hadassah Medical Center
Hannah Urbach	Eliezar's sister
Iris Pinchover	Yehuda's wife, a painter
Lewis Kerr	Talya's husband, a storyboard artist
Nechama Fraenkel	Ruth's sister, a senior supervising clinical psychologist
Nehami HaCohen	Yotam's wife, clinical psychology researcher
Ofra Broshi	Yaron's sister, classical pianist, headed a musical conservatory
Rami Pinchover	Ruth's older brother, a mechanical engineer
Sam Thrope	Tehila's husband, a journalist and Iranian studies scholar
Talya Ezrahi	Ruth's older stepdaughter, a filmmaker
Tehila Ezrahi	Ruth's younger stepdaughter, an artist and teacher
Yehuda Pinchover	Ruth's second-oldest brother, a professor of mathematics
Yotam HaCohen	Ruth's son, runs a boutique consulting firm

PROLOGUE

A starry night in the Judean desert. I'm lying on my back, cocooned in a sleeping bag, and staring up at the sky, trying to figure out a way to bring even an atom of the peacefulness of this place back to Jerusalem. It was the first of many long visits over ten years, and Jerusalem was where I'd planted myself. But on this night an old acquaintance had invited me to join his family and a friend for a short camping trip on one of Israel's phenomenally frequent national holidays. The excursion was an annual tradition for everyone but me, and most of the group, but especially my friend, had slightly romantic feelings about the moonlike desert landscape where we pitched camp.

Elsewhere in the desert rose the site of the fortress of Masada, the cave in Qumran where the Dead Sea Scrolls were found, the amazing St. George's monastery carved into the crevices of the Judean hills, and the large settlement of Ma'ale Adumim, but our rocky campsite was surrounded on all sides by—nothing. It looked like a setting for a Beckett play: A cool, stony whiteness with chalky cliffs stretching into treeless, plant-less infinity. A wind so strong that my friend's two strapping boys had a difficult time setting up their crazily flapping tent. Supposedly the landscape was teeming with life, particularly night creatures. There were rumors of striped hyenas and caracals, wolves, foxes, gazelles, ibexes, and hyraxes—small furry creatures that look a bit like earless rabbits and, like the many desert reptiles, use the rocks to regulate their body temperatures. But none crossed the rocky terraces and escarpments around us. Nor in the deepening twilight did we glimpse a single hawk or buzzard wheeling overhead, nor, later, any nocturnal bird making its way across the darkening sky. In a certain way, the landscape extended one aspect of Israel's complex persona that seems inescapable—its hardness. Particularly Jerusalem's, with its hard stone walls, hard stone houses, hard marble floors, and a citizenry conflict-hardened and militarily trained to be tough.

For a while, I also tried to imagine the flight of Muhammed, who according to Islamic tradition descended across this quadrant of star-speckled sky to Jerusalem from Mecca and went back on his winged steed Buraq, and to summon forth the ancient Hebrews, Babylonians, Persians, Hasmoneans, Macedonians, Seleucids, and Romans, who, whatever disputes engaged them, like me surely gazed up appreciatively. In these imaginings, too, I had limited success.

Back in Jerusalem, with its crowded streets, malls, and high-density housing, you are all too aware of the country's smallness—Israel is only slightly larger than New Jersey, the fifth-smallest state in the United States. But in the long, open prospect of the desert you can easily imagine the land as a place of dreams and longing—and, it goes without saying, of contention. At that point, for me, the dimensions of the conflict looked as unencompassable as the horizon.

Over the course of the evening, I peppered my companions with questions that reflected how new my encounter with the country was, though many of them had been ratcheting around in my brain for years—especially those that turned on the country's rightward drift. My outsiderness stood out nakedly in this conversation, but I hoped I could eventually arrive at a useful perspective. As a secular, diaspora Jew raised by parents who weren't particularly political but, to the extent that they were, were liberal, I had an intense desire to understand how the Israelis' history had led the country to where they were. After a while, escaping what must have seemed like a never-ending barrage of questions, my friends' friend bid goodnight to her teenage daughter, who was sitting next to her, turned definitively in her bag, and zipped herself into sleep position. An Israeli developmental psychologist, she had worked alongside Palestinian colleagues on a project about early childhood for years, she said, and everyone got along fine, and a cordial, even warm relationship prevailed. But in times of violent Israeli-Palestinian hostilities, those relationships turned frigid because no foundation of trust existed, despite their long history together, and nothing ever said at a conference or meeting or expressed in a document had ever changed that. Just before shutting her eyes, she shot me a somewhat pitying look and murmured, "Wake me when the Israeli-Palestinian conflict is over."

My own upbringing in relation to the early history of the country probably didn't differ greatly from that of many other young US-born American Jewish children who grew up in the 1950s. It was a place I knew little about, and what I did know was distinctly one-sided. My earliest sense of a place called Israel bloomed largely in summer camp when I was about nine years old. Though my parents were secular Jews—to put it more precisely, flapper, lawyer (my mother) and small-town New England, factory manager (my father) Jews—they didn't forget that they were Jewish, but their Jewishness defined them less than their Americanness. That summer my parents enrolled me in a moderately religious camp in the Berkshires, chiefly because my mother's older sister, my formidable aunt Dodo, sent her son there. Run by the same people, the girls' camp was across the lake from the boys', and separate Sabbath services for girls and boys were held each weekend.

I was not particularly interested in the religious content of the liturgy, but the singing and formality of the stately religious rituals fascinated me, and at no point in the proceedings did I feel more enthusiastic than at the end of the service, when, with the scent of pines wafting headily in through the windows of the barn-like, raw wood structure where the services were held, all the little girls in their dark green shorts and crisp white polos joined together for a top-of-the-lungs rendition of "Hatikvah" ("The Hope"), Israel's national anthem, laboriously taught to us by our counselors. Few of us had the slightest idea of what the Hebrew words meant, but we knew somehow that they were connected with years of worried parental murmurings about the disasters befalling Jews all over Europe, and that, mournful as the Italian melody of the song was, "Hatikvah" represented and celebrated a happy ending. I believe my family's good wishes for the young state of Israel, yoked as those feelings were to their knowledge of the Holocaust, the wartime death of my aunt's beloved older son who served in France, and the state of mind of some refugee relatives from Berlin—the saddest people I had ever known—constituted the Alpha and Omega of their attitude toward Israel.

Of the actual physical realities of the country, I believe that they, like me, had only the thinnest notion, derived chiefly from newsreels. What we imagined, more or less, was a giant kibbutz, blanketed with orange groves overseen by wholesome-looking young women in summer dresses and equally wholesome-looking, mop-headed young men wearing short-sleeve shirts and shorts. And David Ben-Gurion, the founder of Israel? A powerful grandpa and member of the wild white-haired genius tribe, like Einstein, a heroic innovator, like Freud—a man whose radical vision would change lives. But I can say with some degree of certainty that though they were alert to human rights abuses and civic unfairness, solid Roosevelt Democrats who despised Joe McCarthy, a sense of wrongs done to the Palestinian people never reached their radar, focused as it was on the wrongs done to the beleaguered Jews across the ocean.

If my parents were alive today, I wonder if their ingrained disapproval of injustices would complicate their appreciation and sympathy for today's Israel, now two decades into a right-wing government. Or would they, like so many others, retain a reflexively uncritical, loyalty-born view of the country? When I think about them, I can't help remembering the words of a Hasidic man I interviewed when I asked what he considered to be his chief obligation as a Jew—"To treat others as you would like to be treated." He hadn't hesitated for a millisecond, and he clearly believed his response required no further elaboration. When he said it, I understood that, whatever the ambiguities and religious shortcomings of my upbringing, and whatever Old Testament evidence might be brought forward to complicate the story, *that* had been the taken-for-granted core, our secularism notwithstanding. And that was probably why, even as a non-Israeli, I felt *implicated* by the way the Palestinians were treated and could never quite shake the conviction that the country's antidemocratic moves, whatever else they were, were so contrary to the Jewish values I was raised with. The Hasid's answer was, of course, a gloss on the famous injunction of Rabbi Hillel, "That which is hateful to you, do not do to your neighbor. That is the whole Torah. The rest is commentary."

That is the central concern, I believe, in the growing disaffection with Israeli policies among younger American Jews, and it is at the heart of why so many of them disagree with the contention that there is no true Judaism without Zionism. As for the related contention of the otherwise admirable A.B. Yehoshua, one of Israel's most distinguished novelists, that American Jews are somehow shirking their tribal obligations because they are only "partial Jews" compared with Israelis, I can only add my voice to the protesting chorus of those who have rejected his formulation. Yehoshua and I both love our homelands (and worry about their defects), but who we are and where and how we live our lives are our own business.

———•———

But around our campsite, insider or outsider, we all could share the collective sense of relief that our rocky desert campsite was so blessedly far removed from the everyday din of Israeli experience—even in more peaceful times—and feel grateful for the distance between us and the pressure-cooker jitteriness that characterized life back in Jerusalem. No young citizen-soldiers with guns here, no news of rockets raining down in the south or of yet more demolished Palestinian houses, no religious brawls or contentious national politics. The terrain of our little patch of the desert looked so unyielding, furthermore, that it was difficult to imagine the loud incursion of the bulldozers or tractors long associated in the Israeli imagination with growth and fecundity and in the Palestinian mind with destruction and displacement. (As Steinbeck observed in another context in *The Grapes of Wrath*, a tractor can reverse the conversion of swords into ploughshares.)

Jerusalem-as-spiritual-locus has inspired generations of people of all faiths with exalted feelings, from which, wandering along the time-burnished stone pathways of the old city, I too felt echoes, despite their enthusiastic commercial exploitation. It's impossible not to be dazzled by the city's immense repository of icons, architecture, sculpture, reliquaries, and ancient manuscripts that are testaments to its ongoing significance to the three Abrahamic religions. And considering the tensions that bubble just beneath the surface in Jerusalem, tourists are somewhat surprised by the general air of normalcy that prevails. In part, this might be because Israelis and Palestinians alike have been released from the framework of the papers and evening news into the realm of ordinary daily living and ceased being represented in their stock roles. And if visitors arrive at a time when there are no large-scale overt hostilities, the vendors of souvenirs along the Via Dolorosa will be hawking their souvenirs, the tourist throngs will be surging through the heavy doors of the Church of the Holy Sepulchre, and everyday life will seem to be moving along in a fairly uneventful way. Alas, this is an illusion.

Of course, normalcy, whatever a country's struggles, is what most people crave, and after hostilities die down for a period, the boon of feeling safe is gratefully welcomed. In my two favorite small Jerusalem cafés, the Coffee Mill on Emek Refaim Street in Israeli West Jerusalem and the Patisserie Suisse (which isn't Swiss and serves no patisserie) in Palestinian East Jerusalem just off the main artery of Saladin Street, it is easy for their respective Israeli and Palestinian patrons to forget about the "conflict." The cafés' owners—Rosie and Debbie at the Coffee Mill, Hilda and Teddy at the Patisserie—are capable, welcoming people, and their regulars settle into their chairs as though they were old slippers. Day in and day out, the two establishments buzz with conversation, except when there's some big trouble—a bombing or threat of an imminent violent confrontation, and then everyone scurries home. The West Jerusalem streets, in particular, become hushed, except for the intermittent clamor of sirens and helicopters.

Shuttling back and forth over the years between East and West Jerusalem and between Israeli cities and Palestinian ones, as I got to know two families (one Israeli and one Palestinian) who shared their histories with me, a different picture altogether emerged in which the smooth surface of normal life gave way to deep civic unrest engendered by the Occupation. Some readers will object that there is no such thing as a typical Israeli or Palestinian family. I agree. There is no such family, just as there are no typical American, French, or Japanese families—yet this truth shouldn't serve as an obstacle to grasping what it feels like for a family to live in the maelstrom of the conflict for generations. Even with a plethora of dogged reporting, searching novels, and scores of thoughtful books about the subject, too many top-down political accounts and insider political assessments abound, in which those most affected seem like mere chess pieces and little is conveyed about their ongoing lives.

My goal has not been to try to unravel the Gordian knot that keeps the country's never-ending problems seemingly and confoundingly unresolvable, as so many before me have. Instead, I hope to register the conflict's effect on the lives of successive generations on each side, the people who are the cogs of history, and who, after all, reflect its impasses and long for the peace that would push past them. How had the families survived the dislocations and losses that defined their lives? How, in a region where war and its threat were part of the very air they breathed, were children given hope for their future? How did the adults think about their place in the conflict? How did their sense of what was happening in the country evolve over time? What kept them from leaving? And what was the consequence of an unarmed (since ancient times) minority becoming an armed majority, and how did that experience affect its democratic ideals?

Even in relatively peaceful times, rare as they are, Israelis live with a background fear of obliteration—a state of mind based on history, on not so distant memories (in the 2000–2004 second Intifada, 150 bombs blew up on Israeli streets), on the puffed-up but not empty declarations of their enemies, and on paranoia. (This last, however much it may be confirmed by history, has played a particularly oversize role in the country's affairs.) But by any measure, the Palestinians have seen more innocents perish, have made little progress in their desire for restitution of property, identity, and nationhood, and bear the overwhelmingly greater burden, a conclusion confirmed by seeing up close what politicians and diplomats like to call "facts on the ground."

Moving outward from West to East Jerusalem and on to the West Bank is a bit like plunging through the cleanly demarcated layers of an archaeological dig—in this case, the farther along you go, the more visible the signs of degraded everyday life and the realities of the social and political geography of the land. Violence may haunt the average Israeli and loom large at the funerals of its soldiers and terrorist victims, but for too many Palestinians its threat is a menacing, day-in, day-out presence.

In order to better understand the ongoing effect of the conflict

over time, drawing on the major historical markers of the creation of
the state of Israel in May 1948, the Six-Day War of June 1967, and the
years after the Oslo Accords and two intifadas of 1987 and 2000, I
talked with each of these extended Jerusalem families about their lives
during those pivotal times. Following in the footsteps of recent Israeli
and Palestinian historians without whose work this book would not
exist, I set out to see what members of three generations in each family, each surviving in an extreme situation, made of the fraught eras
that defined so much of their lives. And the more I learned about
them, the more evident it became how intimately their individual
destinies were entwined with the times they lived in. I talked with
young people and old, religious and secular, men and women. My
closest contacts in each family were two extraordinary women—in
the Israeli family, Ruth HaCohen, a professor of musicology at Hebrew University, and in the Palestinian one, Niveen Abuleil, a speech
pathologist—but my picture of the families' lives would have been
incomplete indeed without the contributions of many other family
members, as well as a host of scholars, writers, businesspeople, and
scores of others I came to know well or in passing, and I am grateful
to them all.

INTRODUCTION

In or out of war, Jerusalem's melancholy beauty endures. Despite its antiquity and modest population of less than a million, it is a recognizably modern city, country cousin though it is to Tel Aviv. A far cry from the quiet backwater once occupied by the British, modern Jerusalem is lavishly landscaped and densely built up. Its twentieth- and twenty-first-century architecture is unremarkable but consistent. Except for the city's old, venerated churches, mosques, and biblical shrines, most of its buildings, high-rise and low-, are faced with the same bright Jerusalem limestone, a requirement of local law. Older neighborhoods are architecturally distinguished by small, private houses with elegant arched entrances and beautiful tile floors laid by their former Arab owners. West Jerusalem, with its busy cafés and theaters, well-maintained cultural and religious sites, and abundantly stocked markets, sustains a bustling populace and throngs of tourists who disappear when things heat up but reappear during more peaceful interludes, and everywhere bulldozers and cranes signify the confident thrust of major municipal and private construction.

The busy cosmopolitan atmosphere, however, is a bit deceiving. Jerusalem may be Israel's officially designated capital (if unrecognized by the rest of the world—until President Donald Trump recognized it at the end of 2017; most of the rest of the international community's embassies are in Tel Aviv), and a place of important spiritual significance to Christians, Muslims, and Jews alike. It is also Israel's poorest city. According to one survey, it is its least livable metropolis—fast becoming stratified into decidedly un-Zionist rich/poor enclaves. You might be lulled into mistaking Jerusalem for a normal city until—especially after periods of increased violence—you notice plainclothes but armed security guards inspecting everyone's belongings at the entrance of numerous West Jerusalem restaurants and malls. Most of the time these inspections are not cursory. Suicide bombings still play a starring role in people's memories; intermittent bloodshed is never unexpected, and the oscillation of the war needle too often trembles from warm toward hot. Still, when you're at the excellent Jerusalem film festival, meeting friends for drinks at the lush garden of East Jerusalem's colonial-era, unapologetically old-fashioned American Colony Hotel, or strolling along at night under the cooling cypress trees, you might take this for any other small, pleasant Mediterranean city.

Even blindfolded, though, with the exception of that singularly cosmopolitan American Colony Hotel located just past the East-West border, you know when you're passing from West Jerusalem to Arab East Jerusalem by the abrupt shift to barely maintained, bone-rattling roads. You know it by the crush of too many people (370,000 crowded into a small and ever-diminishing patch of land) and inadequate housing. And you know it by the absence of parks, the piles of garbage awaiting pickup (East Jerusalemites pay the same municipal tax—the *arnona*—as their West Jerusalem neighbors and are entitled to but don't receive the same services), the clusters of unemployed men standing around (76 percent of East Jerusalemites live below the poverty line), the intermittent presence of IDF (Israeli Defense Forces) soldiers manning permanent or "flying" (temporary) checkpoints, and, since 2003, the presence of the unignorable reinforced concrete wall or Security Fence as the Israelis call it. Upon completion the wall is supposed to be about 712 kilometers (442 miles) long—more than twice the length of the 320-kilometer (nearly 200-mile) Green Line (the boundaries of Israel established as part of the 1949 armistice at the close of the Arab-Israeli War) and twice as long and three times higher than the Berlin Wall. Symbolically and actually, the 25-foot-high wall built by descendants of a population once itself segregated and decimated behind walls is a nearly unabsorbable phenomenon. An estimated 80,000 Palestinians who lived outside the wall have migrated to the Israeli side, chiefly into East Jerusalem, making its already overcrowded spaces all the more unlivable.

Palestinians with the blue Jerusalem ID cards that signify permanent residency status have access to the city's excellent medical facilities and in this respect are the envy of their West Bank compatriots, but in other ways they're worse off. Fully participating citizens of neither the Palestinian nor Israeli political system, East Jerusalemites live in a closed city. East Jerusalem is shut off not the way battered Gaza is (under siege and barely surviving), but friends and even relatives with ID papers from the West Bank or surrounding villages can't enter it. The wall, which the government has in places painted with imaginary bucolic landscapes—presumably to conjure scenes that would be visible if the wall didn't exist—also dramatically curtails business. Being cut off from the West Bank has effectively severed East Jerusalem from its chief economic hub and separated many Palestinians from their own businesses. Nonetheless, the East Jerusalem streets still exude an aura of nervous vitality, which in 2015 exploded into violence, with young Palestinians knifing Israelis and driving cars into them throughout the city and the Israeli Army responding by shooting most of the attackers. This level of aggression wasn't confined to Jerusalem. In one instance the Israeli army, rolling into a refugee camp, atypically identified itself as the "Occupation army" and announced over a loudspeaker, "You throw stones, and we will hit you with gas until you all die. The children, the youth, the old people—you will all die; we won't leave any of you alive." A video of this event scorched the Internet, but the violence continued. Fearful Israeli parents began to accompany even their older children to and from school. And some Palestinian parents tried to keep their children from attending school altogether, terrified that they might join their friends in throwing stones when classes were over—and be shot.

Driving out from East Jerusalem proper and heading north for the first time, I felt only confusion: I had passed through a checkpoint, but was I really in the West Bank? High on hill after dusty hill, the vast white settlements blazed in the hot sun. It wasn't that I hadn't been fully aware of their presence—who wasn't? But that knowledge hadn't adequately prepared me for their look of permanence. Somehow their solidity, dazzling whiteness, and height presented a different picture from what I'd imagined. Unlike the Palestinian houses, which are for the most part folded into the hills, the settlements have by and large been built by shearing off the hilltops and radically altering the face of the landscape. They have also inspired the term "hilltop youths" as shorthand for violent young settler thugs known for their attacks on Palestinian orchards, mosques, flocks, olive groves, and schoolchildren. It's been estimated that since 1967 some 630,000 Israeli Jews have settled on the West Bank or in East Jerusalem. The numbers reflect steady growth despite the government's empty private assurances at endless, fruitless diplomatic encounters that expansion was being curtailed. Seeing the settlements looking so, well, settled, dotting the horizon so ubiquitously in what is supposed to become a viable contiguous Palestinian state, unmoors one's sense of the possible.

The roads between the larger West Bank cities curve past small Arab settlements of two or three houses, a goat or two, and some olive trees. Surrounded by miles of rocky hills and an immense sky, these isolated dwellings, some of which are enlivened by patches of yellow broom, look tentative and exposed. As late as the 1970s, according to the Palestinian civil rights lawyer and writer Raja Shehadeh, the hills of the West Bank countryside "were like one large nature reserve," but the settlements have radically changed that. Not only have the hills been flattened to make way for quasi-suburban enclaves, but the wadis (valleys or ravines) have been tunneled through for roads and infrastructure.

In September 2016, Israeli prime minister Benjamin Netanyahu appeared in a nationally broadcast video in which he said that those who advocated removal of the settlers from the West Bank were guilty of pushing for a form of "ethnic cleansing"—a statement that for sheer gall might plunge anyone paying attention to the ongoing conflict into a state of stupefaction. At the United Nations, efforts over the years to condemn the West Bank settlements were consistently foiled by US vetoes of Security Council resolutions. Then, just before leaving office, in December 2016, President Obama approved US abstention on a Security Council resolution demanding that Israel end settlement construction in occupied Palestine, allowing the resolution to pass—the first such resolution to pass since 1980.

The approach roads to the settlements, smooth as raceways, are highly restricted or forbidden to Palestinians. Palestinians are compelled to drive along far less direct and well-maintained ones, which is particularly maddening when emergency medical care is needed.

Along with the settler roads came a complex sheltering infrastructure: police, IDF soldiers, public transportation, water and sewer systems, and post offices, all of which absorb many millions in state funds. The world has become aware, too, of the proliferation of unlawful outposts whose diehard settlers with some regularity harass and attack local farmers. These outposts also require the presence of IDF soldiers, sometimes to serve as escorts for the schoolchildren. Implausibly, an estimated 20 percent of the settlements will have to go if there is ever to be a two-state solution.

In Ramallah, along with the huge villas that mark the well-guarded part of the city where the Palestinian Authority's (PA) government officials live, there are scores of offices of nongovernmental organizations (NGOs) charged with improving the health, education, and general welfare of the Palestinians. The NGOs are the city's second-largest employers after the PA. Outside Nablus, a name associated in the West mainly with terrorist cells but to Palestinians the place where the best olive oil comes from, are mile after mile of terraced olive groves—a landscape of pastoral grace. You can usually tell when the house you are looking at belongs to an Arab by its black water tower, and when a group of Palestinian houses are built next to each other the tanks dot their collective rooftop line like black Chiclets. The tanks are necessary because so much of the country's underground water has been diverted to the settlements. (In general it's been estimated that the average Israeli is allotted three times as much water for household use as the average Palestinian.)

In the 2015 uptick of violence, attacks on settlers became more frequent, but suicide bombings and the threat of them have been rare since then. Knowledgeable students of the country's security history, including members of Shin Bet, Israel's internal security service, credit Hamas's declaration of a truce and the Palestinian leaders' decision to cease attacking Israelis at the 2005 Sharm el-Sheikh conference. Israeli security forces additionally credit the checkpoint system and the numerous military operations that have been initiated inside the West Bank, along with a not inconsiderable network of informers, for the strategic shift.

Since 2000, the year the second Intifada began, Israelis have been forbidden from traveling to the Palestinian-ruled parts of the West

Bank and discouraged from going to its other parts. And most Israeli taxi drivers are even reluctant to drive to East Jerusalem. So in order to get to Ramallah, say, or Birzeit, to attend a lecture at the university, I had to find a Muslim, West Jerusalem-based driver who would be willing to drive me first to East Jerusalem. There I'd catch another cab to the Qalandia checkpoint (then a temporary, ramshackle affair, today a more impregnable-looking military station), gateway to the northern West Bank and for Palestinians always a source of delay, misery, and dread.

No one cared when I walked over to the somewhat chaotic, densely littered, and potholed Palestinian side, but I was sometimes challenged coming back. The idea of free, harmless movement from "the other side" was nonexistent. Past the checkpoint on the West Bank side, a robust trade of fruit sellers and young boys hawking cold drinks flourished on the margins of the approach road, alongside a rogues' gallery clump of taxi drivers awaiting passengers and calling out to potential customers.

I tried to pick my driver carefully because I would be altogether dependent on whomever I chose—have I mentioned that I speak neither Arabic nor Hebrew?—and was unfamiliar with the places I was visiting. No one had told me, moreover, that West Bank buildings do not display numbered addresses and that directions to your destination, even to important institutions, are served up with rather hilarious vagueness—"Oh, we're near the electric company, across from the watermelon stand, a bit beyond the big mulberry tree"—and always require a last-minute verifying call. Back in New York, my husband's uncertainty about my whereabouts when I traveled to the West Bank, particularly in times of violence, drove him crazy. By my third trip he was coming along with me. While I worked, he didn't accompany me but remained in our Jerusalem apartment, usually working himself (he's a painter) on the pocket-size terrace of our studio, ready to spring to my aid at a moment's notice should I get into trouble.

However much the terms of the Occupation are hated and fought against by individuals and communities, some important aspects of it go unchallenged by official Arab leaders in Ramallah. The West Bank is divided into three zones established by the Oslo Accords (which were considered an interim arrangement that was supposed

to expire in May 1999). Area A is theoretically under the civil and security supervision of the Palestinians, though there are constant IDF
incursions into it that cause riots and make the Palestinian security
forces look like collaborators. Area B is under the supervision of both
Israelis (security control) and Palestinians (civil control), and Area
C, which comprises 60 percent of the West Bank, is under the civic
and military rule of Israel alone. The zones were supposed to function temporarily until a permanent agreement could be reached, and
it was understood that Israel was to gradually move territory from
Areas B and C to Area A. That part of the agreement wasn't honored—most of Area C has been slowly annexed by Israel. When PA
president Mahmoud Abbas announced in 2015 that the Oslo agreement was effectively dead because Israel had not lived up to its prom-
ises (Israel had already, during the second Intifada, declared that the
accords were "null and void"), many people expected this arrangement
to end, but so far it hasn't, possibly because, along with the zones, the
presidency and the Palestinian Authority that Abbas heads, which
were created by Oslo, would also be no more. A new municipal election planned for the fall of 2016 was canceled.

Traveling between the zones could have been majorly confusing
since there weren't always clear demarcations for them. I only occasionally glimpsed them. But after a chance call to a local cab company
brought Fuad Abu Awwad to me as a driver, I never worried about
where I was because he had a clear mental map of allowed and forbidden places. Fuad, a multilingual gentle bear of a man who was
in his late thirties when we met and lives in an Arab village on the
southeastern outskirts of Jerusalem, was willing to drive me anywhere
I wanted to go. He had one eccentricity—a striking one considering
the nature of his job: on long-distance trips he would never consult
a map. When GPS technology came along, maps became irrelevant,
but when I first started riding with him, GPS was still uncommon.
It usually didn't matter because he knew his way around so well, but
it occasionally resulted in our getting a bit lost. I rarely minded. He
had so much to say that was interesting that I adjusted to the possibility of unforeseen dead ends and blind alleys and left more time
than I might have otherwise allotted for our trips. Eventually, I knew,
the moment would come when he'd pull alongside another car with

a friendly looking driver—"*Habibi. . .*" (loosely, "bro")—and get directions. Fuad was not a "fixer"—a professional liaison with strong local contacts who works for a fee to connect journalists and other researchers to sources—but he had intimate knowledge of Jerusalem and its inhabitants and also knew more about caution than I ever would. By my third extended trip to the country, he and I had established a warm friendship. I eventually met his wife, children, and other members of his family, and he became my guide and sometimes counselor. There is a certain local cliché of the journalist and his or her special Arab taxi driver who is possibly the only Palestinian the journalist comes in frequent contact with. You'll have to take my word for it that our friendship spilled over those boundaries and continues, via phone and email, even when I'm back home. After the Israeli soldier Gilad Shalit was captured in 2006 by Hamas, and several foreign citizens who never made the international pages had been grabbed and released, Fuad, usually ready to drive me to the farthest reaches of the country, cautioned me against attempting to visit Gaza or any West Bank destination for a while and was unmoved by my pleading professional urgency.

"But we could just drive there at some early hour?" "Not now, really," he said, not looking at me. "They'd probably consider you a great hostage."

At the time I suspected Fuad of being overprotective and thought he was exaggerating the danger, but he wasn't, as I learned after reading Ghada Karmi's forthright, moving memoir, *Return*. The book chronicles the stubborn but futile attempt of the author, a doctor, academic, and 1948 Palestinian exile living in London, to ignore the Palestinian Authority's ineptitude and corruption and nudge along the peace process by lending her services to the all-but-atrophied Ramallah government bureaucracy (she worked as a consultant to the Ministry of Media and Communications). On a trip to Gaza, Karmi happened to be nearby when two foreigners, friends of hers, were kidnapped, though eventually released. "Capture of foreigners," she writes, "particularly Europeans and Americans, was rife for a variety of reasons: most often to force the release of Palestinian prisoners . . . to secure jobs for the kidnappers, or to settle some dispute with another family or political faction. The idea was that Western countries

of which the victims were nationals would accede to the kidnappers'
demands by putting pressure on Israel to comply or forcing the PA
to do the same. The ploy hardly ever succeeded, and most of the hostages were released within a day or so, but still it went on happening."

The 2015–16 period of violence in Jerusalem, which soon spread
sporadically to the rest of the country, like earlier ones was not a game
changer. Its chief long-term result was to jack up inflammatory rhetoric and push any pale prospect of peace further away. As the death
toll mounted, all parties to the conflict made fiery speeches, but Prime
Minister Netanyahu raised the stakes highest, declaring that "at this
time we need to control all the territory for the foreseeable future" and
"if I am asked if we will forever live by the sword—yes." By December
2015 the Israeli police had been authorized to use lethal force as a first
resort against boys using slingshots or throwing firebombs or fire-
works, or, perhaps using mind reading, against those who appeared to
be *about* to do those things. But the violence continued on both sides.
At the end of June 2016 the world learned that a Palestinian man
had stabbed and killed a thirteen-year-old girl asleep in her house in
the West Bank settlement of Kiryat Arba, near Hebron. Two months
after such knife attacks began, two-thirds of all Palestinians believed
that a third Intifada was coming, and many of the city's residents believed they were already in a third Intifada's early stage.

At one point in the hostilities, on the eve of Rosh Hashanah,
Jewish New Year's Eve, the Israeli police used rubber bullets and tear
gas to attack a crowd on the Temple Mount and chained the doors of
the al-Aqsa Mosque shut, throwing stun grenades and tear gas can-
isters at the young Palestinians inside the mosque. President Abbas
declared his support for the young Palestinians, but it was hard to
find anyone, on either side, who didn't believe that the Palestinian Authority and its leaders, primarily President Abbas, had at that point
run their tank dry. For too long they had expected Europe and the US
to come up with a plan that would rescue them. The new level of violence, however, stemmed not only from the ongoing intransigence and
all-too-apparent bad faith of the Israeli leaders but also from what
Palestinians considered Abbas's depressing lack of a nation-building
vision or strong connection to his constituency. No one in a position
of leadership apparently had the will to mount a popular protest akin

to the movement that finally resulted in change in South Africa. As a result, as knowledgeable Israeli and Palestinian observers alike have long predicted, the calcifying lack of hope has led to an increased willingness to turn to violence against random Israeli civilians.

In a further aggravation of this serious situation, in July 2017, two days after the fatal shooting of two Israeli policemen outside the Old City compound known to the Palestinians as the Noble Sanctuary and to the Jews as the Temple Mount, the Israeli government installed new security cameras and metal detectors at the compound's entrances. Until then, metal detectors had always been used at the entrance for non-Muslims, never for Muslim worshippers. Their installation resulted in widespread protests, with thousands of worshippers choosing to pray on the streets outside the Old City rather than go through the detectors on the grounds of the compound, their usual location for Friday prayers. A few of the protests devolved into violence, which resulted in hundreds of injuries and the death of three Palestinians. Since 1967, the site has been administered by the Waqf, an Islamic trust, in coordination with Jordan. By installing the metal detectors, Palestinian and other Muslim officials said, the Israelis were violating long-established agreements relating to the site's governance. By late August 2017, the Israelis were temporarily not permitting any male Friday worshippers under the age of fifty into the Old City. But by the end of the summer the new metal detectors had been taken down.

A friend familiar with Abbas's senior leaders remarked as the death toll rose (between the beginning of October 2015 and the end of October 2016, 235 Palestinians and 35 Israelis had been killed in what the Israelis were calling the "Intifada of the Individuals" and the Palestinians were calling the "habba," or "outburst") that "the PLO [Palestine Liberation Organization] leadership is not ready to struggle beyond staying in five-star hotels. It has lost the trust of its people." The assertion echoed the oft-quoted, innovative Palestinian American businessman Sam Bahour, who characterized Ramallah, the most cosmopolitan of the West Bank cities and de facto seat of the Palestinian government, as "a five-star Occupation."

In the cyclical way that Palestinians and Israelis alike have grown accustomed to, things quieted down for a while, and the level of violence subsided. Then, on December 6, 2017, in what many observers considered one of the more astonishing of his diplomacy-be-damned unilateral moves, President Trump announced that the US would henceforth recognize Jerusalem as Israel's capital and planned to move its embassy in Tel Aviv to Jerusalem—a reversal of almost seven decades of US foreign policy. This challenged the long-standing international consensus that the status of Jerusalem should be decided as part of the final phase of any peace agreement between Israelis and Palestinians. The declaration predictably set off a new wave of violence, with bloodshed, fatalities, protests on the Palestinian streets, and, in Arab and Muslim countries, the widespread burning of Israeli and American flags.

Trump plunged ahead with his radical policy shift despite impassioned pleas from many US allies and some of his own advisors. His reaction to the UN General Assembly's subsequent (nonbinding) 128-member vote to condemn the new US position was uncompromising. Doubling down, Trump threatened dire consequences for those who had opposed his move. His UN representative at the time, Nikki Haley, echoed the threat, and within weeks it was announced that the US would make a $285-million cut in its 2018–19 UN budget. In the weeks that followed, Iran declared its recognition of Jerusalem as *Palestine's* capital, while Yisrael Katz, Israel's transportation minister (known as "the Bulldozer" for his many successful infrastructure projects across the country), announced that a planned station of the country's new high-speed rail line, inside the Jewish Quarter of the Old City and near the Western Wall—perhaps the most sensitive and contested site in the country—would be named after Donald Trump because of the president's "historical and brave decision to recognize Jerusalem, the eternal capital of the Jewish people, as the capital of the state of Israel." The Palestinians had already tried to stop the line, since some of it would run through occupied land, but their efforts had failed, and both Trump's announcement and the plans for the station were greeted favorably by most Israelis. The transportation minister was far from the only official to rush to name a local project after the US president. One Jerusalem city council member proposed changing the name of Saladin Street (named after the revered twelfth-century Muslim military and political leader), the main East Jerusalem artery that leads to the Muslim Quarter, to

Donald Trump Street. The mayor of a northern Israeli city said he planned to name a new park after the president, and the city council of the coastal city of Ashkelon passed a resolution naming one of its roads Trump Declaration Street.

Five weeks after the president announced his decision to relocate the US embassy from Tel Aviv to Jerusalem, on the seventieth anniversary of the creation of Israel, the embassy opened. The opening event was officially attended by his daughter Ivanka, her husband and White House advisor, Jared Kushner, a sizeable number of evangelical notables, and some Republican congressmen. Officiating at the inaugural ceremony was the US Southern Baptist pastor Robert Jeffress, a close Evangelical advisor to the president, known for his bigoted remarks about Mormons and—wait for it—Jews.

At the same time that many Israelis were celebrating the relocation of the embassy, the ongoing clashes and protests in Gaza, called by the Palestinians the Great March of Return, became exponentially more lethal. The Great March began along the Gaza-Israel border on March 30, 2018, as a general protest against the region's blockade and to demand that the Palestinian refugees and their descendants be allowed to return to their families' houses in Israel. Most of the estimated thirty thousand protesters were unarmed and demonstrated peacefully, but groups of young men and some women near the border fence rolled burning tires toward it, launched kites bearing incendiary devices over it, and threw Molotov cocktails at Israeli soldiers stationed on the other side. The Israelis fired tear gas, rubber bullets, and live ammunition. The day of the embassy opening, more than 60 Palestinians were killed, bringing the total number of fatalities during the Great March to 111, with over 12,000 injured. By late fall the number of fatalities had climbed to over 180, a number that included the killing of Razan al-Najjar, a twenty-one-year-old woman working as a paramedic for the Palestinian Medical Relief Society. Some 5,800 had been injured from live fire. One Israeli soldier had been killed and hundreds of acres of Israeli farmland scorched. Before that year was over, the US cut more than $200 million from aid to Palestinians, including $25 million for East Jerusalem hospitals, and ended all funding for UNRWA, the United Nations Relief and Works Agency for Palestinian Refugees in the Near East. As a tough measure to supposedly encourage the Palestinian leadership to agree to some future peace plan devised by President Trump's son-in-law, Jared Kushner, the administration also ordered the closure of the office of the Palestinian diplomatic mission in Washington.

By then, it was taken for granted that the president's decisions to move the embassy and defund the Palestinians had political origins at the expense of diplomatic concerns. Specifically they satisfied the wishes of his evangelical base and of his major supporter Sheldon Adelson, the casino billionaire and generous Republican donor, for whom absolute fealty to Israel was a central tenet. Adelson contributed $25 million to a political action committee that supported Trump's election campaign and gave an additional $1.5 million to the Republican National Convention. By the time President Trump made his announcement about Jerusalem, most of the world had ceased being shocked by the president's inflammatory language and actions, though it was still difficult for international leaders of every stripe to understand how the president, like a boy with a match—no, a blowtorch—sitting atop a mountain of incendiary history, could so flagrantly disregard the region's realities. It was far from difficult for the people most affected by it to wrap their minds around, however, since imperious political gestures made by figures in power had been their lot for over a hundred years.

In Jerusalem

CHAPTER I

THE GREEK COLONY

The street Ruth HaCohen lives on is quiet and leafy. Tall, well-established trees shade prosperous-looking houses, and the pale blue flowers of plumbago bushes spill over weathered walls. It's a mere three or four blocks from the neighborhood's busy main thoroughfare where, three years earlier, in 2003, a suicide bombing destroyed a coffee shop. The bomb killed seven people and injured more than fifty, but there are no visible scars left from that event anywhere in the neighborhood, called the Greek Colony after its early twentieth-century settlers, most of whom fled in 1948. As I walked along, I noticed a number of plaques on the facades of buildings. It hadn't taken me long to recognize that there is scarcely a patch of Jerusalem that isn't ornamented with a plaque bearing the name of a donor who financed the construction of a building or the landscaping of a park or a street that isn't glorified or burdened by a name drawn from the city's history.

In New York, where I live, the city's landmarks, like the Statue of Liberty and the Empire State Building, are a familiar backdrop, rarely in the foreground of anyone's mind. For most of the city's population, they are a notch above but not more preoccupying than Grand Central Station and Yankee Stadium—hazy components of one's sense of the metropolis. But in Jerusalem, the Dome of the Rock, the Wailing Wall, and even the Church of the Holy Sepulchre (where the various denominations sharing its candlelit recesses are often at odds) are ongoing, active sources of contention and sometimes violence and can rarely be relegated to anyone's mental archive of the ignorable. Most of the city's residents take this fact of their lives for granted and accept it stoically; for others it creates a disquieting mental buzz.

Ruth HaCohen's house, with a tall blue gate and tidy garden, is

1

near the end of the street, and, like most of the neighboring houses, it looks solid and secure. Except for the intense lushness of the vegetation, you could imagine you were in a European city. There's a pomegranate tree outside the front door and bougainvillea in profusion nearby. I first met Ruth on a cool summer evening; the day had been sweltering, but I had quickly learned that the temperature plummets every evening, a reminder that now and forever this hilly city is perched on a desert. She had just returned from attending to a number of administrative duties at Hebrew University, where she teaches. Her schedule is crowded, and I could see she was tired, but she was warm and welcoming and spoke with animation. Her pale blue eyes, emphasized by an artful streak of blue under each lower lid, were a bit red in the corners. We had agreed beforehand that this would only be a brief meeting, and before much time had passed she interrupted herself to say that really I should meet her parents soon, since it would be impossible to understand the trajectory of her life without linking it to theirs. They lived, she said, only a few blocks away. So, several days later, I paid her parents, the Pinczowers, a visit, which turned out to be mostly a chat with Ruth's mother, Esther. Her father, Eliezar, an erect, rangy man, was in failing health, and his capacity for conversation was limited, though a perceptible aura of goodwill all but trailed after him when he excused himself and left the sparsely furnished living room. He was ninety. Esther, seven years younger, carefully guarded her husband's dignity. Barely five feet tall, scoliotically stooped and also slowed by age, Esther could nonetheless describe in the minutest detail, and vividly, her pre–World War II upbringing in Munich, as the granddaughter of the city's chief rabbi, as well as her childhood's ugly finale. She could describe in equal detail her early days and transformed life in Palestine, the challenges of her adopted country, and the quirks of the airy and surprisingly pleasant old-age apartment building on the Hebron Road where since 2003 she and Eliezar had been moored.

A little over a year later, shortly before I returned to Jerusalem, I learned that Eliezar had died peacefully after an uneventful day in which, as usual, he had prayed, eaten a light meal, and taken his daily constitutional. Esther sorely missed her husband of fifty-seven years, but by then so much of her life had been defined by radical upheaval that she weathered the change with admirable fortitude—or at least the appearance of it.

Ruth was the third of Esther and Eliezar's four children (she has two older brothers and a younger sister). She was born in 1956, and like many of her compatriots she marks her birth by its proximity to one of Israel's wars. In her case, it was a month after the Suez-Sinai conflict waged by Britain, France, and Israel against Egypt (with diplomatic input by the US and the USSR) after the Egyptians nationalized the Suez Canal—or so the war was generally advertised in the West at the time. Britain and France had owned the Suez Canal Company since the canal was finished in 1869, and those countries wanted to regain control of the canal. It was chiefly an old-fashioned colonial war, joined by Israel, which was facing ongoing problems of border infiltration by Fedayeen guerrillas. The Egyptians had also closed the Straits of Tiran (the narrow passages connecting the Gulf of Aqaba and the Red Sea between the Sinai and Arab Peninsulas) to all Israeli vessels. Though the war was launched for a constellation of reasons—among them Britain's reaction to Egypt's strengthened ties to the Soviet Union and its refusal to join the Western Cold War alliance and France's anger at Egypt's support for the FLN (Front de Libération Nationale) in Algeria—its chief if unsuccessful object was to bring down Egypt's powerful president, Gamal Abdel Nasser.

A well-established scholar and beloved professor of musicology at Hebrew University where she holds the Artur Rubinstein Chair, Ruth is married to one of the country's leading political theorists, Yaron Ezrahi, and she and Yaron have dazzling academic résumés, replete with many awards and honors. Both were married before; she has a son from her previous union, and he has a son and two daughters from his—all married. One oddity of their living arrangement, which demonstrates that Jerusalem real estate pressures are not that different from those in London or New York, is that Yaron's ex-wife and her second husband live in half the house, though their wing is definitively separated from his and Ruth's and has its own entrance.

The first time I met her, Ruth was dressed completely in pink—pink shirt, slacks, and elegantly draped scarf. Tall and slim, she has short, honey-brown hair and the kind of lips often described as bee-stung. It obviously gave her pleasure to expound on her family's history, and she spoke with the assured cadences of someone comfortable with making sense of complex subjects. Altogether she presented an interesting combination of pink-cloud softness and no-nonsense, absolute competence—an attractive marrying of old Europe and swashbuckling modern intellectual. Over the years that followed I rarely saw her at rest. Whether lecturing to her students or welcoming friends and family to her home, she was a woman in motion. On this day, wine and slices of carrot cake were already set out. The house's comfortable modern furniture, tasteful folkloric bric-a-brac, and good paintings, including a small, accomplished abstract one executed by her husband when he was young and considered becoming a painter, place it securely within the parameters of what might be called the international tenured professor style.

Before long, Ruth brought out a large album filled with photos of many generations of her mother's family and some of her father's as well. There was Eliezar, a tall, optimistic-looking young man. She was proud of her father, as she is of her entire family, with its seven-generation lineage of scientists, scholars (like her father and mother), well-to-do merchants, and doctors. One detail of a family portrait makes her shake her head. Her maternal great-grandmother was in the photo, but "she was ... very pregnant at the time, so they hid her because it was not OK to show a woman's belly. It's showing the source of it all. You want to have it immediately if you can. But you cannot, so ..." The story of her father's arrival in Palestine in 1934 is a tale that, like so many told about the lives of early Zionists, has a strong idealistic cast, and she tells it with evident admiration.

The young man from a religious family came from Breslau. They were originally from the town of Pińczów, in Poland, but moved to Silesia in the eighteenth century and specifically to Breslau (now Wrocław, Poland) in the late nineteenth century. Inspired by the ubiquitous nationalistic youth groups of the era, Eliezar decides at the still-wet-behind-the-ears age of eighteen, just after the Nazis came to power, that he is going to immigrate to Palestine and become a teacher, heading toward the teachers college founded by the respected municipal leader David Yellin. With the blessing and support of his family he pursues his youthful vision, setting off for Palestine as soon as he finishes his *Abitur*, the German secondary-school exam, pausing briefly for a grand tour of Italy.

"Was the Italian part of the trip perhaps an opportunity for some wild oats sowing?" I asked, and Ruth blinked.

Then she laughed. "*Never* did they talk about such things. They were *never* part of the conversation."

At the gymnasium (secondary school), Ruth's father had been a top student, and his German mentor and mathematics teacher took a dim view of his immigration plans and goal of teaching young children and tried hard to discourage him. He believed that his student, whom he knew as Ludwig, should stay in Germany and aspire to more elevated things—demonstrating that high-minded Germans could be as blind about what was about to befall their country as most Jews were. "Zu niedrig" ("too low"), he tells his student. "You can do better. This is not an ambitious enough life plan for someone of your caliber." But Ludwig never hesitates. He comes from a religious family, and the idea of living in a place with so much rich religious history moves him. He is overcome with joy when he sets foot on Palestinian soil.

"Ludwig" was left in the dust. Henceforth, he would be Eliezar—the Hebrew name he had previously used only in his private Jewish life. When the state of Israel was in its infancy, all civil servants were encouraged to shed their Diaspora-friendly names and change them to Hebrew ones, usually drawn from the Bible. This helped expand what one modern historian calls "the sacred trinity of Bible–Nation–Land of Israel"—that trio so central in interpretations of Jewish history that focus on the Bible as the North Star of Jewish consciousness. In his memoir, David Ben-Gurion put it another, rather homelier way: "Hebraicizing one's name seemed to my generation a way of underlining our feeling for the country and our affinity with our ancestors. We were, in effect, indicating our purpose of taking up where they left off." But Eliezar had not shed his old name for a simply programmatic reason; he was a new man embracing a new life, and his name belonged with that life. Little is said in this fond daughter's recounting of the effect on the gently raised city boy of the harsh landscape, scorching, sun-dazzled days, or the stripped-down, electricity- and plumbing-deprived reality of his new country—probably because the

young man had thought so long about his dream, and now he was living inside it. Of the Arabs who lived in the land and the already deep
antagonisms that had developed between them and Jews, nothing
was initially said. Eliezar was a man of peace, and the drama of bloody
conflict that preceded and followed his arrival—for example, the massacre of unarmed Jews in Hebron by their Arab neighbors and others
in 1929 and subsequent bloody clashes of the British and Jews with
Palestinians, in which some twenty Palestinians were killed who had
not participated in the attacks on Jews, or the momentous 1936–1939
country-wide Arab revolt and bloody general strike, which was both a
protest against Jewish immigration and a rebellion against the policies
of the British Mandate in general—occupied only a shadow backdrop
in his personal history.

     After a few years Eliezar finished his seminary studies and be-
came first a teacher, then a founder of a new school—so much new-
ness everywhere!—and then the developer of innovative teaching
methods and institutions for furthering the education of the under-
schooled immigrants from North Africa, who from the outset of the
Zionist project were allocated poorer housing and land than their
Ashkenazic (Jews from northern Europe) brethren, socialist ideal-
ism notwithstanding. Eventually he became a teacher of teachers. His
father, a doctor who served in the German army in the First World
War and received the Iron Cross for bravery, was also an amateur
singer of lieder and Yiddish and Zionist songs. He and his wife, the
librarian of Breslau's Jewish Theological Seminary, regularly hosted
Sunday string quartet afternoons. They, too, were ardent Zionists.
They had even journeyed to Palestine in 1912 for their honeymoon
and named one of their sons Theodor after Theodor Herzl, Zionism's secular founder, whom they, like so many nationalistically in-
clined Jews of that era, considered a kind of prophet. Still, unlike their
sons (Eliezar's brother also immigrated to Palestine), they stayed in
Breslau along with their daughter, Hannah, until the Nazis made it
impossible to remain there. Eliezar's father treated mostly gentiles in
his practice but saw fewer and fewer patients after it became forbidden for Jewish doctors to treat non-Jews. Eliezar's mother lost her
job when the Nazis closed the seminary, so there were big economic
troubles. Even after they understood that they would soon have to

leave, it cost money to get out of the country and to live: how would they support themselves once they landed in Palestine? But in time, the dangers that grew closer and closer swept aside all other considerations. The British Mandate's refusal to grant the certificates that were needed for immigration became the family's biggest worry. Eliezar and his brother had been given student certificates, and, as it turned out, Eliezar's earlier arrival and the crucial certificate he possessed attesting to his full-time residence in Mandate Palestine helped save his family. These enabled them to eventually join him, since family enlargement was one of the permissible exemptions of ever-tightening Mandate immigration restrictions.

Eliezar's mother was the next to leave after she managed to secure a job as a high school head in Jerusalem, but she did so with trepidation since her husband and daughter, Hannah, had still not received their certificates. A resourceful and cultivated young woman, Hannah had been striving to adapt to her future Zionist, possibly kibbutz milieu by acquainting herself with the mysteries of agriculture. She had taken seriously the Zionist exaltation of physical labor in general and farming in particular as a central tenet of the creation of the "new Jew"—one emancipated from the bourgeois financial and commercial culture Jews had long been a part of and essential to the hands-on building of a new country. For several years, gentrified city girl that she was, she spent summers, pitchfork in hand, at first without incident, in Lower Silesia with a German farmer, learning agricultural practices for her life to come. During the non-farming months of the year, after graduating from a Jewish elementary school, she studied first at a Nazified secular high school and after that at the Jewish Theological Seminary before the Nazis shut it down— originally with the object of teaching Jewish history in the German school system. In 1938 her farming days abruptly ended. The farmer's son, a member of the Gestapo, was warned that because of Hannah's presence his family would soon all be arrested, precipitously ending Hannah's pastoral apprenticeship. After that, she moved to a Zionist youth group training center in Cologne, where she continued to work with young people hoping to immigrate to Palestine. She hadn't been there very long when, a few days after Kristallnacht (November 9, 1938), her father, who had been living with relatives in Breslau since his wife's emigration, was grabbed along with thirty thousand other men—one-quarter of all the Jewish men then living in Germany—and sent to a concentration camp. Hannah learned this from the Breslau relatives with whom he had been staying. They sent her a postcard with an agreed-upon coded message: "Your father, too, has left for vacation."

Hannah learned that her father had been taken to Buchenwald when she received another postcard that he had somehow managed to mail her from the camp. Its message told her nothing, but the postmark, Buchenwald, told her everything. She immediately sent her mother and brothers in Palestine a telegram telling them that they needed to urgently increase their efforts to secure a certificate for their father—at that point, late 1938, Jews who managed to acquire a certificate were still permitted to leave. Possibly because of the father's early Zionist association, the family finally managed to get him one and sent it to Hannah. Terrified, she ran with it to the huge Gestapo headquarters—with its notorious cells and basement torture rooms that prisoners themselves had been forced to build—submitted it, and left, half-convinced that she would also be arrested.

But ten days later, to the family's enormous relief and amazement, her father was released. Almost immediately he boarded a train to Trieste and from there sailed to Palestine. By then, however, the wear and tear of his experience had badly affected his health. Although he declared to his family that he was the happiest man in the world to have arrived in Palestine safely, he died just three years later. Hannah was then twenty years old. It was Hannah who recounted these details to me, filling in what Ruth had broadly sketched out for me. Hannah was ninety-three when I met her at her comfortable, book-lined apartment in Jerusalem, and when she recounted the details of her struggle to free her father and of her own subsequent escape, she did so with characteristically German-Jewish lack of drama, despite the accompanying exclamations of her grown daughter who was present ("Imagine—her guts!" "Into the Gestapo fortress!" "Such a young girl and so brave!").

Of course, many of the elements of Hannah's story are by now all too familiar and have been echoed with different permutations by refugees from all over the world. But looking at the elegant old woman with translucent skin so matter-of-factly telling it, I was both awed and aware of a kind of lowering alertness to the reality that similar, mostly untold acts of bravery are certainly taking place wherever governments hold absolute power.

The reason she had been left behind after her parents left Breslau, Hannah explained, was that at that point children over seventeen were not included in "family" certificates. However, earlier in the thirties her enterprising mother had made a journey to Holland and visited her brother (who was later shot somewhere in Europe; his wife and children were sent to Theresienstadt and then to Auschwitz, where they died). There she had met some of her brother's English friends, who promised to send a written invitation for Hannah to work for them as an au pair in London—an invitation that made Hannah eligible for an official British work permit.

The British papers had arrived in a fat envelope that Hannah hadn't even bothered to open while she was struggling in the waning months of 1938 to rescue her father. Now, with the invitation, she could pretend she was going to England via Palestine—although this was a nearly impossible feat to achieve by then, the beginning of 1939. Frightened but determined, she made her way to the British embassy in Berlin before dawn. It was early January and icy cold.

Though it was still dark, a frantic mob scene greeted her outside the embassy gate—hundreds of desperate people were trying to leave the country, but only those with official papers like hers were admitted. As soon as she acquired her visa for England, she stuffed it in her purse, found a sign that said "The Colonies," and spoke to a clerk about wanting a visa to visit her family in Palestine. There was no line outside that office because—regrettably, the clerk said—at that point no more visas were being issued for Palestine; he suggested she begin working at her job in England first and visit her family at a later date. Oh, but that would be impossible, she said, trying to exude sincerity as far as a squirrel could leap, because she couldn't just begin work and then abandon her employers, could she? And she missed her family so much … A naturally straightforward young woman, Hannah considered the duplicity she summoned at that moment the high point of her efforts, and, as the years went by, never ceased to look back in wonder at the bold girl she had been.

The clerk gave her a long, indecipherable look and asked her to sit down while he went into another office and spoke with his superior, someone Hannah could not see. Nor could she hear what was transpiring in the office, though it was nearby. But when the clerk emerged, he held the miraculous Palestinian visa in his hand. "I don't remember my feet touching the ground after I left—I believe I flew home!" A few days later she left the country. Later still, as her boat was docking in Haifa, she tore up her British work documents and threw them overboard. Decades on, she would learn that her invisible bureaucrat-savior had been Frank Foley, a British spy who had once considered becoming a priest and who was hiding in plain sight as a passport official in Berlin. Foley not only managed to acquire intelligence about Germany's essential military research but also time and again found ways to sneak thousands out of Germany, forging passports, hiding Jews in his own house, and even entering internment camps (as documented in Michael Smith's *Foley: The Spy Who Saved 10,000 Jews*). At the 1961 war crimes trial of Adolf Eichmann in Jerusalem, one witness characterized Foley as a "Scarlet Pimpernel" for his many dangerous intercessions on behalf of Jews threatened by the Nazis, frequently at the risk of his own life.

CHAPTER 2

FRENCH HILL

I was introduced to Niveen Abuleil, a young, energetic speech pathologist, by a friend of her family who worked for the UN. At that time, late spring in 2010, Niveen still lived with her parents and sisters in a northern East Jerusalem neighborhood, French Hill, near Hebrew University. On the phone she sounded friendly, if cautious, but several phone conversations later she invited me to meet her at her family's house. Her parents, Zaineb and Abdallah, had finished building the house in 2000, though they had lived in the neighborhood for more than five decades.

French Hill is one of the areas ruled by Jordan until 1967, when it was occupied by Israel in the Six-Day War and then annexed under Israel's Basic Law: Jerusalem. The UN Security Council declared the annexation a violation of international law and to this day does not recognize its legitimacy, and an advisory opinion of the International Court of Justice issued in 2004 declared that all Israeli settlements in East Jerusalem, including French Hill, constituted a breach of international law. Nonetheless, over the decades, the neighborhood has been heavily built up by Israelis, and most Israeli Jerusalemites consider it an Israeli neighborhood. The post–Six-Day War settlement of Jews in the neighborhood was strongly encouraged by the government, beginning with Ben-Gurion, the country's aged former prime minister, who at that point had retired from government but not from politics. Shortly after the 1967 war, when Jerusalem's municipal boundaries expanded to Palestinian neighborhoods and extended the government's economic, political, and demographic reach, Ben-Gurion declared—despite his general objection to the Occupation and stated opinion that all the territories conquered should be returned (*except* for Jerusalem)—that "Jews should be brought to East Jerusalem at any cost.

Thousands of Jews should settle soon. Jews will agree to settle . . . even in shacks. We should not wait for the construction of proper neighborhoods. The important thing is that they will be there."

Some eight thousand Israelis now live in the neighborhood, along with a small but tight-knit core of about five hundred Palestinians, a good many of whom, like the Abuleils, are 1948 refugees from the village of Lifta, three miles to the northwest of the city. The Palestinian families who live there do their best to ignore the hostility of their Israeli neighbors and maintain a strong if unwelcome presence. The name "French Hill" has been attributed to various institutions and historical persons (including a British army officer named French), but most of these attributions do not bear scrutiny. In any case, the Palestinians call it Ard al-Samar, "Black Soil," a reference to the dark earth of the surrounding area. On a busy intersection at the border of that part of the city, which adjoins the Arab neighborhood of Shuafat, many bombings and other attacks by Palestinians took place during the second Intifada, including, on March 19, 2004, the shooting of George Khoury, the twenty-year-old son of Elias Khoury, a Christian Arab and respected human rights lawyer.

The younger Khoury, an international affairs student at Hebrew University, was jogging on French Hill when he was shot from a car by a member of al-Aqsa Martyrs Brigade, the military branch of the Fatah movement, which later revealed that he had been shot in error. The shooter, who had mistaken Khoury for a Jew, apologized. His father later said, "I am against all violent attacks on innocent civilians, whether it be against Israeli civilians or Palestinian civilians." He also called on the Palestinian movement's leaders to denounce such acts "in a loud and clear voice" and added, in a radio interview, "Terrorism is blind. It does not discriminate between Jews and Arabs or between the good and the bad." Eulogizing the young Khoury, one of Yasser Arafat's advisors described him as a *shaheed* (martyr) for the Palestinian struggle, but George's mother interrupted him. "My son," she said, "was an angel, not a martyr." This wasn't the Khoury family's first brush with violent death. In 1975 Daoud Khoury, Elias's father, was killed along with thirteen others in Zion Square in central Jerusalem, by a bomb in a booby-trapped refrigerator.

A few weeks before I met the Abuleils, at around three o'clock one morning, someone slashed the tires of all the Palestinian residents of their street—including those of Niveen's VW Golf. One of her brothers called the police, and they came but said that it would be too difficult to try to find the culprit or culprits. This surprised nobody. "What can we do?" Niveen's outgoing second-oldest brother, Maher, said to me about the event when I met him a few weeks after my first visit to the neighborhood, "We are no big concern of theirs." Settlers' slashing of tires on Palestinian vehicles is far from a rare occurrence. In some cases, the vandalism is accompanied by graffiti, as was a slashing I walked past in Sheikh Jarrah, another East Jerusalem neighborhood, where "Death to Arabs" had been scrawled on the cars and nearby walls.

The Abuleil house is approached via a tall, locked heavy iron gate with gilded trim connected to a buzzer system. The gate is filigreed and rather splendid looking—you would not be surprised to find a consulate within—though the multistory family structure it opens onto across a sun-filled courtyard is plain as pie. Both the depth of the courtyard and the height of the gate and surrounding wall reinforce an architectural awareness of security concerns. After several years of approaching the house via the nearly always deserted, sun-bleached street, I realized I had never once seen a child playing on it. The children are held close by their families. In some ways, the street reminded me of certain nondescript thoroughfares in New York, streets where there was neither commerce nor any discernible clues to the sorts of lives lived within the buildings and you couldn't tell if the residents had lived there for fifty years or fifty minutes. The outside of the Abuleil house on the street side, like many Arab houses, was bereft of ornamental planting when I first saw it, but the next year Maher landscaped it with rose bushes and small trees. The street in front of the home was pitted and potholed, but it, too, got a facelift several years later. There is a small, grassy garden out back where family celebrations are occasionally held. Above the entrance a blue plaque indicates that someone within has made the hajj to Mecca.

It took the Abuleils nearly a decade to acquire the necessary papers to build their house, partly because of a shortage of money and partly because the government makes the process of building-permit acquisition for Palestinians next to impossible. (Palestinians represent 40 percent of the city's population, but only 7 percent of building permits were issued to them between 2010 and 2015.) The permit dilemma is by now well-known: delays, evasive responses, and other bureaucratic stalling greet the would-be Palestinian house builder. Finally, in frustration, he or she goes ahead and, permitless, builds a house. And then that fact is discovered, the authorities are shocked—shocked!—and the bulldozer appears and the house is destroyed. Before the Abuleils' new house was built, all eleven members of the family lived in a small, two-room structure next door built by Niveen's grandfather in the 1930s, and in it her parents raised their four sons and five daughters.

One of the sons, Monzer, a lawyer, died suddenly at thirty-five in Jerusalem, possibly from complications from a heart attack he suffered while in Amman on a business trip. No one in the family is absolutely certain about the cause of his death. There was no medical evidence of anything suspicious, but because Monzer was interested in nationalist issues and so much violence swirls around them, the Abuleils have not ruled out foul play. The remaining three sons are all married and live with their families on a separate floor of the house, as do Monzer's widow and her children. Niveen's brother Mazin is a dentist whose practice is now located in the little house next door. Her brother Maher's popular falafel shop around the corner (and across the street from Hebrew University), Falafal Hajj Liftawi Abuleil, is frequented by Israelis and Palestinians alike. And brother Muhammed studied in Russia and earned a PhD there in civil engineering. When I remarked to a Palestinian artist friend that extended family living arrangements seemed to be quite common among Palestinian Jerusalemites, he responded with a somewhat cheerless smile, "You think it's about family togetherness, but it's not. It's about economics." Most other people I asked about this thought that perhaps both factors were at play.

Traffic between apartments and especially into Abdallah and Zaineb's is heavy, so the families are constantly thrown together. When I first met them, four of the sisters, Sana, Nisreen, Ruqaya, and Niveen, shared two pocket-size bedrooms, and a married sister, Khawallah, the second oldest daughter, lived nearby. When overnight visitors slept in the apartment, Niveen, the youngest of the sisters, gave up her bed and slept on the couch. At any time of the day and long into the evening, one or more of the Abuleil sons, several of their daughters or daughters-in-law, visiting relatives, neighbors, and friends can be found settled on one of the senior Abuleils' overstuffed living room chairs or sofas, placed more or less in a small circle (an arrangement ubiquitous in Arab homes), nibbling on homemade savory or sweet pastries, dried fruits and fresh ones, sent forth from the kitchen by Sana, the eldest daughter.

Tall and efficient, with cheeks often flushed from her culinary efforts, Sana has an air of someone not easily thrown off course. I have watched her oversee the care and feeding of her parents and play hostess to the multitudes wandering in and out of the apartment, a not unusual role for unmarried oldest daughters in this part of the world and one that I at first thought she must resent. But as far as I could tell, she doesn't. She knew that her parents, both far from healthy, could depend on her and were grateful for her attentions, that everyone loved her excellent cooking, and that in her way she was essential to keeping her family, a powerful machine, going. Once she worked as an office manager, but if she showed signs of missing that life I never detected them. When I asked her directly about it, she shook her head slowly. She missed it, she said, not at all.

The Abuleils' visitors nearly always included a steadily flowing stream of small children who, as is the custom, took Abdallah's hand, kissed it, and brought it to their foreheads when they came into the room. Several of Maher's children were there the first day I visited. Abdallah, who was seventy-five, drifted off to sleep now and then and seemed pleasantly surprised to see the throngs in his living room when he woke up. The room's decorations, apart from the sofa and chairs, include a frosted crystal chandelier, a framed photo of Monzer, a big dining table, and a breakfront filled with knickknacks. The family does not expect advance notice from visitors, and the front door remains unlocked. Because of a stroke Abdallah had suffered a few years earlier and his generally poor health, the pace of visits had increased. People came to pay their respects to him, cheer him up, and keep him company, and the sisters made arrangements to give Sana a break from her role as chief caretaker of their parents. I'm sure there must have been times when visitors weren't around, but Niveen and her sisters appeared surprised when I once said something about the impressive number of visitors. To them it was a central part of their lives, nothing special. In Abdallah's boyhood in the village of Lifta before 1948, family rooms, he told me, were filled in much the same way.

The day of my initial visit to the Abuleils, Niveen happened to arrive late, but Zaineb was there to greet me along with Abdallah, Sana, and her ailing and rail-thin Aunt Fatima, Zaineb's youngest sister. Fatima usually lived in Ramallah, but she was staying with the Abuleils because she, like Abdallah, was recuperating from a stroke. Some of the family spoke English, but some didn't, and my knowledge of Arabic was limited to a handful of polite phrases, so conversation between us rode along awkwardly for a while on slow-moving clouds of "so glad to meet you," "you're most welcome," "salaam alaikum," and "shukran" (thank you). Niveen's mother was not among the household's English speakers but was fluent in the ubiquitous Arab language of extravagant hospitality and made sure that a steady stream of coffee and pastries flowed my way. Sana, busy in the family's modern, well-equipped kitchen, offered brief moments of linguistic rescue (she had traveled alone on a sightseeing trip in the US years before and retained a working knowledge of English). But for the most part the family sent friendly nods in my direction, and I nodded back and tried my best not to look panicky.

The women smoothed their long robes and spoke quietly to each other. Two of Niveen's brothers, Muhammed, the engineer, and Mazin, the dentist, both large men, wandered in, noticed me, greeted me hastily, and quickly left. Pace my late colleague Edward Said, as I sat there in my New York "office" clothes, sleek tape recorder on my lap, I couldn't help but feel that I must have seemed like a character in a play called The Occidental—especially when I continually stumbled pronouncing names, my tongue tripping over the emphatic, unfamiliar Arabic stresses.

Luckily, shortly before Niveen showed up, help arrived in the compact, eager form of then-eleven-year-old Abdallah—Maher's sharp oldest son, a good English student at school, who came up from downstairs with his sister and two younger brothers and translated for his family and for me. When Niveen, an intense, pretty young woman with dark, deep-set eyes and high cheekbones, showed up with apologies about half an hour later, the children followed us into her bedroom, where she had hoped we could talk privately. But the children were in our laps as soon as we sat down, magnetized by my tape recorder, and it soon became evident that if we were ever going to have a quiet conversation it would have to be elsewhere or when the children weren't at home. Niveen's English is excellent, and she immediately took over young Abdallah's translating duties. After a while she pulled off her hijab, revealing a mop of shiny black hair—a Palestinian birthright, or so it seemed. When I brought up the tire-slashing incident, she shrugged. "We're never surprised about things like that. They don't want Arabs to live in this area. They hate us. All these years, and we have no relationships with our Jewish neighbors."

The Abuleil children all attended private schools. Young Abdallah told me he went to St. George's, run by the Anglicans, among whose distinguished alumni is Edward Said. The family was far from rich, but everyone agreed that the Arab public school system was inadequate—too many schools had no yard, no lab facilities, no library, and sometimes no heat, and in general they were overcrowded and undersupported (the government spends two times as much on the Jewish schools as it spends on the Arab schools). From the family's point of view, those schools could not provide children with a satisfactory education. Abdallah-the-elder, Niveen's father, had long ago become convinced, he told me a few days later, when the children were at school and the house was relatively quiet, that a strong education was the chief way, the *only* way, for his children and grandchildren to push beyond the harsh circumstances of their lives and to grow and prosper.

Abdallah and Zaineb, I also learned that afternoon, were distantly related. Back in Lifta, he told me, there had been five main *hamulas* or clans: Gabaa, Sofran, Sa'ad, Mekbel, and the one the Abuleils (as well as his wife's family, the Odehs) belonged to: al-Aeda. Even today, the clans maintain close networks around the world.

Before 1948, Lifta was among the most prosperous of the Arab villages, and Lifta residents also owned extensive lands throughout Jerusalem. Abdallah's father owned one thousand dunams (a bit less than 250 acres). Jerusalem today may be the poorest of Israel's cities, but in the twenties and thirties, while Mandate Jerusalem wasn't as

prosperous as Jaffa or Haifa, it was bustling and expanding and pro-
viding new social mobility for the Arab middle class. This was fertile
ground for a lively circle of Arab professionals and intellectuals—like
the educator, poet, and nationalist Khalil Sakakini, who along with
many forward-looking doctors, businessmen, lawyers, and other professionals moved out of the Old City to Jerusalem's southern neighborhoods. The British also made Jerusalem the seat of the mandate
government, which added to its luster. When the intellectual leaders
of Palestinian society were forced by the war to leave, they took with
them the most promising articulations of a still-forming Palestinian
cultural identity.

As Jerusalem prospered, Lifta's fortunes grew along with it. Its
stonemasons cut and moved their pale limestone from local quarries
to the city to supply the metropolis's growing building needs, and
Lifta farmers brought tomatoes, cucumbers, peaches, almonds, bar-
ley, wheat, and olives to the city's markets. Until the conclusion of
the 1948 war, when Israeli, Jordanian, and Egyptian boundaries were
drawn, though not finalized, as part of a peace treaty, the people of
neighboring villages had a far more fluid sense of the reach of their
villages. Land formerly owned by Liftawis stretched, for example, to
central Jerusalem not far from where the Knesset now stands, as well
as to the Central Bus Station at the northwestern entrance of the city,
Hadassah Medical Center, and parts of Hebrew University in northeastern Jerusalem. Elderly villagers will accompany you on far-ranging
tours, pointing out various sights throughout Jerusalem, repeating,
"That was Lifta," "And there," "And there too." Some of these claims
have been challenged by local historians, and few of the oral archivists
have access to proper deeds to confirm their claims, since, along with
nearly everything else owned by Liftawis, many of those documents
were destroyed during the war. Even those *with* proper deeds have for
the most part been legally outmaneuvered so that their land rights
have been nullified. Nonetheless, the old villagers are unyielding in
their insistence that they know to the last dunam the boundaries of
their former neighbors' former lands.

Along with the rest of their neighbors, the Abuleils fled their
home in panic during the early days of the Nakba, or "Catastrophe,"
as the 1948 war is known in the Arab world. (Jewish Israelis refer

to it as the War of Independence.) In one respect, Abdallah's family was far luckier than thousands of others. The Abuleils owned land in Jerusalem, and there they continued to grow some of their own fruits and vegetables. Part of the family had already been staying in the little Jerusalem house since it was built in the mid-1930s. The majority of their Lifta neighbors were not so fortunate. They were small-farm cultivators who suddenly found themselves homeless and without any way of making a living. Although the Abuleils were disoriented, dispirited, and frightened, they managed to keep going on their Jerusalem land, then ruled by Jordan, but their luck was not to hold. Though they were sure that the worst that could happen to them had already happened, another blow awaited them: the largest portion of their land, except for the plot their house stands on, was expropriated after the Six-Day War in 1967, when the Israelis conquered the neighborhood. Today, just around the corner, along with Maher's falafel shop, a Hebrew University dormitory, a Hyatt hotel, and an elementary school stand on land the family once owned. In the new, reduced situation they found themselves in, with fresh losses compounding the old ones, Abdallah told me, it was impossible not to feel discouraged and angry, but they somehow kept going and, crucially, kept together. The strength of that cohesion has been the bedrock of their life. About the family's massive loss of land, Abdallah shook his head and said, "It was ours, wasn't it. Not the Turks' or the Jordanians' or the British, not the Israelis'—*Khalas* [That's it]. We'd lived there for hundreds of years, and it was our life, but this was swept aside."

One of the major events of the war years that still remains burned into the family's collective memory occurred during the first phase of the conflict, the 1947–48 Civil War, an attack whose ferocity so alarmed the Abuleils and their neighbors that it prompted a spate of late-night discussions about possible flight from their village, with its famous communal spring and rich skein of life. It was the gunning down on December 28, 1947, of six civilians and wounding of seven others in a Lifta coffeehouse, by the Irgun, Menachem Begin's right-wing paramilitary fighters, along with the militant Zionist group Lehi (Fighters for the Freedom of Israel), also known as the Stern Gang. The event occurred one month after the announcement of the UN Partition Plan for Palestine terminating the era of the British

Mandate. Passed as a resolution by the majority of the UN General Assembly, the plan was not illegal, as most Arabs considered it to be, but whether it was fair was another question altogether. The plan was swiftly accepted by the Zionist leadership but rejected by the Arabs, who, though constituting the majority population of Palestine—67 percent—were allotted 43 percent of the land. This was one occasion when it looked as if the US would side with the Arabs. The US Department of State at first considered the Partition Plan unfeasible and thought the country should be governed under a UN trusteeship, but, bowing to lobbying pressure, President Truman allowed the US to vote for it. At that point, Jews owned only 7 percent of the land, but, of the new territory they were being allotted, 84 percent of that represented the best suited for agriculture. A year later, they had captured 76 percent of all the land. After the coffee shop attack and subsequent military assaults on Lifta by Jewish militia trying to break an ongoing siege of Jerusalem and strategically clear the western exit of the city and the crucial Jerusalem–Tel Aviv road, the supply route on which Lifta lay, there were few villagers who weren't persuaded that remaining in their homes was no longer safe.

Several weeks after our first meeting, recalling the upheavals of that time, Abdallah, whose long, thin face seemed to have become more gaunt in the short interval since I'd last seen him, and his slender mustache a bit sparer, said, "We'd heard by then about the terrible things that had been done to the Jews in Europe but we couldn't understand why *we* were being asked to pay for it—*we* hadn't been their enemies." At first, the women and children were sent away, and some of the men tried to defend the village, but by February 1948, all remaining villagers, some twenty-five hundred people, had fled on their own or been trucked to East Jerusalem. "The AHC [Arab Higher Committee] tried to insist that we stay, but really how could we? Our position was hopeless. Did you know we had *no* weapons factories, so we were trying to fight mortars, submachine guns, and modern bullets with homemade bombs?" Abdallah's father saw early on that his fellow Liftawis were severely outmatched. They did have rifles, Abdallah added, but not many, and the ones they had were old and in bad shape. It was hard not to see, too, that the growing strength of the Zionist movement, coupled with the lack of strong Palestinian leadership, made the long-term odds against them discouraging indeed. "The point is," Abdallah, who was wearing a white knitted cap and striped robe, went on to say, trying to convey the temper of that time, "we had nobody to ask about what was happening, and, as much as anything else, that frightened us." While Abdallah's immediate family and his relatives and neighbors speculated about the degree of support they might expect from their Arab brethren across the border, those countries were engaged in a complex jockeying for power that had little to do with the needs of the Palestinians.

After the UN General Assembly voted, on November 29, 1947, for the partition of Mandatory Palestine into two independent states, one Jewish and one Arab, the Palestinian Arabs, the Arab states, and the seven-member Arab League were united in their rejection of the partition as illegal, impractical, and immoral, and all-out war seemed inevitable. "And this gave us some hope," Abdullah said. "There were all these official statements issued on our behalf. And for a while we kept hearing that our militia had blocked most of the big highways and won many battles."

Abdallah's information about the initial phase of the war was accurate, but, as we have learned, the unanimity needed by the Arabs to *win* a war was absent. King Abdullah of Transjordan was interested in becoming master of all Arab Palestine, and within the Arab League itself there was little agreement about the future of the land. Its members, other than Transjordan—Egypt, Iraq, Lebanon, Saudi Arabia, Syria, and Yemen—were more focused on thwarting King Abdullah's desire for dominance. And they were all probably most united in their strong distrust of the Grand Mufti of Jerusalem (the "Grand" part of his title was an invention of the British), Haj Amin al-Husseini. Husseini, who led the AHC, was a maximalist in terms of territorial ambition and was (and still is) popularly admired for his vision of an independent state over the whole of Palestine. But he was feared for his murderous dealings with opponents (of whom there were many among Palestinian leaders) and shifting allegiances—to the British before he turned against them, to the Germans in Nazi Germany before they abandoned him. Bizarrely, in 2015, in the midst of the violent period of clashes, Prime Minister Netanyahu attempted to lay the entire blame for the Holocaust on the Mufti's useless supplications

to Adolf Hitler, even insisting that it was he who planted the idea of
the total destruction of European Jewry in Hitler's mind. The Arab
League steadfastly refused the Mufti aid in the crucial period leading
up to the war—not only declining to help him set up a government in
exile but even refusing him money for administrative support. In any
event, by the time the war began on May 15, 1948, as the Oxford professor of international relations Avi Shlaim points out in his excellent
2009 reexamination of the conflict, the Palestinians, in contrast to
the Israelis, did not have "a responsible government, an administrative
regime, or a unified military command."

There were naturally some Liftawis who suffered under the mis-
apprehension that they would soon return to their homes. This was
fitfully encouraged by a handful of earnest militia fighters and the
Mufti and later by rumors of a mighty invading army of five of the
seven members of the Arab League—Syria, Lebanon, Transjordan,
Iraq, and Egypt—who officially entered the war after Israel declared
its establishment as a state. However, news of the death in a fog-
shrouded battle of one of their most beloved and courageous military
leaders, Abd al-Qadir al-Husseini, the Mufti's nephew, and, a day
later, of the infamous April 9, 1948, massacre at Deir Yassin, coupled
with the swift demolition of villages and rapid resettlement of Jews in
formerly all-Arab districts, shocked them into a new and heretofore
inconceivable possibility—the possibility of the loss of their homes,
all their worldly goods, and the reassuring interconnectedness of their
village life, perhaps forever. For many Palestinians, the events of Deir
Yassin, a small village three miles west of Jerusalem whose inhabitants were mainly stonecutters, marked the crucial turning point in
their conflict with the Jews. One hundred ten to one hundred twenty
villagers (estimates vary), including women and children, out of a total population of seven hundred, were killed during the attack, and,
though accounts of it vary slightly, all concur that there were instances
of rape and other barbarities, that many of the 107 were summarily
gunned down, and that others were killed by hand grenades tossed
into houses. There were reports, which turned out to be correct, of
unarmed quarry workers, who had already surrendered, being shot
where they worked and their bodies dumped into the quarries after
being paraded through the Jerusalem streets.

It was also later revealed that Deir Yassin had been one of several villages that had signed a nonbelligerency agreement with its neighboring Jewish towns and that, as International Red Cross delegates reported afterward, the attack was carried out "without any military reason or provocation of any kind." The latter was partly inaccurate, however, as the village lay on the supply route to Jerusalem, which at that point was under siege, so there was a "military reason" to capture it. Nor were the villagers only victims, as they are nearly universally portrayed—at one point forty of them waged a pitched battle with a far larger number of Israeli forces for eight hours—though that was not a justification for brutalizing its civilians. Members of the Haganah (the "Defense," the pre-state military force that, after Israel was created, would become the Israeli Defense Forces) had also participated in the attack and blamed the Irgun and Stern Gang militias for its excesses.

Word of the carnage at Deir Yassin spread rapidly, and a flood of refugees from other villages soon abandoned their houses. Debate has followed ever since about the scope or degree to which planning preceded what would later be called the ethnic cleansing of the Arab population by the authorities of the Yishuv, as the pre-state Jewish community was called. Some Israelis who disapprove of what transpired at Deir Yassin and of the Jewish treatment of the Palestinian people in general at that time—in that era the name conferred on it was "transfer"—nonetheless proffer the argument that ugly things happen in war and that even normally decent people commit brutal acts in wartime—unpremeditated acts triggered by fear and confusion. Unfortunately, most archival materials on the Palestinian side were either confiscated, bombed away, scattered, or are held closely by the Arab nations humiliatingly involved in the war. Earlier records are lacking, including those confirming land ownership, since the British Mandatory government never finished its accounting of land in Palestine, so the Palestinian side of its own history is all too blurry. There were no state records because there was no central government machinery charged with keeping them, and the problem was compounded when the Israelis destroyed or confiscated all Palestinian publishing houses, libraries, the land registry, hospitals, printing presses, municipal councils, and cultural centers.

But archival Israeli material unearthed over the last decades by the "revisionist" Israeli scholars (collectively referred to as the New Historians), drawn from the Israeli Defense Forces Operations Branch and the Haganah and other Israeli sources, including documents made available by the 1997 thirty-year declassification rule that opened up state documents to historians and other researchers, reveal an engaged level of military planning on the Jewish side. Opinions differ as to the intent of the plan called Operation Dalet. One perspective is that all the elaborate preparation was mainly defensive, a way of preparing for the expected pan-Arab assault on the country; the other is that it was designed to guarantee success in driving out the native populations. In any case, the New Historians have established that, from 1940 on, elaborate preparations were made that ended up expediting the expulsion of more than seven hundred thousand Palestinians from their land. Included in these preparations were detailed instructions about the methods to be used when evicting people from their homes, laying siege to and bombing villages, demolishing houses, and working with a registry and inventory of all Arab villages, compiling what came to be known as "The Village Files." These entailed a complex compendium of each village's topography, access roads, landholdings, water sources, sociopolitical makeup, religious affiliations, names of leaders, ages of its male population, and even an index that estimated the villagers' degree of hostility toward the Zionists, based on the level of their involvement in the 1936–39 Arab Revolt.

Although the revolt was chiefly directed against the Arabs' colonial ruler, the British, the Jews had been recruited by the British and were heavily involved in its suppression. The Columbia University historian Rashid Khalidi believes that the revolt and the 1936–39 general strike were the chief determining factors in the outcome of the 1948 War for the Palestinians, and he persuasively demonstrates "how the failures of their leadership, and the absence of structures of state, contributed to their military and political defeat in both cases; and finally how this heavy legacy affected them thereafter." Apart from such core issues, the revolt's blow to the male population of the Palestinians was devastating. Fully 10 percent were killed, wounded, or exiled, and a disproportionately high number of the Arab casualties included the most experienced fighters and military cadres. By 1939, when the revolt ended, most of the high-ranking political leaders and thousands of other fighters were, as Khalidi points out, dead, imprisoned, or in exile.

In the earliest stages of the Village Files project, long before the war, young Zionist scouts pretending to be studying nature gathered material that was the beginning of an intelligence database. Eventually informants and spies were recruited to gather precise information about the number and status of the villagers' weapons, the landholdings of each family, names of shopkeepers, the names and descriptions of each village's imam (or leader), and the number of guards protecting a village—often zero. All of that happened under the mandate, clandestinely, including the taking of aerial photographs of Arab villages, though this was strictly forbidden by the British authorities under the terms of the mandate.

As much as anything else, it was this detailed knowledge of every Palestinian village, along with the superior military organization gained from their experience with the British, especially in World War II, that gave the Zionist military leaders confidence and a blueprint for conquering the region. In addition, the Yishuv had a military already organized, the so-called Jewish Settlement Police, twenty thousand strong, with a secret underground army of thirty thousand. On the other side, after the British decimated the Palestinian leaders' organizations at the end of the 1936–39 uprising, there remained little military infrastructure. And as for the much-vaunted attack of the five invading Arab armies, the David-versus-Goliath version of events that still lingers as an article of faith in some quarters, archival research by historians over the last thirty years has shown that between Arab declaration and Arab execution lay a vast abyss. Lebanon, Iraq, Jordan, Syria, and Egypt would declare war against the new state in 1948, and there was at first fierce fighting that didn't look as if it were going the Jewish fighters' way on soil that had been promised to the Palestinians by the mandate. But in the end, only the Egyptian army waged a full-scale war across the territory of the new state.

None of this should downplay the ferocity of the war or the loss of life suffered by both sides. At the beginning of the war the Jewish population was 650,000, and the Arab population was 1.25 million. After it was over there were 1.2 million Jews and 159,000 Palestinians living in the country. The postwar figures reflect the huge influx of Jewish refugees from Europe and the massive exile of Palestinians. There were thirteen thousand Palestinians killed in the war, four thousand from the Arab coalition, and six thousand Israelis killed.

For Niveen's father (Abdallah was thirteen at the outbreak of hostilities) and his family, the overwhelming strength of the Jewish fighters and absence of any sense of security became unignorable as the bullets and bombs came closer to their doorstep. "The women became frozen; they just sat staring for hours in silence, and nobody slept much at night. We were living in fear." Some of Abdallah's memories of that time would blur. Historians, among them Walid Khalidi (Rashid's cousin and a preeminent member of the first generation of Palestinian exile scholars) and his team of researchers, concur that the attack on the Lifta coffee shop took place in December 1947 and that by early January there was a severe shortage of bread, and women and children had begun leaving the village. Though Arab legionnaires still remained in the area, and in mid-January some of the villagers were told by them to return to the village (and some did), by February 1948 the village was depopulated.

In a number of long conversations I had about the war with Abdallah, whose health continued to be poor and sent him in and out of the hospital, he several times cited the events of Deir Yassin as being a major precipitating reason for his family's rapid departure, though the Deir Yassin massacre actually took place in April 1948, months later. The unofficial historian of Lifta—Yaqub Odeh, a relative of Zaineb who was trained as a lawyer—told me that there were still fighters around after February 1948, trying to stave off the inevitable in Lifta, but he acknowledged that most of the villagers were no longer in their homes then. About the general feeling of fear and the devastation being wreaked throughout the Palestinian villages however, there was no confusion. The 2004 revision of the historian Benny Morris's groundbreaking *The Birth of the Palestinian Refugee Problem*, first published in 1988, included information about this from newly declassified archival documents. It revealed, Morris writes, that "there were both far more expulsions and atrocities by Israeli troops than tabulated" in his book's earlier edition, as well as "far more orders and advice to various communities by Arab officials and officers to quit their villages or at least send away their women, old folk, and children." But Morris's history excludes interviews with people like Abdallah; in Morris's view the unreliability of memory makes personal interviewing futile. Here is his explanation for his methodology: "After careful thought I refrained almost completely from using interviews, with Jews or Arabs, as sources of concrete information. My brief forays into interviewing had persuaded me of the undesirability of relying on human memories 40–50 years after the event to illuminate the past."

The rightness of his decision was confirmed, he writes, by the answer given to him by a well-known archaeologist many decades after the war, when Morris asked him about the mass expulsion of Arabs from Lydda and Ramla in July 1948, which is sometimes referred to collectively as the Lydda Death March. It is estimated that fifty thousand to seventy thousand Arabs were forced from the two towns, making them two of the biggest sites of transfer of the war. Many deaths occurred as the marchers struggled along the dusty road in the intense Mideast summer sun. The strategic point of the march was to keep Arab fighters off the route the marchers were blocking and prevent a threat to Tel Aviv. The archaeologist had during that time served as the Haganah/IDF head of operations, and thus, Morris goes on to report, was the de facto chief of general staff, so there would have been no way he wouldn't have known about the expulsions, but, when questioned about them forty years later he responded, "What expulsions?" Morris goes on, "He did not deny that an expulsion had taken place; he merely said that he could not remember."

Morris's confidence in the reliability of written contemporaneous documents is from a certain traditional point of view—academic, scholarly—unassailable. Archival period documents add a necessary, solid dimension to forages into the past. Yet what is left out of this formulation is the magnitude of the emotional basis for people's lapses or rearrangements of memory. While it's important to ascertain as best we can the sequence of the war's events and their military and political causes, isn't it equally crucial to understand the impact of those events on people's imaginations? The cost to their families and their communities? The massacre at Deir Yassin loomed so large in the local population's minds that it became a black shadow over their lives. Small wonder that Abdallah—and many other refugees—could not help but consider it key to their understanding of the upheavals that afflicted them. This too constitutes evidence.

Similarly, even in the clinching example Morris cites about the archaeologist and former chief of operations who "forgets" about the part he played in the bloody events in Ramla and Lydda, which resulted in even more casualties than Deir Yassin, who is to say what dark thoughts he may have had over the years about the disappearing line between civilians, soldiers, and regular militiamen during the war? Especially since Morris's interviewee, whom he doesn't name, was probably Yigael Yadin, an archaeologist and the IDF's head of operations at that time, who was celebrated as a military hero and who, in his later political life, was considered a domestic moderate and a dove in foreign affairs. Yadin was not one of the principle commanders involved in Lydda, but, as Morris notes, it would have been impossible for him not to know about the operation. Isn't the "forgetting" worth scrutinizing, especially since Yadin was far from being a forgetful old man at the time of the interview? (He was only sixty-seven when he died, in 1984.) Isn't individual moral struggle—or at least recognition of the two sides' differing perspectives in the long, painful history of this conflict—bound up with remembrance and forgetting, even on the part of a loyal soldier? Surely the two ways of reconstructing the events we later on call history—memory and archival documentation—are complementary.

The issues embedded in these questions are not simply about the value of competing forms of historical evidence. They are directly related to the more elusive question of what constitutes history and will in the future play a major role in the country's accepted narrative about its beginnings—and ambiguities. The stories people tell about their lives strongly shape the way a culture imagines itself. Both sides of the conflict are certainly attached to mythical as well as factual versions of their own history, but if no account is heard from the people "cleansed" from Ramla and Lydda, the temptation to make skewed, vainglorious assessments of the event is opened. A notable example can be found in Ari Shavit's *My Promised Land*. Shavit focuses on the moral anguish felt by the commanders who carried out the operation and concludes, nonetheless, that "if Zionism was to exist, Lydda could not exist. If Lydda was to exist, Zionism could not exist," words that themselves exist in a moral vacuum. It's also true that oral histories alone, adopted by some younger historians, can seem incomplete. The military positions of soldiers that Morris tells us about, the winning and losing of battles and the documents of field commanders, however revealing, are in a sense a reality of *every* war, and the cumulative sense derived from them is that they are neither right nor wrong but simply necessities of bloody conflict. Absent the testimony of everyday victims of the war, it becomes far easier to discount subsequent claims to land. And easier, too, not to question the stereotype that Palestinians can be reduced to one of two things: a problem or a threat.

Morris considers himself a man of the Left and his books achieve an admirable degree of evenhandedness in dissecting the course of events in the war, but there's another vein altogether in his conclusions, proffered somewhat casually at the very end of *The Birth of the Palestinian Refugee Problem* but not at all casually in several interviews he gave after his revised publication came out, in which he said that there are "circumstances in history that justifies [*sic*] ethnic cleansing. I know this term is completely negative in the discourse of the 21st century, but when the choice is between ethnic cleansing and genocide—the annihilation of your people—I prefer ethnic cleansing." And in another interview, speaking about Ben-Gurion, Morris criticized him for only carrying out a partial expulsion plan during the war.

"If he had carried out full expulsion . . . he would have stabilized the State of Israel for generations." Like Shavit, whose self-described liberal credentials are an established part of his personal history (though David Shulman, the Hebrew University scholar of Indian languages and poetics and activist, has more precisely characterized him as part of "the wishy-washy center"), Morris rests his conclusion squarely in the iniquitous realm of ends-justify-means.

If one of his country's leading researchers and historians, after carefully recording the losses suffered by both sides in the bloody history of the war, can complacently offer up such a devastating assessment, where are we? But surveys have shown that many Israelis share Morris's either-or postulation. As the Israeli government migrates ever rightward, a sizable proportion of the general population has followed along. Some would say it has been the other way around. According to the result of a 2016 poll conducted by the Pew Research Center, nearly half of Israeli Jews favored "transferring" Palestinians out of Israel proper. In 2006, though what was admitted to be a "quiet deportation policy" had supposedly been rescinded, the number of Arab Jerusalemites losing their residency status increased sixfold, and, according to one professor of international law, from 1964 to 2011, Israel revoked the "permanent resident" status of more than fourteen thousand Palestinian Jerusalemites. Recent governments have been particularly zealous in doing this. Of all the Jerusalem Arabs who have lost their residency rights, 35 percent lost them in 2008, twenty-one times the average of the preceding forty years.

The unshakeable assumption of the Israelis who support this policy is that no diplomatic solutions can ever override the fact of an implacable, virulent anti-Semitism that abides in every Arab heart. It precludes ever seriously pursuing avenues that might provide a modus vivendi for peace and in no small part underlies the government's support for the illegal spread of settlements in the West Bank, the uprooting of families in East Jerusalem, and an implicit policy of looking away as settlers uproot Palestinian trees, fill in their wells, and terrorize their children.

That the history of the Jews in nearly every corner of the globe is a story of humiliation, expulsion, persecution, and genocide, and that there is a bedrock of ambient anti-Semitism in the world in general and in the Arab world in particular is undeniable, and in western Europe there are unignorable signs of a growing number of active anti-Semitic groups, even apart from the barbarities of ISIS. The resurgence of terrorist attacks aimed at Jews is equally troubling. As Howard Jacobson writes in his sly Booker Prize–winning novel *The Finkler Question*, about Jews and their attitudes toward Israel and their Jewishness, "anti-Semitism was becoming again what it had always been—an escalator that never stopped, and which anyone could hop on at will." The 2012 shooting at a Jewish school in Toulouse, the 2014 one at the Jewish Museum in Brussels, and supermarket murders in Paris in 2015, along with the spike in attacks on US Jewish institutions, neo-Nazi marches that followed the 2016 election, and the horrendous 2018 Pittsburgh synagogue massacre bear witness to the ongoing presence of a generalized anti-Semitism. One has only to tune in to some of the Internet's uglier hatred-spewing sermons of certain mullahs—the current Mufti of Jerusalem, for example—or the diatribes of the more militant functionaries of Hezbollah and other groups to appreciate the ongoing toxicity of hatred of Jews. Its myths, which reach across the centuries in pamphlets, plays, sermons, histories, and pogroms, also attest to the tenacity of anti-Semitism's greatest hits: Jewish abduction of Christian children, Jewish poisoning of Christian wells, "blood libel," emasculation of Christian men, and a global greed-driven conspiracy to rule the world. And let us not forget the latest wacko addition to this sorry list—charges of Jewish culpability for 9/11 and pre-attack secret evacuation of the World Trade Center by its Jewish office workers.

Unfortunately, Mahmoud Abbas's claim to a statesmanlike lack of animus toward Jews in his single-minded focus on establishing a state for his people was seriously discredited when he declared at the late April 2018 opening of the Palestinian National Congress that the Holocaust was not caused by genocidal German hatred of Jews but by frustration over the Jews' financial activities. It was the Jewish peoples' "social function," not anti-Semitism, he said, specifically "usury and banking and such," that brought about the Holocaust. Abbas later apologized for his remarks, but the damage had been done. The speech merely added more poison to the already teeming cauldron of distrust that fed the Israeli view of the Palestinian leaders.

Nonetheless, the facile charge of anti-Semitism has been too programmatically aimed at Israel's critics, and the democratic, inclusive, tolerant state envisioned by Herzl seems to have little relation to the country that in recent years has become crueler and crueler toward its Palestinian population and increasingly less interested in their human rights. It is definitely not the country imagined by the generation of the 1920s and 1930s. Walid Khalidi, drawing on Israeli as well as Arab military accounts, estimates that more than four hundred Arab villages were destroyed or depopulated during the 1948 war. Several years before Khalidi's melancholy book about the destruction of the villages—*All That Remains: The Palestinian Villages Occupied and Depopulated by Israel in 1948*—was published in 1992, I happened to attend a lecture he delivered in a university auditorium in Connecticut at which he displayed a large map of Israel, filled in—crowded—with small dots representing the vanished or all-but-vanished villages that were emptied of their inhabitants during the war. The audience was not particularly friendly, but Khalidi, an elegant figure whose British-accented English is marked by old-fashioned rolled r's, was obviously used to speaking to groups who were resistant to the reality portrayed on his map. Following his talk, he answered each skeptical audience question with a scholar's exactitude. Khalidi's lecture and map revealed the depth of my lack of awareness of the extent of the depopulations. The map became permanently lodged in my brain, and the flyer announcing his lecture, "The Palestine Problem: Causes, Current Status and Prospects of Settlement," now yellowed, its edges curled, has remained pinned to the bulletin board in my study.

Travels with Fuad I

▶ Over the years, as we drove between the neighborhoods of Niveen Abuleil's family and Ruth HaCohen's family (and around the country), Fuad Abu Awwad and I logged hundreds of miles together. I learned fairly soon that though he was no snob, he was keenly aware of status and had an old-fashioned respect for educators. No amount of cajoling, even with the passage of time, would persuade him to call me, in the American way, by my first name. Instead, he insisted on calling me Doc*tor*, emphasis on the second syllable, because I teach at a university. When, helping me with my luggage one day, he saw that the approach to my pocket-size studio was via a dim, labyrinthine garage with a certain resemblance to the mob rub-out site in the film *Some Like It Hot*, he made it clear that he didn't consider my housing arrangement suitable.

There seemed to be few people in Jerusalem Fuad didn't know or at least know about. Customarily, one of the names parents are given in that part of the world, called a *kunya*, incorporates the name of their oldest son (as in Abu Mazin, or "father of Mazin," for Mahmoud Abbas, and Umm Mazin, or "mother of Mazin," for his wife). People are identified not so much for what they do or who they are as by who their parents are, and Fuad had apparently committed to memory the life stories of a prodigious number of them. Before I met the Abuleils, I had been meeting for several years with another family who were among the *ayan*, or elite families of the city that have traditionally dominated life there. That family had been part of the city's power structure since the twelfth century, and *fellaheen*, or farming families, like the Abuleils were no part of their experience, though they would sometimes dutifully extol them for their traditional ways and perseverance. That family and I parted company because of a messy divorce a key couple in the family was going through, a struggle that transformed the family saga into too much of a telenovela. By then I had been writing about them for more than three years, so it took me a while to decide to move on, but when I told Fuad what had happened, he wasn't too surprised, as he believed, along with F. Scott Fitzgerald, that the rich were different from you and me and consequently behaved in unconventional ways.

Fuad was also familiar in a broad way with the histories of nearly all the families I began contacting next. By then, the first Gaza War (2008–2009), called by the Israelis "Operation Cast Lead," had taken place, with its heavy death toll and massive destruction of the territory's infrastructure. Most of the Palestinians I spoke with were more disgusted than usual with what they considered the Western nations' indifference to their fate and were in no mood to talk with outsiders like me. Young professionals were particularly unwilling to participate in a venture they thought might get them in trouble with the Israeli authorities, even when their parents were game. One entire fruitless summer went by and half of another, with Fuad correctly understanding, from my forlorn expression when he pulled up in front of yet another East Jerusalem home to drive me back to my own, that I'd failed in my quest yet again.

Then one afternoon, to my astonishment, he announced that he'd phoned Nasser Eddin Nashashibi on my behalf, for help. A member of one of Jerusalem's oldest and most prominent patrician families, Nashashibi was a journalist who had also served as secretary to the Palestinian delegation to the Arab League in 1945 and another time as the league's roving ambassador, as director general of the Jordanian Broadcast Service, and as a contributing editor to the popular Egyptian weekly *Al-Ahram*. Members of his family had held high positions under the Mamluks, Ottomans, and British. Nashashibi lived in a huge villa in the East Jerusalem neighborhood of Sheikh Jarrah and owned retreats in London and Geneva. Perhaps centuries of familiarity with the custom of having elites like the Nashashibis solve local problems played some role in Fuad's decision to contact him. Fuad certainly hadn't met him or known anyone who had, but, convinced that I could use the advice of someone connected to a lot of people in the city, he proceeded to ignore the social taboos bred into his bones and rang him up. This was more or less equivalent to your local yellow cab driver phoning one of the Rockefellers, but Fuad, contrary to everything I knew about him, made light of it, and, wonder of wonders, Nashashibi had agreed to see me that very day! What a generous man, I thought, and what openness to a fellow Arab!

An elegantly dressed older woman led me into a soaringly high-ceilinged room, and Nashashibi, who was then eighty-eight, apologized for not standing. He had stayed up too late the night before, he said, and was tired. He didn't look his age. He had carefully groomed silver hair, was wearing a burgundy silk dressing gown, and had a fleshy face, a strong nose, and, despite his fatigue, a booming and rather commanding voice. Surrounding him were hundreds, perhaps thousands of mementos from his long career: photos of himself with presidents and sheikhs, beautiful women in elegant gowns, beaming celebrities of various nationalities, diplomats, and relatives, all in silver frames; a virtual warehouse of elaborately carved antique tables and chairs; and a desk covered with unstable-looking piles of paper and numerous brass trays piled high with paperweights, letter openers, and other bibelots too numerous to mention. With Nashashibi at the center of all this, the effect was akin to seeing a faded, slightly damaged portrait within an ornate, jewel-encrusted frame.

As it turned out, he had neither advice of any kind nor a single thought about my dilemma. He looked bored and was quick to change the subject, when I briefly brought it up, to one he very much did want to talk about: his uncle, Ragheb Nashashibi, a moderate Palestinian politician and longtime (1920–1934) mayor of Jerusalem, about whom he had written a biography that had been published fifteen years earlier. "Storrs [the British military governor of Jerusalem at the time] called my uncle 'the ablest Arab in Palestine,' and he was," Nashashibi said. In his uncle's era, there were two main political factions, one led by his uncle, the other by Haj Amin al-Husseini. Both men opposed the Zionist project, but, as portrayed by his nephew, his uncle believed in negotiated efforts and artful persuasion, which he hoped would eventually succeed in moving the British to reject the Jewish homeland idea and support the handover of the institutions of government to the country's rightful indigenous leaders. Unlike many references to his uncle, which tend

to characterize him as over-conciliatory and ineffective, the word
"moderate" is generously applied by his nephew throughout the text,
and the broad picture is of someone humane, clever, and diplomati-
cally skilled.

His uncle's rival Husseini is portrayed in Nashashibi's book as
a fervent nationalist and an uncompromising zealot who sometimes
expressed his displeasure with those who held opposing points of
view, like Ghada Karmi's uncle, a father of eight, by assassinating
them. The book offers a stout defense of his uncle but leaves out a
reality that over time had a far more malign effect on the progress
of the Palestinian people than the rivalries of the two major political
factions—that Nashashibi and Husseini were *both* cleverly manipu-
lated by the British. Husseini, no less than Nashashibi, despite his
inflammatory rhetoric, was for a time extremely obsequious toward
his British overlords, who appointed both men to their positions,
sustained them financially, and made it possible for Husseini to gain
the power he did—power that eventually gave him standing when
he became the premier anti-British, anti-Zionist nationalist leader.
In general both factions tended to negotiate politely, even fawningly,
with the British privately, while showily denouncing their policies
in public. Nonetheless, for more than a decade and a half, both men
appear to have been unaware that they were being used as pawns
in the familiar British colonial strategy of distributing favor and
patronage to discourage rebellion and sowing dissention among
leaders so they were unlikely to remain unified in their desire for
self-determination.

After many hours of excavating the vagaries of old Jerusalem
political cabals, during which I fell into a kind of stupor, Nashashibi
suddenly sprang to life. He'd just had an idea that he thought was
inspired, he said, though somehow the studied way he said it made
it clear that he'd planned to say this all along. "My chauffeur quit last
week and I have no one who can drive me around. Do you think
that, um . . . Fuad might like to be my driver?"

"Well, I don't know. . . . Why don't you ask him?" I said, hand-
ing him my cell phone after calling Fuad, who had just driven up
outside the villa's electronically controlled gate. They subsequently
arranged for Fuad to drive him somewhere the next day. I thanked

him, and we took our leave. Fuad had a thoughtful expression as we drove along the busy highway linking East and West Jerusalem. His wife, Kivo, had recently lost her job when the medical supply company she worked for underwent a downsizing spasm. Nashashibi was clearly a very rich man, and Fuad allowed himself to imagine a plummy sort of sinecure, one that might even replace his current job with its long, exhausting hours.

But some days later a downcast Fuad let me know that the whole venture had turned into a disaster. Apparently the old man had asked Fuad to drive him around for several days and required him as well to transport the older woman who'd shown me into the living room (and whom he later introduced as his niece) for several hours as well. Neither of them could be coaxed at any point to discuss money, and the woman even seemed irritated when Fuad brought the subject up. "Look, I have a wife and three children. I have to know that I can take care of them," Fuad told me he'd finally said to Nashashibi.

It then emerged that the job would additionally entail traveling with Nashashibi to London and Geneva when he visited his residences in those cities, and where Fuad would be expected to more or less always be available, and the salary offered was laughable. Fuad told me he had shaken his head in disbelief and was about to decline the offer but never got a chance to. At that point, Nashashibi had ended the conversation abruptly, saying he wouldn't be requiring his services any longer. And that was the end of Fuad's cross-class caper and liveried fantasies.

"Oh, and by the way, what do you think they paid me for all that driving around?" he asked a few days later, when he had arrived at the point where he could laugh at his experience.

"Nothing, can you believe it, zero, not a single shekel!"

CHAPTER 3

SHELTER

E sther Pinczower's family, the Fraenkels, played a strong leadership role for generations in Munich's thriving Jewish community, her daughter Ruth told me. Religious but also enthusiastically
attached to German culture, their identity, like that of the Pinczowers, was dual. Esther's mother was born in the waning years of the
nineteenth century and was encouraged by her grand rabbi father
(who taught Talmud to Gershom Scholem, the great scholar of
Jewish mysticism) to attend university, which was rare not only for
a young woman in her circle but even for young Christian girls of
that era. There she studied (O tempora! O mores!) Germanistics—
the culture and philology of Germany. Later on, married and in her
own household, she prided herself on her modernity and was in the
vanguard of young wives who enthusiastically acquired the accoutre-
ments of the new age—a refrigerator, a telephone, a phonograph. But
the Fraenkels were slow, very slow, to draw logical conclusions from
the devastating effect the National Socialist Party was having on Jewish lives. Esther was ten when the Nazis came to power. Before then,
she'd studied only at a Jewish school. She had learned to read Hebrew
before she learned to read German, but her German was excellent
(Esther spoke only German with her parents at home until their dying days), and in 1935 they decided to send her to a secular German
girls' lyceum, St. Ann's, that was part of the same excellent secondary school system that they themselves had attended decades earlier.
There she could study Latin and Greek and expand her knowledge
of German literature and history. That their daughter would be isolated and humiliated as a result of the school's already solidified fealty
to National Socialism was something they were blind to. Cultured,
well-educated, and sophisticated though they were, her parents were

for too long inadequately alarmed by the inroads Nazification had already made in Munich. When Esther told me this, I was at first unable to grasp how that could have been possible, especially in Munich.

Since 1924, Munich had been the National Socialists' headquarters. Hitler became chancellor on January 30, 1933, and through the Enabling Act of that same year he assumed dictatorial powers. The city was considered the Nazi capital. Storm troopers had already been terrorizing Jews all over the country, and Munich's nineteenth-century neoclassical square, Königsplatz, was a site of massive Nazi rallies and book burnings, and the square itself became the National Socialists' "Akropolis Germaniae." Jewish professors had been ejected from the city's universities, and in 1933, the same year as the infamous boycott of Jewish shops, the Nazis also organized a boycott of all Jewish doctors and lawyers. What was happening then has been widely described by historians and has become a staple of World War II books, articles, and films: Nazi toughs stopping people from entering stores and marking their facades or windows with a yellow star or the word "Juden"; Jews only being allowed to sit on certain designated park benches and seats of buses and trains; and the firing of Jews working in museums, broadcasting, or on newspapers.

For the post–World War II generations, this story, like Hannah's, is an all too familiar one. But for Esther's culturally assimilated family, though history was rushing toward them with gale force, there was until the closing of Jewish shops the fervent wish, hope, or fantasy that if the family went stubbornly about its business, prayed, repeated their rituals of ordinary life with enough fortitude, they could somehow hold on to that cherished existence, a life that, as Esther put it, "We couldn't imagine not going on forever." Perhaps this is not so strange. Who, living in close proximity to some horrible event has not had the self-protective reaction, "Oh, that happened on the *south* side of the street; luckily, I live on the *north* side." And though what was taking place in Munich in the 1930s was of an entirely different order, for a long time a form of self-hypnosis did not permit Esther's family to fully acknowledge the impossibility of their situation—even though bit by bit (in the same manner chillingly chronicled in the diary of the Romance language scholar Victor Klemperer, writing in his

case about Dresden) the world of Munich Jewry was on the verge of
annihilation. They were, of course, aware that it was only because of
Esther's father, who, like Eliezar's, had served with distinction in the
German army in World War I, that their daughter was even allowed
to attend an elite German school.

But somehow they remained blind to what their daughter faced at
that school. Esther was an excellent student and always shone in her
studies—the family was proud of her ability to recite whole chapters
of the Bible—but now the curriculum as she described it more than
half a century later, peering intently at me over a bowl of grapes on
a table in her tiny light-filled living room, was "full of Nazi rubbish."
There was only one other Jewish girl at the school, and she and Esther
were completely frozen out by the other girls—all Bund Deutscher
Mädel (BDM), the girl's wing of the Hitler Youth. "Every day we were
taught about the glory of the Reich and forced to sing terrible Nazi
songs along with the other girls—songs like 'Today Germany belongs
to us. Tomorrow the whole world.'" The other students shunned Esther and the other girl, behaving as if their two Jewish schoolmates
didn't exist. Her three brothers and her sister, all younger and still attending Jewish schools, were spared similar experiences, but as things
got worse, nearly all Jewish parents began to take their children out of
German schools, which the Nazis proclaimed to be proof that Jewish
children were lazy. (Recounting one of the exquisitely ironic twists of
fate in her life, Esther mentioned to me that sixty years later a group
of young, blond, blue-eyed German girls in the process of conversion
to Judaism—girls who very much resembled her old Bund Deutscher
Mädel schoolmates—were sent to her, in what Ruth would later describe to me as "fear and awe," to learn about Judaism as part of their
preparation.)

Before long, the other Jewish girl at the school departed for the
US. Esther continued to take exams and receive high marks, but now
she was forbidden to raise her hand in class. What did her parents say
about what was happening to her in school? "Nothing—I didn't tell
them." An ironclad combination of Teutonic and religious stoicism
kept her from sharing her daily school pain.

"We didn't complain," she said, shrugging, her plainly arranged

gray wig—an artifact of religious observance, not vanity—shifting
slightly as she shook her head. "That's how it was. In 1925, an uncle of
my father's—eight years *before* Hitler came to power—he was beaten
for being Jewish, and he was wearing ordinary clothes, and he was a
leader of the community. But nobody told us about it 'til years and
years later. Denial. Perhaps it had some biological function."

Compounding the isolation and confusion Esther felt about
what was happening around her was her parents' "not in front of the
children" habit of discussing all important events, including the deepening political crisis, out of her earshot. So she had the sense that
she alone understood the momentousness of their situation, callow
twelve-year-old though she may have been, and the darkness and fear
she absorbed over that period, she told me, would linger through her
whole life. There were, of course, whispered conversations after the
boycott of Jewish shops, and all familiar goods—food, shoes, clothing—ceased to be taken for granted. Before that, there still was some
stubbornly clung-to familial idea, as Esther saw it, "that these were
things which happened *outside* . . . not inside." But eventually what
was happening outside became impossible to ignore. There were
nonetheless, mind-bogglingly, two more painful years for Esther to
endure at her school, but the alarm bell had sounded. "It was a given,"
Esther went on, "that . . . we would have to leave, and there was this
terrible undercurrent of fear. But even then there was still a sense, too,
that it was all a terrible dream. We'd grown up thinking everything
around us was permanent."

"Shelter" is a word that came up often in Esther's conversations
about her childhood—the shelter of her family, residents of Munich
since the second decade of the nineteenth century; the shelter of her
home; the shelter of Munich's close-knit Jewish community; and the
kind of sheltered childhood religious children in particular were accustomed to. "But the Nazis were so forceful and powerful that our
parents couldn't shelter us from that. My parents always told us it
was important to learn as much as possible about the world. Now my
father said, 'Don't mention what you know.'"

Finally, her father, who earned his living as a wool merchant in
a business he inherited from his father, established a beachhead in

Palestine, and by 1937 the whole family had arrived safely in a town
just south of Haifa. As far as she knew, there had been no discussion
before they left of going to any other country, Esther said, because no
other place would allow them refuge. A few months later the family moved to Haifa itself. (Esther counts her family lucky because
they "only" lost one member, her mother's brother, who'd emigrated
to Belgium in 1933 but was eventually interned and killed in Auschwitz—his wife and children survived.) Her parents chose Haifa
to settle in because it was a thriving port. Esther's father hoped to
continue his life as a wool merchant by buying wool from local Arab
shepherds and selling it in Syria and Lebanon, but because of what
Esther mildly described as "bad relations" between Arabs and Jews—
and later because of the war, when most of the city's Arab population
fled—this was not to be. About what the Arabs in Palestine were
experiencing in those years, she and her family knew next to nothing.

And about what was unfolding at that point in Germany, she
knew even less—though they were aware from newsreels of the general turn of events in the Pacific, no word reached them from Munich.
Much later they found out that their Jewish teachers had all perished,
but they heard not a word of the bustling community they'd left behind. "It was like an earthquake," Esther said, "like something that
happens and you don't know what happened and who was involved
in it, just that something terrible is occurring but you have no special
information, how or where. Only very slowly during years of reading
did I come to an understanding of what really happened." Over the
next decades Esther read accounts of the nightmare of the camps, of
babies being thrown alive into burning pyres, of carloads of people
suffocating on the trains to mass extinction, and everything she read
persuaded her that a safe place for the Jews had to be possible. All
around her, a considerable number of the people moving along Haifa's
hilly streets, and in the markets, were refugees. The collective trauma
of a population afflicted by deep depression and even derangement
from their experiences with the Nazis served as a somber counter-
point to the hopeful ethos of the kibbutz orange groves and pioneer-
ing youth groups for decades to come.

The average Palestinian, unpersuaded by the Jews' claims to a land
they inhabited several thousand years ago, continues to question why

his or her land was chosen for resettlement, first for Russian pogrom refugees and later for those from Nazi-ruled Europe. The answer, as far as it goes, is that all other suggested alternative places of refuge considered—Australia, Iraq, Libya, and Angola—were met with stiff opposition (a kind of global NIMBY reaction) or intra-Zionist dissention and rejection because of perceived impracticability. One early exception to the overall failure of other schemes was helped along by the American banker Jacob Schiff, himself a German immigrant, who brought Jewish refugees to the US Southwest. Between 1907 and 1914 some 9,300 Jews were successfully relocated in the region. Esther's mother had been far from eager to settle in Palestine; she would have preferred the United States, which she believed to be the only place with the same degree of modern technological advancement and cosmopolitanism—and cars!—as Germany. But the United States had ceased welcoming European refugees in the 1920s and failed to change its immigration policies in response to the situation in Europe. And though the British curtailed Jewish immigration numbers severely, it was still easier to settle in Palestine. Nonetheless, once they arrived, her mother was far from pleased with what she saw. True, she'd agreed with the rest of the family that Palestine was probably a better bet for ensuring the continuance of the Jewish culture so central to their identity. But the place looked primitive, with mules and camels clomping by, like an illustration from her childhood Arabian Nights book, and for a while she was miserable. Grateful to have been "saved," of course, but dubious about what her future life might hold.

The sparkling water of the Haifa port, exotic date palms, beautiful mosaics and gardens of the Arab landholders, and sultry Mediterranean nights provided little reassurance. Plucked from a well-to-do milieu in an urban setting where she had played a dynamic civic role, then thrust into an exotic Middle Eastern backwater about which she knew next to nothing except what she'd read in the Bible, Esther's mother was appalled by the oppressive heat and uneasy with the polyglot throng around her. Their apartment had no running hot water (a woodstove sat in the bathroom), but with considerable ingenious maneuvering she had managed to have most of their family furniture and a refrigerator, phonograph, and bathtub shipped to Haifa. There were other brand-new German appliances as well, which the Nazis, for a steep price, had allowed the Jews to purchase before permitting them to leave.

Securing a modern stove proved nearly insurmountable at first. Esther, taking pleasure in recounting what was clearly a bit of family lore, said that her mother somehow persuaded the electric company to give her, gratis, an electric stove if she would recommend it to her friends, a promise she was happy to make. Her mother's forebodings about her social status turned out to be groundless. Before long she had connected with the swelling Haifa German Jewish community and became one of its leaders, just as she had been in Munich.

The vast majority of refugees arriving from European cities were forced to make rapid downward adjustments. Former owners of large shops became peddlers, and many strapped families found it necessary to send their children to work. Esther's parents were struggling, too, but they desperately wanted to have their children continue their education. Esther's father had managed to hide enough money in his foreign accounts to provide them at first with a small cushion. Esther was fourteen when they immigrated to Palestine and still experiencing the aftershocks of her German school trials, but neither the trauma of the move nor the adjustments that needed to be made clouded her joy. A precise woman who chooses her words carefully, Esther unfailingly spoke in a measured way, but not about this. For her, she said, her arrival was "a resurrection." The curtain had fallen on humiliation and fear.

"I was so happy to be here. To see the sea, blue. To see the wonderful flowers. It felt secure, and ... not to have always this horrible sense of inferiority." A shadow on her family's relief was the gradual arrival of bad news, always bad news, of the expanding war in Europe. They lived with growing fears about the fate of those left behind. After a while money began to be in short supply, and like thousands around them they had little idea how they were going to live. Their way was eased by a relative who had immigrated earlier, in the 1920s, a professor of mathematics, medievalist, and well-known public figure who was among those officiating when Hebrew University was founded in 1925. He was Esther's father's cousin and often took his younger cousins along when he went hiking. For Esther's family he became a central reassuring figure, helping them find ways to settle in. "He was the model," Esther says. "He showed us you could leave everything behind, swallow your pride, move on."

This theme and its variations have been associated with Jews since ancient times, as has the idea that the hostility that followed them wherever they settled inspired an enormous adaptive capacity, which the historian Paul Johnson, among others, attributed to the need to figure out modes of survival in ever-changing circumstances. Certainly since the advent of the industrial age and in post-industrial times, the capacity to adapt and change has been a crucial survival skill. Some years ago, the Berkeley history professor Yuri Slezkine went so far in his provocative and over-the-top *The Jewish Century* as to argue that the Jews (along with other groups who are also good at adapting—he mentions Indian traders in East Africa, Irish tinkers, and Chinese businessmen in Indonesia) even *define* modernity because "modernization is about everyone becoming urban, mobile, literate, fastidious and occupationally flexible." This perspective stands in distinct contrast, of course, to the centuries-old cultural prejudice against Jews as rapacious, threatening vagabonds.

The difference for Zionists was that now they were on a path toward creating their own national home, though one whose dimensions and viability would continue to be repeatedly redefined.

The 1917 Balfour Declaration was an outgrowth of the post–World War I British and French carve-up of the Ottoman caliphate in the Middle East (itself sketched out by the secret, sphere-of-influence-creating 1916 Sykes-Picot Agreement, which it is tempting to visualize as the handiwork of a desiccated grande dame in an old, once-elegant dress, cutting up a map of the Middle East with long, spidery fingers). Thanks to the declaration, the French acquired Syria and Lebanon and the British Palestine, and it established in principle the Jews' right to a national home. In its lordly colonial manner, the Balfour Declaration, as Arthur Koestler wrote in the late 1940s, was a document in which "one nation solemnly promised to give to a second nation the country of a third nation."

A more passionate condemnation was offered by Edward Said. It was, Said writes in *The Question of Palestine*, "made (a) by a European power, (b) about a non-European territory, (c) in flat disregard of both the presence and wishes of the native majority resident in that territory, and (d) it took the form of a promise about this same territory to another foreign group, so that this foreign group might, quite literally, *make* this territory a national home for the Jewish people." Long-standing interpretations of the reasons behind the Balfour Declaration (issued by Prime Minister Lloyd George's government) emphasize the Christian beliefs and biblical romanticism of certain pockets of the British government, and it is beyond dispute that philo-Semitism was a key component for British cabinet ministers Arthur James Balfour, Lord Milner, Robert Cecil, and Jan Smuts. But the journalist and historian Tom Segev has argued that a contrary element also played an important role and that support for the declaration had far less to do with Lloyd George's (or his cabinet's) religious beliefs or a friendly attitude toward the Jews than with an exaggerated and basically anti-Semitic notion of the Jews' immense power in the world. Jewish world power at that point was, in fact, practically nil.

Thus encouraged, between 1919 and 1923, 35,000 Jews immigrated to the country; 80,000 more arrived between 1924 and 1928; and 250,000 poured in between 1929 and 1939 as the European situation became more dire. But despite the dogged endeavors and diplomatic skills of Zionist leaders like Chaim Weizman and David Ben-Gurion, the reality and viability of that national home was far from secure. The Balfour Declaration promised a home for the Jews, but it did not promise a state. Much depended on the predisposition of whatever British government was in power over the decades, as well as other ever-changing political considerations.

The Arabs in Palestine were understandably furious about what they considered a rapacious tide of new colonial intruders in their land and rejected all blueprints for dividing it up. They rejected the Balfour Declaration, which had only the vaguest assertions of protection of Arab rights, and in one grand gesture gave majority power to a minority population. And they rejected all blueprints that followed it: the Peel Commission's plan for partition (1937), which took Arab rights into greater consideration but would also have caused the transfer of hundreds of thousands, as well as the White Paper of 1939, a nearly complete disavowal of Balfour policy. Clearly reflecting major reconsideration of the official British line in London, the White Paper severely curbed Jewish land purchases as well as immigration despite the ugly turn of events in Europe, and it further promised Arab independence within a decade.

Until World War II, when Haj Amin al-Husseini threw his lot in with the Axis and even traveled to Berlin in the vain hope of enlisting Nazi support for his nationalistic aspirations, the British treatment of Arabs and Jews oscillated toward one or the other's interests, though the Jews definitely profited more from British help. This reflected attitudes that indeed grew out of romantic biblical religious notions of various British leaders as well as their anti-Arab biases. Officials in Palestine, historians have noticed, tended to be more pro-Arab than those making policy in London. The fluctuations, rumors, and vacillations of British policy then and the subsequent vagaries of US policy would contribute mightily to the history of what the Middle East policy scholar Aaron David Miller has so aptly characterized in his book as "The Much Too Promised Land."

Earlier Western travelers were by and large put off by the place, and it's hard not to agree with the Palestinians who have observed that the land most Western travelers describe in their writings is something of a chimera, or, as Raja Shehadeh puts it, not "a land familiar to me but rather a land of these travelers' imaginations"—often, their biblical imaginations. Mostly, even when they credit it with lofty spiritual significance, they do not like it. Shehadeh mentions, among others, the travel writings of Thackeray and Twain. Thackeray, in *Notes of a Journey from Cornhill to Grand Cairo* (1846), writes, "There is not a spot at which you look but some violent deed has been done there: Some massacre has been committed, some victim has been murdered, some idol has been worshiped with bloody and dreadful rites." Likewise, Mark Twain in *The Innocents Abroad* (1869): "Palestine is desolate and unlovely. . . . Palestine is no more of this work-day world. It is sacred to poetry and tradition—it is a dream-land."

By the time World War II came along, the gradual apprehension of the enormity of what was transpiring in Europe, coupled with a cumulative disgust with the confused contradictions of British policies, had transformed the Zionist idea of a national home into something quite different. The Jewish community in Palestine now had one overriding goal: sovereign statehood. And the underground paramilitary force, the Haganah, and its more militaristic offshoots, the

Irgun and the Stern Gang, were charged with far broader aims. Some thirty thousand Palestinian Jews fought alongside the British in the European war, giving them invaluable skills in their own future war for independence. But the 1939 White Paper restricting Jewish immigration to Palestine, which the British, in the midst of the war and worried about antagonizing the huge Arab population of the Middle East, threw as a sop to the Arabs of Palestine, had convinced Ben-Gurion, then the chairman of the Jewish Agency (the pre-state arm of the World Zionist Organization) and later Israel's first prime minister and minister of defense, that the British were trying to sabotage the Zionist project.

More than anyone it was Ben-Gurion, a revolutionary leader and statesman, who transformed Herzl's vision into a visible reality and plan of action. He set himself the task of leading the Zionist masses away from their focus on sacred texts, partisan ideologies, Holocaust trauma, and refugee problems so that they could apply their energies as a community to the military, social, political, and economic issues and actions that were so urgent and central to the establishment of a modern state, and he largely succeeded. A concerted effort was made after the White Paper's publication to oppose the British with determination and force. The doubleness of the Zionist position was best summed up in Ben-Gurion's much quoted remark, "We shall fight the war against Hitler as if there were no White Paper, and we shall fight the White Paper as if there were no war." Because his mother worked at the Tel Aviv Museum of Art, Ruth's future husband, Yaron Ezrahi, then eight years old, was present on May 14, 1948, when one of its rooms was chosen as the site for Ben-Gurion to formally declare Israel a state. It was a thrilling moment, but Yaron could not help but notice that, young as he was, he was nearly as tall as the Father of the Nation.

CHAPTER 4

IN AND OUT OF WAR

As the 1948 war went on, Abdallah's family had only the vaguest sense of the scope of the devastation being visited upon villages like theirs throughout the country, devastation that Walid Khalidi and his team—including some Israelis—would so scrupulously document. "We kept hearing rumors from different people about certain villages being leveled," Abdallah told me one evening not long after he'd spent another few days in the hospital with problems related to his diabetes. "But," he continued, "we didn't know if they were true, and we had nobody to ask about them. *Yani* [that is to say], as much as anything else, that was what frightened us." He was wearing his white knitted cap and long robe over pajamas—more or less his standard outfit in those days of convalescence. He did not look well. As on previous visits, Sana, her cheeks flushed from her ministrations over the stove, brought us delicious Turkish coffee and a bowl of fresh fruit. A few minutes later she reappeared with a plate full of shredded wheat pastries and for me another plate piled with watermelon.

I braced myself. The family's prodigious hospitality begot responsibilities. If you didn't finish eating whatever was placed in front of you, I'd learned from earlier visits, the assumption seemed to be not that you were inadequate to the great mountain of food you'd been offered but that it was somehow not to your liking, and very soon a substitute mountain would appear. This, I soon discovered, was a lose-lose situation. Though I soldiered through more delicious offerings than I thought myself capable of, there often was—did I imagine it?—a little look of disappointment cast my way, like the one Sana shot me that day, folding her hands in front of her apron and remarking as she sailed back into her domain, "Not much appetite today?"

After the war ended, Abdallah told me, Lifta was one of the rare

Palestinian villages with some of its buildings left partially intact, though most of their roofs were destroyed to discourage residents from returning. Nonetheless, 395 of its 450 houses were demolished, particularly those in which nationalist fighters lived—they were immediately blown up. And it did surprise people, Abdallah said, that the soldiers seemed somehow to know just where those houses were. The question of what would become of the villagers' lands had been a subject of debate for the Zionists well before the war. A 1940 diary entry of an official from the Jewish National Fund (JNF)—a still-powerful organization founded in 1901 to acquire and develop land for Jewish settlement—affords a good sense of the more uncompromising thinking about the subject. In a conversation he had with the JNF's land value and surveying engineer, who wanted to talk about how they were going to deal with land expropriated from the Arabs, the official wasn't reticent about discussing the goal of "transferring" the refugees. In his diary entry about the conversation, he was explicit: "It should be clear to us that there is no room in Palestine for these two peoples. . . . Without the Arabs, the land will become wide and spacious for us; with the Arabs, the land will remain sparse and cramped. . . . The only solution is Palestine, at least Western Palestine, without Arabs. There is no room for compromises."

By the end of May 1948, the same official wrote in his diary, after many thousands of Palestinians had fled their homes and lands, that their flight had created "a complete territorial revolution" and that the new state was "destined to expropriate their land." As the Jews began rapidly settling into the Palestinians' homes and news of widespread looting of the contents of other homes began to reach the outside world, there was an international public outcry. But it had little effect on the leaders of the new state. The first US ambassador to Israel, James McDonald (who was something of an expert on the subject of refugees, having served as the chairman of the US President's Advisory Committee on Political Refugees from 1938 to 1945), brought the matter up at a meeting with Israel's first president, Chaim Weizman, but Weizman reacted coldly: "What did the world do to prevent this genocide [the Holocaust]? Why now should there be such an excitement in the UN and the Western capitals about the plight of the Arab refugees?"

Even before the last of Abdallah's father's remaining farmland was confiscated after the 1967 Six-Day War, the number of cultivatable dunams left him after 1948 was already inadequate. He had worked for a while selling textiles in California and made more money there than he was able to earn back home, but living apart from his large family seemed less viable as he got older. (He actually had two wives—Abdallah was the child of his second, who had been his brother's wife and as was the custom his father married her after his brother's death). As his sons grew older they pitched in to help support the family, but with so many mouths to feed—Abdallah had seven sisters and three brothers—money was still short. Abdallah was sent to a technical training school, which helped later on when he served in the Jordanian army and when he opened a car repair shop after he quit the army in 1967, disgusted with the military's inability to help his people. "I could see by the time I was in my twenties," he told me, returning to a subject he often revisited, "that education would be the only way for my own children not to be left behind and to fit into the modern world." Abdallah strongly encouraged his daughters no less than his sons to find a professional métier and to acquire as much education as they could, Niveen told me, and they did. Ruqaya had recently received her master's in Islamic history. Nisreen has a degree in social work and worked at the infamous Shuafat refugee camp, where she struggled valiantly to help hold together the lives of its residents and aid in their ongoing battles with poverty, overcrowding, domestic violence, underemployment, and despair—afflictions that only got worse as the years rolled on. Khawallah has a bachelor's degree in special education and was planning to get a master's soon; Sana had attended a business school; and Niveen has a master's degree in speech pathology. The many certificates and licenses that Niveen has had to acquire, earned via English and Hebrew exams, seemed neverending. I mostly saw Nisreen and Ruqaya on the fly, as they were often rushing to or from work or school, respectively.

Niveen's mother, Zaineb, has lively, rather searching eyes, a welcoming presence, and is usually dressed in a dark, beautifully embroidered *thobe* (or traditional long robe) both inside and outside her home. She was born in Lifta the same year as her husband—1935—and, like him, was thirteen when her family was forced to leave.

Zaineb, too, suffered from diabetes and has hearing problems, but she was in better shape than her sister Fatima, who looked paler and even thinner the second time I saw her. She was continuing to convalesce at her sister's house. Zaineb was extremely solicitous of Fatima, bringing her small plates of fruit and trying to make her comfortable with extra pillows. No matter how ill she felt, however, Fatima always wore a beautiful silk hijab and cut an elegant if fragile figure. Zaineb is unsure of the exact date of her birth, as most family documents, photographs, furniture, keepsakes, and family treasures were left behind when her family fled Lifta in 1948, but in any case, she said, Palestinians of her parents' generation often didn't register births (nor were birthdays celebrated in the Western way, although this has changed in recent decades). Unlike the Abuleils, her family—the Odehs—had nowhere to go in 1948 and no option other than to join the more than seven hundred thousand other Palestinians—about half the total Arab population of the country—who became refugees. Various members of the large Odeh clan went to Jordan, to Lebanon, and the United States.

In general, the wealthier urban-dwelling Palestinians found refuge in the nearby Arab cities of Beirut and Cairo. They left behind houses filled with costly furniture as well as factories, warehouses, shops, and financial assets held in local safe deposit boxes, hoping that their new homes were just temporary sanctuaries from the exigencies of war. Zaineb's immediate family, including her father's brother and his family and her grandparents, with more limited resources, fled to Ramallah together. Her memory of the departure is made up chiefly of confused images of women crying and men staring grimly at the passing landscape. The more well-to-do middle-class tradesmen and bureaucrats from Jerusalem and other cities were sometimes able to find satisfactory housing in Ramallah, but most families, like hers, were packed into tent camps in the eastern part of the city. (More than four million Palestinians, descended patrilineally from the original 1948 refugees, still live in camps today.) Eighteen Odehs struggled to adjust to their new, rootless, cramped way of living. Sometimes, in late-night conversations, the men talked about trying to recover some of their belongings from Lifta, but they were discouraged from doing so when word reached them that people had been killed attempting to return to their homes. Every member of the family I talked with who lived through that time remembers it as shattering. "There was a huge shortage of food to eat and we shared terrible, frightened feelings about what the future might hold," Zaineb said. "We kept waiting for the grownups to fix everything," she added, "but they couldn't." Like Abdallah's father, Zaineb's was unable to find enough work to support his family. He'd earned a living as a farmer and stonecutter, but there were few jobs available in Ramallah.

He tried and failed to sell textiles and small goods in a storefront, but eventually he, too, was forced to leave. He found work in the United States. For over a decade he would remain mostly separated from his family, sending money home steadily and making occasional visits. He even acquired a green card. After a while the Odehs were able to move to a modest house. Zaineb grew up alongside three sisters and a brother (now deceased), and both her grandfather and uncle, who were left in charge of them, were extremely conservative about the girls' upbringing. For a long time, like many of the other refugees, they kept hoping that somehow a miracle might restore them to their old homes and lives. But after a while the reality of their new circumstance began to sink in. After the new state of Israel was officially declared, it was not uncommon for it to be referred to as "the unlawful entity" or "the alleged state of Israel."

On one of his home visits, Zaineb's father plucked away his only son, Mustapha, and brought him back to Michigan. The father had settled in Detroit after finding a job as a baker. Mustapha attended US schools, studied psychology in college, taught it as a lecturer for a while, and went on to open a restaurant in Jackson, Michigan. The girls' education wasn't considered important or even necessary. About the particulars of their father's life in America, his daughters know next to nothing, just as Abdallah's father conveyed little to his family about his life in America. As far as they were concerned, it was a tragic circumstance to be separated from your family, particularly from your father, and the less said about it the better. The young Odeh girls continued to live a strictly supervised, closed-in life with their mother, whom Zaineb describes as an increasingly sad, remote figure, "always weeping." Her mother could neither read nor write, a not unusual phenomenon in that era when the literacy rate for women in

Palestine was 3.3 percent. The bias in favor of men is apparent in their 25.5 percent literacy rate in the same period. But this disheartening fact—especially considering all the young women who needed to find fresh ways to survive in such blasted circumstances—would change radically over the next decades. Today the literacy rate is 95.6 percent for women and 98.6 percent for men, and the Palestinians currently head the region in gender parity in education. But, as one UNESCO report puts it, despite the fact that Palestinian women are considered the best educated in the Arab world, their degree of education does not necessarily indicate a vast improvement in their social status.

Zaineb loved school. She was a bright, lively student whom her teachers doted on and thought showed excellent academic promise. Her grandfather took her out of school anyway before she turned fourteen. He expected her, as the oldest girl, to help around the house. And no one was able to persuade him to change his mind—it was the custom of the time and not considered particularly harsh. Zaineb and her sisters missed their father and seethed about their upbringing but mostly saw little they could do to change it. An exception was Rasmea, the second-oldest and most rebellious of them, who openly complained and rarely submitted quietly to the strictures imposed on her. When she asked her mother when her father was coming home, her mother answered, "When our land and home are returned to us. Meanwhile, he will remain in America." Rasmea became obsessed with this explanation and as a toddler repeatedly sought out people in the neighborhood to ask, "Where is America? Where is America?"

Travels with Fuad II

▶ Until 2000, Fuad worked as a waiter and at other jobs at Jerusalem's luxurious King David Hotel. He was so obviously competent that the management offered to send him to a Swiss hotelier school, but then the second Intifada broke out, and he began to feel uncomfortable in his role as "the good Arab," ministering to the needs of rich Israelis, so he quit. A Jerusalem taxi driver earns very little, but Fuad's education has been so limited that, like many Palestinians, few alternative professional avenues are open to him. In a less caged-in situation, he would probably be running his own small business or managing a thriving hotel. Despite his modest income, he somehow saved enough to buy a small parcel of land near his village where his two sons and daughter would have "a nice little green place to play," but the wall came along, cut directly through his property, and made it off limits. The land seizures for the wall have an especially diabolic feature. In order to justify the process for its always elastic security needs the government cited the law passed in the 1950s allowing the state to expropriate property abandoned by Arabs who fled the country during the 1948 war. Since the Security Fence separated Fuad's seized property from where he lived, he was now considered an "absentee landlord"—though his real-life nearby presence earned him a special and by now well-established, Kafka-esque designation: "Present-absentee."

Once Fuad was driving me back to Jerusalem with an elderly Palestinian woman I had gotten to know, who wanted to show me the crumbling remains of a house in Jericho. (She had spent a good part of her life fighting her brothers in court because they refused to allot her the 50 percent of their father's inheritance she was entitled to under Sharia law, and the house represented one of her few legal successes.) Upon our return, we were privy to an unfortunately not

uncommon example of Israeli-Palestinian civic encounters. Fuad
had slowed the car to point out several buildings on a street near
the Old City that had once housed a number of well-known East
Jerusalem businesses. In the waning late-afternoon light, the white
stone buildings had taken on a pinkish glow, and the passing throng
seemed to float by them. I caught a quick glance of a wonderful
pomegranate juice vendor, with his huge, elaborate, Rube Goldberg
brass dispenser slung over his chest. Fuad never stopped the car, only
slowed it, but we were immediately pulled over by an Israeli policeman (obviously working with a plainclothes partner, a Peter Lorre
look-alike, staring balefully at us from a parked car across the street)
who accused Fuad of stopping in a "no stopping" zone. As it turned
out, this charge was merely an opening sortie.

He proceeded to bait Fuad for nearly half an hour. He showed
no interest in the car's two passengers (the old woman and me—and
Fuad gave us a warning look that said, "Don't involve yourselves in
this"), and he proceeded to examine the car's every nut, bolt, nook,
and cranny, goading Fuad—an obvious attempt to get him to react
so he could upgrade a small, concocted infraction to something that
might allow him to throw Fuad in jail. Fuad carefully avoided getting
suckered into the policeman's game, and that apparently made the
policeman angrier. "Why are you doing this to me?" he asked at one
point; the policeman gave him a sharp look but answered only with
a smirk.

Both of them, of course, knew the answer. This scene was part
of an all too familiar pattern of harassment in East Jerusalem. Its
manifestations can be minor, like stopping a car for no apparent
reason and toying with the driver, or major, like denying requests for
house building permits and then tearing down houses because they'd
been built without permits. Or making it impossible to reunite
families. Or offering 1,761 tenders for new Israeli houses in East Jerusalem in 2008 while making concurrent official assurances to international mediators that the attempt to Judaize East Jerusalem would
cease. But major or minor, to the city's Arab population all these
maneuverings, policies, and sleights of hand plainly spell out an
unambiguous message: PERHAPS YOU'D RATHER LEAVE.

CHAPTER 5

A NEW COUNTRY

Who am I in this strange country? And what is my place here? are two vexing questions every disoriented immigrant must grapple with. Esther thought about both of them from the moment her feet touched Palestinian soil, and they would be pondered no less seriously by her daughter Ruth, though she was born in Israel, for much of the time she was growing up. Both experienced significant changes in the way they answered them. It was one thing for Zionists to say they were creating a new kind of Jew—unshackled, as Herzl envisioned, from subservience to a hostile dominant culture and the humiliations of anti-Semitism, de-ghettoized, and community minded—and quite another for people to transform themselves to accommodate the new program.

And by the late 1930s, when Esther's family, the Fraenkels, arrived, there *was* a program, spoken and unspoken: the achievement of the Sabra ideal. The word "Sabra" has evolved popularly to mean any native-born Israeli, but in its original sense it applied only to a small nucleus of people, perhaps a few hundred (with names almost certainly unknown today outside Israel), who came of age in the pre-state country. They were the children of the "pioneers" and personified the goal of *hagshama*, the realization or consummation of the Zionist mission. This passionate band created the template for the generations that followed, a template that Esther and her family at first had difficulty adjusting to. In his book *The Sabra*, the sociologist Oz Almog likens the sense that his generation had of themselves to promulgators of a new civil religion. Embodying the yearnings of their forebears, they considered it their personal destiny to create a new state—one that exalted not only agriculture but also other forms of manual labor (like road building and construction), all but deified the heroic soldier, and was openly contemptuous of the Diaspora

57

Jew as effete, constricted, and hopelessly egotistical. Beyond that, the Jews were a people in a hurry, as one former British official put it in a virtually self-parodying English way: "If after waiting for nearly two thousand years an impetuous people are suddenly informed that they may return home, they will arrive pardonably keyed-up to expectations of high immediacies."

The Jews who settled in Palestine even before the Sabra ideal coalesced tended to diverge radically from the model fantasized by Herzl and embodied in his utopian, German-Romantic buddy novel *Altneuland*, in which Arabs and Jews live amicably side-by-side (partly because the Arabs imagined by Herzl understand "the beneficent character of the Jewish immigration"). For Herzl, who was secular, assimilated, and did not speak Hebrew, the idea of abandoning Europe was supplanted with that of creating a new Europe in another place and in an independent form—"an outpost of civilization as opposed to barbarism," as he writes in *The Jewish State*, "a rampart of Europe against Asia." In his vision all religions would enjoy freedom of worship, and the state's Arab citizens would have equal rights and be active participants on the country's political stage, but *Altneuland's* inattention to the reality of the Arabs' resentment and deep-seated fears about the plans of the Jews is one of its major flaws.

Another early Zionist and slightly older contemporary and rival of Herzl, Ahad Ha'am—whose name, at least for non-Israelis, has faded into the mists of history—believed that Europe and the baggage of the old model of the nation-state was a problem, not something to be preserved. Sometimes referred to as the founder of Cultural Zionism, Ha'am had a wholly different vision of what his people should be striving for in Palestine and was one of the few early travelers to the country who warned against the asymmetrical relationship of the Jewish settlers and the native population. Reacting to Herzl's portrait in *Altneuland* of the Arabs' smooth integration into what Herzl called the New Society, with no mention of their growing displacement from their land or the frustration and anger it engendered, Ahad Ha'am wrote in a scathing review of the book, "Peace and brotherly love reign between them and the Jews, who took nothing from them and gave them so much. A delightful idyll indeed." Ha'am was by no means centrally focused on this worm in the golden apple of Zionism, but from his first trip to Palestine in 1891 through all his many subsequent trips and after he settled permanently there in 1922, he consistently sounded warnings about it. His alarms became more substantive as he grew older, when it became painfully obvious to him that the relationship of the two peoples was a major problem. As early as 1891, when Jewish travelers to Palestine by and large tended to ignore the presence of the Arabs, Ha'am observed that most of the country's arable land was already being tilled by them, and, deploring the way he'd seen some settlers treat the Arabs, he urged his fellow Jews to behave with more respect. "Yet what do our brethren do in Palestine? Just the opposite. Serfs they were in the lands of the Diaspora. Now, as they suddenly find themselves enjoying unconstrained freedom, they become despots themselves. They treat the Arabs with hostility and cruelty, deprive them of their rights, offend them without cause and even boast of the deeds, and none among us oppose the despicable and dangerous trend."

Neither Herzl nor Ha'am lived to see the birth of the Jewish state (Herzl died in 1904, Ha'am in 1927), but Herzl labored throughout his later life in impassioned negotiations to bring it about. Ha'am, a cranky, reclusive, rather taciturn man, attended few international conferences, declined invitations to most public events, and rarely missed an opportunity to bitterly attack established Zionist leaders, especially Herzl. When World War II came along, its depredations and the Jews' desperate need for some haven tended to obscure the fine points of Zionist disagreement, just as they made irrelevant the vehement opposition of the orthodox rabbis to the establishment of a Jewish state *before* the advent of the messiah. Nonetheless, Ha'am's vision had an enduring effect on Jewish nationalism, so much so that Ernst Pawel's definitive biography of Ha'am's bête noir, Herzl—*The Labyrinth of Exile*—is somewhat subversively dedicated to "the spiritual heirs of Ahad Ha'am." Despite his worries about the relationship between the Jews and the Arabs, Ha'am envisioned Jews living *among* the Arabs, not separated from them, and creating communities based on the wisdom of Jewish teachings emphatically not religious in content but grounded in Jewish culture and traditions and in the binding ethical values of the past.

Herzl, in contrast, was an Anglophile, and he imagined the leaders of the new Jewish national homeland would be urbane, idealistic, secular "gentlemen." So firmly was a basically British model embedded in his mind that he insisted that the delegates to the first Zionist Congress show up in white tie, and they did, though many of them, especially those who came from eastern Europe, had never before encountered anything remotely like it. One of *Altneuland*'s characters, speaking to a cluster of villagers before an election, urges them to "hold fast to the things that have made us great: to liberality, tolerance, love of mankind"—a credo shared by both of Ruth's parents and, it seemed, their entire family, though initially its application to the Arab population occupied no place in their cosmology.

But if Herzl's ideal new Jew was modeled on the bourgeois world of western and central Europe and its emphasis on honor and respectability, and Ahad Ha'am's on secular, intellectual values that united liberalism and the moral and spiritual wisdom of Judaism, two additional and contrasting strains of thought made their way to Zionism's cultural table. One was the idea of the new Jew as a Nietzschean hero, creating his own history with his will and strength, more interested in power than in rationalism and daring to ignore conventional morality in favor of self-interest. The other was the socialist model in which individual destinies are subordinated to collectivist goals. In Israeli living rooms and university corridors, indeed throughout Israeli society itself, echoes of all four cultural strains are part of an ongoing national debate today, with different arguments offered for which strains dominate. The historian Anita Shapira in her excavation of this subject suggests that it is the last two.

In her first years in the country, Esther was a teenager. That posed the usual passel of identity challenges, which were only compounded by her having come from a culturally sophisticated religious family and the need to adjust to an unreligious society monumentally less focused on the fine points of a European education. Goethe—shmerta! As she strode along the steep streets to her school, Esther wondered who her friends would be. How would the young girls in shorts and shoulder-baring blouses ever be welcomed by her family? The cultural identity her family claimed as its own didn't serve them particularly well in their new milieu—though they had no interest in abandoning it. The Jewish organizations supporting the schools wanted their students to understand that they had a crucial role to play in building the new state, and the curricula reflected that. Plenty of religious people were naturally lapping up on the country's shores, but the dominant culture was secular. The ubiquitous youth movements that were proliferating were also mostly secular and even, it seemed to Esther, antireligious. In the clamorous Haifa public high school Esther attended, being religious, she told me, was considered behind the times, "an oddity . . . something that belonged to the gulag." Her long skirts and modest ways occasionally drew mocking remarks. Nonetheless, the one thing she was sure of was her religious identity. Over the years, I have thought about Esther and her relation to her religion, and about her progressive political views. (In the elder home she lived in, with the liberal *Haaretz* tucked under her arm as she sailed through the lobby, she had been known to draw disapproving glares from her fellow oldsters.) I came to believe that in her case—unlike those of too many religious nationalists—the closely held, old-fashioned moral grounding of religious belief, coupled with her strong sense of justice, shielded Esther from the excesses of supranationalism.

A lesson in instant democratic socialization came along with her new milieu. Her Munich schools, whatever else they were, had been elite institutions. In her new school, the father of one of her classmates was a mule driver, and even in her own religiously oriented youth group most of the young people were from Poland or other East European countries, and they too seemed totally unlike the people she had grown up with—"even in their religious behavior."

But Esther had to wrestle with another, far more insidious private struggle. After one late afternoon of extended conversation with me, with evening shadows darkening her apartment, Esther confessed that she'd had to work quite hard to come to terms with the degree to which her German education had subtly and damagingly infected her own thinking. The Nazified school that had caused her so much humiliation, she said, had in a way successfully pushed her to feel exactly as they wanted, pushed her "to a state of non-existence, nonhumanness." The ostracized girl mocked for her non-Aryanness had in some lasting way absorbed the racism leveled at her, taken it into her very core. Though she herself was dark-haired and brown-eyed,

for a long time, she said, "The first thing I thought when I saw someone was 'Has he blue eyes? Is he or she blond? Does he belong to
the European part of mankind?' There were many long years when
I had to fight with myself about this.... It seems impossible, even
laughable."

Oddly enough, the pointed divergence the pioneer generation
insisted on from earlier Diaspora models (the "over-timid Jews" who
burdened Herzl's thoughts) subtly encouraged a certain complement
to Esther's unwitting elevation of gentile looks. Over and over, Zionist writings of the 1930s described the Native Son—the wondrous
soldier-civilian or pioneer kibbutznik is rarely described in any terms
that aren't masculine—as robust, self-confident, and full of virile energy. Even allowing for the generally healthy environment of farm
and orchard life and an educational system that emphasized outdoor
activities and sports, these depictions have a decidedly strong bias in
favor of a kind of gentile Jew. No longer admired were the sort of
children who were all around Esther when she was growing up, the
German equivalent of the pale Russian striplings Isaac Babel wrote
so empathetically about, who saw the sun only when they crossed the
street for their violin lessons.

In essays and manifestos, it became clear that just as with other
nineteenth-century nationalist movements, it was not only the body
politic that the Zionists wanted to transform but the physical body. As
early as 1917 they were rejecting what they considered the degenerated
body of the fathers. One Zionist handbook for youth guides portrays
the ideal "new" Zionist youth "as a young, muscular strong-willed Jew,
who thinks like a normal, healthy person, does not debate endlessly or
utter foolish witticisms, is disciplined and obedient with an idealistic
world view, who loves everything fair and beautiful." With its peculiar
admixture of Gilbert and Sullivan and Zarathustrian will-worship,
the handbook's message would become all too familiar in Zionist literature's popular representations. Public notices and posters of the
next decade would feature slim, handsome, straight-nosed, beardless
men bearing a striking resemblance to the figures in Soviet popular
representations. They look different in every way from the stereotype
of the sallow, servile Jew so familiar from anti-Semitic literature. In
1933 one intoxicated Jewish author approvingly commented, "Your

first glance when you meet a young native-born man will reveal a flourishing, muscular, tall body. The hunched back and bent gait that many scholars have identified as almost racial trademarks seem to have vanished, and the anxiety and fear of the 'gentiles' and the feeling of inadequacy and inferiority that were the lot of the young Jew in the Diaspora seem to have been pulled out by the roots." *Many scholars?*

The early nonreligious Israeli youth groups shared with the religious ones a nationalistic ideology focused on joining a kibbutz and building up the country. And Esther couldn't wait to join one. But before she would be allowed to join her own religious youth group, she needed to convalesce. For a long time after her arrival from Europe she had been ill, with a mysterious extreme fatigue, and was advised to remain in bed. Her mother brought her German classics to read, and she remembers the period, in which she sipped lemonade and devoured book after book, as being one of tremendous relief. As she recalled that time, I had a vivid picture of Munich Esther shedding the chrysalis of her European skin and becoming new Esther with Old World markings. Religious youth groups like the one she eventually joined were somewhat less focused on the glories and tantalizing radicalness of kibbutz life, but she nonetheless longed to work on one and would do so twice. Once in her youth, via the Center for National Service, which dispatched her to pick grapes on a kibbutz near Rehoboth, about twelve miles from Tel Aviv, and later, when she was married and the mother of three, she worked on a kibbutz when Eliezar left Israel temporarily to study at Teachers College at Columbia. At that second kibbutz in a village in the southwest of the country, she taught English.

Not long after World War II ended, Esther returned to Germany, to work at a displaced persons (DP) camp. When she told me about this, I was not a little incredulous. "I know, it sounds strange, but it seemed the right thing to do, to help the children who were so lost—they had nothing." She saw returning as a gesture of spiritual activism, and she did it with her parents' approval. Her daughter Nechama, younger than Ruth, believes that it was also a way to cope with survivor's guilt, which she believes colored her mother's entire life and contributed to the "heaviness" both daughters experienced in relation to their religious obligations.

Specifically, Esther had volunteered to work with children in Stuttgart who had ended up in the city's refugee camp. There were mothers in the group but no men—fathers were either missing or dead. On the way to the camp, waiting for several documents to clear, she worked for a few months with other refugee children outside Paris, and, as when I'd inquired about Eliezar's Italian tour, when I asked Esther if she'd made any attempt to seek, in any form, however diminished by war, *la vie Parisienne*, my question was met with a baffled stare. Once she arrived in Germany a not entirely unfamiliar mental disassociation overtook her, similar to that of her parents in the years leading to their departure from the country. What had happened in the past seemed strangely remote from her. Despite the ghostly, bombed-out buildings and terrible destruction everywhere, she was so focused on her mission in Stuttgart—to teach Hebrew to the children and try to ease their distress—that somehow, even as she knew that the tracks unspooling beneath the trains she rode were the same that sped so many to their deaths, she never allowed herself to think about it. This remained true, she maintained, for the entire time she worked in Germany—nearly two years. When, after Stuttgart, she taught for a while in Bavaria, in a town where her family had summered, it was no different, though she was disturbed that so little seemed to have ruffled the village's surface: "Everything was so like it had been. It was as if nothing had happened." It was the same even when she visited devastated Munich, her former mother ship (60 percent of which had been bombed). The place was being rebuilt along the same lines as its prewar grid, but it no longer held anything of the world of her childhood. "I don't know—I had no connection. I didn't feel it belonged to me."

"Even in your own neighborhood?"

"Yes, the same."

Walking around the bombed-out, once familiar streets, she felt little emotion until she came to the place where the city's main synagogue, destroyed early on by Hitler, had stood. A blacksmith was working near the site. He watched her as she circled around and around it, though what was there was only a patch of weeds and rubble.

"What are you looking for here?" he finally asked her. "What I'm looking for," she replied, "I'll never find." Remembering that moment more than sixty years later, Esther said, "That was the only place the full impact of what had happened reached me because that was the place ... of Jewish belonging, of the Jewish community—of Jewish life. Gone." As she continued to describe how at that moment the enormity of what had disappeared forever swept over her, it was plain to see, as Ruth's sister Nechama had suggested, that the shadows of survivor guilt would play a significant role in her life. (Decades later, it impelled her to attend the Jerusalem war crimes trial of Adolf Eichmann every single day.) From that time on, she went on to say, cultivation of a strong Jewish identity became even more central to her.

Esther continued to work in Germany over the years leading up to and during the 1948 war. Until then, her awareness of Arabs had been meager at best. So separate were the lives of her family and those of the Arab population that they might as well have lived on different planets. When her family first came to Palestine they had lived in a place called Zikhron Ya'akov, twenty-two miles south of Haifa. The town is at the southern end of the Carmel Mountains, overlooks the Mediterranean, and was idealistically designed by Baron Edmond de Rothschild toward the end of the nineteenth century (there was a space for farm tools behind every house). From time to time the family passed poor Arab villages on the way to the seaside, and then Esther would be struck by how different the houses looked, especially the Bedouin shelters, from European ones and wonder about the lives within. "There were a lot of dogs everywhere and the special scent of bread baking coming from their *tabuns*." But at that point for her family there was far more unknown about the lives of Arabs than known, which was true for the vast majority of the Jewish immigrants in Palestine. It remained true even when, a few years later, they moved to Haifa, a city shared by Jews (70,000) and Arabs (65,000). During the same years, when the country's leaders were making strategic plans that would shatter the Palestinian world, her family wanted to think there was "no problem. . . . They lived there, that's how it was. There was never a sense of responsibility for them or that we took something away from them."

"Did you ever revise your opinion?" I asked.

"Yes, entirely."

Before the 1948 war, Esther's father, struggling to find his financial footing, established a good relationship with a young Arab from
a nearby village who was teaching him Arabic, and he instructed his
children to be civil and greet any Arab they passed, but there were no
discussions as far as Esther knew about the general Palestinian situation. Her family viewed the attack against Jews in the Arab Revolt
of 1936–39 and the hostilities that followed as further rounds of cos-
mic treachery toward a barely surviving people—"something which
couldn't be, because it's our country." After all, there were international
documents to prove it. Legal, all of it. How, Esther wondered, when
the Jews were still so traumatized from their German experience,
"would anybody try to fight us? We've only just escaped from our terrible enemies." Her ready answer then was, "Somehow we have to live
with that. . . . It was part of Jewish history, Jewish life—that there is
always somebody who tries to kill Jews." For not a few Israelis, this is a
topic that still surfaces often—the historical chain of tribal injury that
stretches all the way back to the Pharaohs in a long unbroken line.

A people recently decimated and existing geographically in a
strange new region could well see all enemies in this light, and the
strategic decisions that created the country certainly did not make
the Israelis any new Arab friends. But to see history only in this way
(as Esther eventually did not) would engender disastrous repercus-
sions and, for its most cynical politicians, become the go-to explanation for acting in diplomatic bad faith. One way to look at what
Ruth's husband, Yaron, has characterized as Israeli's tendency toward
"ontological victimhood" would be to compare the Israeli body politic
not to the vaunted Sabra ideal but rather to a seriously injured person recovering from war wounds, hospitalized, still fearful, and with
the memory of pain still fresh. For such a person *nothing* beyond the
drawn curtain has any meaning, not even the idea that there could
be somebody else beyond it—another seriously injured patient, a
Palestinian.

Who would dispute the fact that there are two traumatized populations in the country? The Israelis have in many ways never fully
recovered from the depredations of the Holocaust, nor from their
many wars and two intifadas, and the Palestinians not only have not

recovered from the events of 1948 and 1967 but are also being traumatized anew by nighttime raids, violent clashes, more and more arrests, and the continuing loss of land. That the Arabs passing before
Esther's family on the road or in villages saw their country being over-
run by Jewish immigrants whose official pieces of paper and stamps
would nullify their pieces of paper and stamps and lived history was a
reality that was then nowhere on her family's radar.

Nor was the family aware of the methods employed by the pre-
state Jewish militias to ensure their strategic success. Historically, the
end of 1937 had brought about radically different tactics on the part
of the underground Jewish fighters. Earlier, various militant Jewish nationalists such as Avraham Stern (who, like Husseini, would
later try but fail to enlist support from the Nazis) carried out isolated attacks against the British. But 1937 ushered in a period of no-
holds-barred terrorist acts, at first against the British, then the Arabs.
Booby-trapped suitcases, the taking and whipping of British officers,
and, in one infamous case, the kidnapping and hanging of two British
NCOs whose bodies were then booby-trapped, were among the new
forms of attack.

It was "the advent," as Morris characterizes it in his book *Righteous Victims*,

> of Jewish terrorism.... Before, Arabs (and, less frequently,
> Jews) had sniped at cars and pedestrians and occasionally
> lobbed a grenade, often killing or injuring a few bystanders
> or passengers. Now, for the first time, massive bombs were
> placed in crowded Arab centers, and dozens of people were
> indiscriminately murdered and maimed—for the first time
> more or less matching the numbers of Jews murdered in the
> Arab pogroms and rioting of 1929 and 1936. This "innova-
> tion" soon found Arab imitators and became something of a
> "tradition"; during the coming decades Palestine's (and, later,
> Israel's) marketplaces, bus stations, movie theaters, and other
> public buildings became routine targets, lending a particu-
> larly brutal flavor to the conflict.

The Irgun bombs of 1937–38 sowed terror in the Arab

population and subsequently increased its casualties. . . . The
bombs do not appear in any way to have curtailed Arab terrorism, but they do appear to have helped persuade moderate Arabs of the need to resist Zionism and to support the
rebellion.

The two main radical paramilitary organizations, Lehi and the Irgun,
were formally disbanded on May 29 and on June 11, 1948, respectively,
but their ghosts hover over the acts of settler extremists.

At her DP camp in Germany, news of the war at home came to
Esther mostly via letters from her younger brothers, who were serving
as soldiers, and from her father, who at that point had been traveling to Switzerland to recover more of the money he'd parked there
and in the hope of reviving his woolen business through old Swiss
business contacts. From Esther's vantage point, as well as that of the
vast majority of new immigrants, the hostility of the Arab states and
their declared intention of occupying both the Arab and Jewish parts
of the country seemed to her like a possible new Holocaust in the
making. The more nuanced revelations of Morris and the other revisionist historians who, like him, worked with official archival Israeli
documents to uncover previously unknown facts about the war, especially about the strengths of the Jewish forces, were not published
until the late 1980s. What *was* known at the time of the war was that
Azzam Pasha, the Arab League's secretary-general, promised a massacre of the Jews to rival the Mongols' destruction of Baghdad in the
thirteenth century. And, Esther said, nobody knew whether the Arabs could make good on his threat. In the spring of 1948, one of her
brothers wrote Esther a letter in which he said, "All the people I loved
are no more." He was referring to friends who died in a famous wartime massacre in Kfar Etzion, a kibbutz south of Jerusalem where
127 Jews (sources differ about the exact figure) were brutally killed
by soldiers of the Arab Legion and irregular forces from Hebron and
surrounding villages. After receiving that letter and more describing
the carnage of the war and ferocity of the Arab attacks from her other
brothers, Esther wrote a note full of sisterly pride to her father, prais-
ing her brothers' valor. "I really must say that what your sons are doing now is so outstanding. They are fighting against wild elements."

But over the next decades, chiefly through reading, Esther slowly and painfully began to comprehend the enormity and breadth of what had happened from the Palestinian point of view—widespread expulsions, one-third of the seven hundred thousand Palestinian Arabs exiled more or less permanently to overcrowded refugee camps, and far more atrocities committed by Israeli troops than she'd had any idea of. But in the midst of war she knew none of this, and neither she nor anyone she knew were thinking about much else but how to recover from their own displacement and survive.

In that same period her father reluctantly acknowledged that he would never be able to restart his old business, and his health began to fail. For a while he tried his entrepreneurial hand at importing straw for mattresses and brooms, but that didn't pan out either. They were still better off than many people around them, but now Esther and her siblings were told that they each needed to contribute five pounds a week to the family. Their life in Palestine was certainly a far cry from the comfortable milieu in Munich they were used to, in which private nurses had been employed to care for the children, but they had arrived with so many household goods as well as extra shoes, medications, and books that their subsequent low expenses in Haifa were at first manageable. When her father succeeded in retrieving a bit more of his money from Switzerland, they drew on that for a while. So many of the European World War II refugees had arrived with larger resources than their predecessors that this wave of immigration—the fifth Aliyah ("Ascent"), as it was called—is sometimes referred to as "the bourgeois Aliyah." But in time the family's modest cushion was exhausted, and her father was adamantly opposed to accepting reparations from Germany (which had not yet actually happened, though it was soon to), even though his health was deteriorating. By the time Esther finally returned to Haifa from Germany, the war was over except for some fighting in Jerusalem.

But the Haifa Esther returned to was noticeably different from the one she'd left. Where, she asked her mother, had all the city's Arabs gone? Her mother told her that they had left. The mayor "asked them to stay," she said, "but they wouldn't. They all fled to Lebanon and Jordan." Esther accepted this explanation at face value as a logical outcome of war, though it left out entirely the bloody particulars

that led to Haifa's de-Arabization. The municipal authorities of the
city, the third largest in Palestine, with the largest deepwater port, did
indeed want peace, but the Haganah had other plans. In response to
the Arab protests over the UN Partition Plan's designation of Haifa
as part of the Jewish state, it broadcast terror messages in the Arab
neighborhoods, planted car bombs; and retaliated after an Arab riot
in an oil refinery. Forty-one Jewish workers had been killed and forty-
nine injured in the riot (itself a response to the bombing and deaths
of six Arab day workers standing in a crowd outside the refinery gate),
and the Palmach, an arm of the Haganah, retaliated by killing seventy men, women, and children of nearby Balad al-Shaykh, where
many refinery workers lived. The battle of Haifa, four months later
(also known as "Operation Passover Cleaning"), was the culmination
of those events, and, by the time it took place, 2,000 British subjects
had been evacuated and many Arab civic leaders and rich Arabs had
decamped, leaving the remaining Arab population feeling vulnerable
and abandoned. At the beginning of the war, 65,000 Arabs lived in
the city. At the end, only 3,566 remained. Many fled in boats in a
mass tableau of panic that might have been drawn from the pages of
Thucydides's *History of the Peloponnesian War*.

On April 22, 1948, the Haganah launched fresh attacks on the
Arab neighborhoods the evening after the commander of the British forces, having come to the end of his Mandate responsibilities,
informed both the Jews and Arabs that he was evacuating his troops
except for a small detachment at the harbor and at a few roads needed
for the withdrawal of other personnel later on. In less than a day the
better trained, better equipped, numerically superior forces of the
Haganah pummeled the Arab population with mortars and machine
guns and took the city. Many decades later, *Haaretz*, drawing on an
account published in 1978 by Israel's Ministry of Defense, filled in
the picture of the episode. When the fate of the Arab population
still seemed unclear, its leaders, using loudspeakers, told everyone to
gather in the market square.

> Upon receiving the report, an order was given to the com-
> mander of the auxiliary weapons company ... and they
> opened up on the market square [where there was] a great

crowd. When the shelling started and shells fell into [the crowd], a great panic took hold. The multitude burst into the port, pushed aside the policemen, stormed the boats and began fleeing the town. Throughout the day the mortars continued to shell the city … and the panic that seized the enemy became a rout.

It has been well established that at the time of the market assault, the city's Arab representatives were holding what were regarded as fruitful negotiations with the city's Jewish leaders about terms for a ceasefire. The Jewish mayor mentioned by Esther's mother, Shabtai Levy, believed that Arabs and Jews could coexist in the way mandated by the UN Partition Plan, and he urged the Arabs to surrender and accept decent terms for remaining in the city. (The Fraenkels kept inside their apartment during this time. Word of the negotiations reached the family, but not until long after the fighting ended did they hear about the Arab side of the battle.) The Arabs were in the process of considering the ceasefire terms when the Haganah, marching to its own drummer, began the shelling of the people standing in the market square—a crowd that included women and children. At that point, the soldiers of the Arab Legion and some Iraqi volunteers had already begun to leave the city, and at Arab military headquarters nobody was answering the phone. An article published that day by Ezriel Carlebach (editor in chief of the newspaper *Ma'ariv*) supplies a likely explanation for the Haganah's willful disregard of the ceasefire negotiations. Stressing Haifa's strategic importance, Carlebach wrote: "At this moment we are fighting for Haifa, which means we are fighting for the state. . . . If Haifa is in our hands both the oil magnates and the naval strategists, both Whitehall and Wall Street and also Washington, will have to take us into account." Translated into less grandiose terms, the Haganah wanted to ensure its complete control of the city, which besides being the country's largest deepwater port was also the terminal for the Mosul–Haifa oil pipeline, and they wanted to feel confident that both would remain open to receive armaments and other supplies. The result of this campaign of realpolitik was what Esther had been so surprised to discover—that only a fraction of the old Arab population was left in the city.

In 1950, Esther moved to Jerusalem to study at a religiously oriented teachers college. It was there, where Eliezar was also living and working, that a romance bloomed between them. They had already met briefly a year before, so they knew each other slightly. At that point, Eliezar was the principal of a local elementary school, and later on he held that same position at a teachers college. They married in 1951, and, because apartments were scarce and they had so little money, they moved in with his parents. The fledgling country was pitied by its citizens for its insufficiencies—but empathetically. As Esther put it, "it had so many problems. Jews from all over the world who couldn't integrate into the society.... In so many places there were no houses, no towns, no villages, no streets, and in many places no electricity, and food was in short supply. These things were never mentioned in the Zionist pamphlets, but we understood that it was a young country, and we felt it was bound to get better."

After Esther's father died, in 1951, the family's circumstances became even more difficult and remained that way until the last part of the decade. At that point Esther's mother decided to accept reparations from Germany. The extra money, which amounted to some $700 monthly for each family member, improved their lives considerably, and in 1960 Eliezar and Esther were finally able to buy their own apartment in the pleasant neighborhood of Rehavia, where Ruth and her brothers and sister grew up—a neighborhood that had become home to so many German Jews that it was dubbed Neue Berlin.

CHAPTER 6

OCCUPIED

As Zaineb and Abdallah's youngest child, Niveen is in a way the most removed from the Lifta that was, but like all the members of her close-knit family she continues to feel a connection to the pre-Nakba place of family memory and to what's left of the actual site, the shade of Lifta—a mere fifteen-minute drive from the Abuleils' house on George Adam Smith Street. One hot summer afternoon she and I, accompanied by an elderly neighbor with a keen memory, tramped around Lifta's overgrown, steeply terraced remains, scattered around a wadi below a modern highway. As the afternoon went on and the already scorching heat grew more intense, I was glad to be wearing a light summer dress, though neither Niveen nor her neighbor, who were covered head to foot in dark, heavy cloth, seemed to be uncomfortable. Half- or fully destroyed houses were all around us, but there were also some mostly intact ones. The Abuleils' former home was among the mostly destroyed ones. Far above us, cars barreled along the route to Tel Aviv that had been so fiercely contested during the 1948 war. The incline was uneven and weedy. We moved slowly to accommodate the neighbor.

As we circumnavigated the remains of the village's crumbling structures, including a fair number of large, impressive, thick-walled houses with their roofs lopped off, Niveen summoned without difficulty the names of many of the houses' inhabitants and their subsequent histories. Her tone was matter-of-fact as she spoke about the lives she'd heard so much about and the world that had flourished there before everyone fled, and there was something akin in it to the manner in which young people in houses of worship recited the drilled-in, repeated words of familiar prayers. The neighbor's recollections had a far rosier hue. Unlike Niveen, a child of the memories of Lifta, the neighbor, a petite woman with papery skin, was a survivor of the pre-war Lifta who had grown up before the Occupation. Listening to them and staring at the architectural devastation all around and at the unloved, weedy patches, I thought about a passage from the poet Mourid Barghouti's clear-eyed memoir of exile, *I Saw Ramallah*. As he contemplated a site of his childhood, he asked: "What is so special about it except that we have lost it? . . . Our song is not for some sacred thing of the past but for our current self-respect that is violated anew every day by the Occupation." Niveen, unlike her neighbor, was looking at an *idea* of the past—though one that over the years had coalesced into a vivid picture.

Few issues are more emotionally loaded for Palestinians than that of the right of return. And it is still commonplace for many of them to express the wish or hope that one day they will be back in the places they came from. But, surprisingly, a survey conducted in 2003 by the Ramallah-based Palestinian Center for Policy and Survey Research found that while more than 95 percent of the 4,500 refugee families polled wanted Israel to *recognize* the right of return, only a minority of them would actually exercise that right as part of a peace agreement. More than half said they would accept compensation and homes in the West Bank and Gaza or land Israel would give up in exchange for West Bank land. The Columbia University–trained political scientist and director of the center, Khalil Shikaki, was about to hold a news conference detailing the results of the regional survey and other matters when a Palestinian mob attacked him at work, and he was forced to lock himself in his office after he was shoved and pelted with eggs. He eventually emerged relatively unharmed from the melee but afterward said that the mob, which had brought along its own news releases testifying to the sacredness of the right of return, was putting government negotiators "on notice" that the right of return was non-negotiable.

Some claimed that the way the survey questions were framed had led to misleading answers. "What the survey showed," Shikaki told me when I visited him in his modern Ramallah office, "was that the refugees were less interested in being "nationalist standard bearers" than in finding solutions to the actual problems of their lives. Shikaki himself grew up in the bleak refugee camp of Rafah near the Egyptian border. He has rejected violence throughout his life although his older brother Fathi, who was assassinated in Malta by two Mossad agents, was the cofounder of the Islamic Jihad Movement in Palestine. About the results of the 2003 survey that so incensed the mob that attacked him, Shikaki told a *New York Times* reporter something that certainly seems to jibe with Niveen's attitudes: though some people clung tenaciously to their righteous ideological dreams, "refugees are human beings with needs. These people want to live their lives." The day I visited him, much of what we talked about was focused on the fading belief in the possibility of a peace agreement anytime soon and the bad faith of political leadership on both sides. I said that it was difficult to see how anyone in his position could hang on to hope.

It wasn't really hard, he answered: "Because what's the alternative?" Lifta's mosque and village club were left standing. Next to the mosque is an old cemetery partly overgrown with wild herbs and spiky grasses, and, in the hills above the wadi, orthodox settlers had built a community. The afternoon we were there Niveen watched in silence as a group of orthodox boys played near the village's famous spring. It's impossible to wander today over the steeply terraced village with its vestiges of old *tabuns*, cross-vault–arched passageways, courtyards, and ghostly, crumbling houses and not think about the lives lived in the place. This is not a "lost" and then centuries later "found" world like Herculaneum or Pompeii, or a monument to past glory like the Acropolis, or kitsch "living history," like colonial Williamsburg. It is history as an unhealed wound, a past that for exiles and non-exiles alike has not lost its presentness and occupies a mental space fired by longing and fantasy. Above all, like so much in Israel, it is a history that remains contested.

In recent years, a plan approved by the Jerusalem Municipality to tear down Lifta's remaining structures and build some 120 new luxury apartments on the site was invalidated by the courts. The plan was aggressively challenged by Israeli human rights groups and former Liftawis like Yaqub Odeh, Niveen's uncle, who would like the buildings left as a historical site. Throughout Israel, nearly half the former Arab villages—or whatever rubble remained of them after they were razed—182 of them, have been left inside the boundaries of the country's nature and recreation sites, and many were planted over by the Jewish National Fund. The signs in the parks focus on their Jewish or Zionist history and provide hiking landmarks, rarely mentioning anything about the Arab villages. Dedicated since its beginnings in the early days of the twentieth century to building the country by acquiring land for Jews and keeping it in Jewish hands in perpetuity, the JNF is associated worldwide with the country's afforestation, but to the Palestinians it represents the chief and insatiable gobbler of their lands. Its role did not come about by accident. As early as February 1948, even before Israel had become a state, Ben-Gurion told JNF leaders, "The war will give us the land. Concepts of 'ours' and 'not-ours' are peacetime concepts only, and they lose their meaning during war." Palestinians say that this thinking continued after the war ended, however. The court decision halting development plans did not comment on Lifta's possible future use, and Yaqub Odeh and his fellow challengers are far from confident that further maneuvers to push the plan forward will not be tried by the developer, but the Save Lifta defenders are prepared to stay the course and hope in the end to prevail.

In another country—in mine, for example—our parents' childhood home sites can elicit all sorts of feelings, but they rarely have the resonance they do here, where so much present history is bound with remnants of the past. Raja Shehadeh points out in *Palestinian Walks*, "In Palestine, every wadi, spring, hillock, escarpment, and cliff has a name, usually with a particular meaning. Some of the names are Arabic, others Canaanite or Aramaic, evidence of how ancient the land is and how it has been continuously inhabited over many centuries." But there is no careless sense of belonging to a place. The threat of the Lifta land being taken over by Israeli developers for expensive condos and a spa are a source of renewed distress for those attached to it, and a plan to build a tunnel that connects the land beneath the Lifta site to the Knesset has already been realized. "We cannot grumble about [Jerusalem] as people grumble about their tiresome capitals," Barghouti, whose family, he tells us, is possibly the largest in rural Palestine, writes. "Perhaps the worst thing about occupied cities is that their children cannot make fun of them," even though they live "in a time of historical and geographical farce." Some of the ex-inhabitants fighting the development plan have said that their protest binds them closer to the terra firma of Lifta. Were there some young people whose families came from Lifta who just didn't care about the issue? Undoubtedly. But I never met any.

Israel unilaterally claimed the Abuleils' Lifta property as "state land" under the Absentee Property Law of 1950. (If you don't live on your land, you forfeit the right to own it—the law applies even to those who have been forced to leave it.) But Niveen's neighbor's mental map still retained the property lines she had grown up with. We continued to walk around and at one point stopped at the mosque and looked again at the spring. The eye-shaped watering place was a hub of village life, the neighbor said, the place where women came to gossip and talk about their troubles. It wasn't difficult to imagine the Lifta the woman described or the weight of its loss to her. But Niveen, I had observed from the first days I spent with her, was rarely overtaken by nostalgia or regret, however much her life has been formed in its shallows. Her gaze was instead focused, you might say perhaps stubbornly focused, on the work she had to do to meet the requirements of her professional career and her family life.

I'd also noticed that Niveen was especially curious about the oddities of human behavior, even aberrant behavior. Ever since she had been a small girl, she said, she had been fascinated by the complexities of people's responses to the trials of everyday life—particularly strange psychological tics and behaviors—and she found it rewarding to teach children to cope with tough physical challenges, though this was demanding work. In a sense, she thought that their struggles put her own—especially the bleak political reality of Palestinians' day-to-day life—in perspective. Four days a week she works with Arab children who have special needs related to speech, working for an institution in the Israeli Jerusalem school system. Until a few years ago, when she quit, she'd also held a similar job in the Arab school system, in the West Bank, in Ramallah. She made her way there twice a week, on Saturday and Sunday, each time dreading the challenge of the Qalandia checkpoint, through which she had to pass.

Palestinians drive miles out of their way to avoid Qalandia, but Niveen didn't because it was the most convenient way to get from her home to her job—if things went well. Sometimes she drove her VW through the checkpoint. Sometimes she took a taxi up to it and then went through on foot. On the Israeli side, a big red sign warned that the checkpoint was the entrance to Area A, the zone run by the Palestinians and therefore forbidden to Israeli citizens, life-threatening and against Israeli law to enter. It was the return trip, however, that gave Niveen trouble. Coming the other way, from the West Bank, for anyone not in a vehicle there is an elaborate and challenging walkway. Besides being under surveillance, the pedestrian encounters stoplights, a metal barrier, and aggressive and often quite young and jittery Israeli soldiers, too many of whom treat the Palestinian multitudes, as Niveen put it bluntly, "like animals, subhumans." The passageway resembles nothing so much as the pre–Temple Grandin cattle conveyor tracks.

If you're driving through Qalandia from the West Bank into Jerusalem, as Niveen often did, you tend to move fitfully and with excruciating slowness in a long line of cars inching toward the checkpoint and its gaggle of helmeted soldiers holding M16s manning it. Sometimes the traffic moves along steadily, but more often it doesn't. People are challenged. Something is wrong with someone's papers. An hour or more can pass for those waiting in line. The sun is hot, or your air conditioning is too cold. Tempers fray. When you finally reach the checkpoint, you are stopped, your identity papers are checked, and the trunk of your car is scrutinized—not just for bombs but for a complicated list of proscribed foods, including dairy products, that cannot be brought back to the other side. When you are at last waved forward, a mad rush of cars endeavoring to jockey their way to a better lane position ensues. According to the human rights organization B'Tselem, there were in 2017 thirty-nine staffed military barrier checkpoints (of which Qalandia is one), fifty-nine fixed checkpoints in the West Bank, and many so-called flying checkpoints, which can pop up anywhere, anytime, often on major transportation routes at rush hour. As of 2017, the UN Office for the Coordination of Humanitarian Affairs counted some 2,941 flying checkpoints. For Palestinians trying to move around, these obstacles are an ongoing source of frustration that is compounded by the policy that prohibits them from driving along sixty kilometers of forbidden or partially forbidden settler roads. Presenting yet more obstacles are the ubiquitous physical obstructions such as dirt piles, concrete barriers, and trenches that block access to and from numerous towns and villages, causing major problems for the old and sick. No one on either side of the conflict was surprised when, in the 2015 uptick of violence, the checkpoints became flashpoints.

If you are unlucky enough to live in the West Bank, and Niveen knew and was related to many people who did, a complicated permit system that varies from locale to locale further constrains your movements, and whether you are headed toward a university exam, a business meeting, or a construction job, this puts you at risk of being turned back at a checkpoint. More than once when I showed up for an Israeli-Palestinian panel discussion in Jerusalem, the Palestinian speaker never appeared because of "checkpoint difficulties." The first time this happened the speaker was supposed to be Yasser Abed Rabbo, the former secretary general of the PLO, someone with international status. This apparently happens so often that some panel discussion and lecture administrators maintain a B-plan, with understudies ready to spring forth from the wings. Even if your work takes you there daily, special permits are required for traveling to the "closed" land between the Green Line and the West Bank, to the Jordan Valley, and, of course, to the settlements—which most often employ West Bank Arabs to build their unwelcome houses. In earlier times, Palestinians worked as nannies and home health aides, but the intifadas brought that era to an end, and Filipino workers eventually replaced them. Nowadays, with some notable exceptions, construction sites, shopping malls, university classrooms, and taxis are pretty much the only places—not counting checkpoints and clashes with the army—where Palestinians and Israelis mingle, a reality that only reinforces their separateness.

Every week, according to a 2018 report of the Bank of Israel, 121,000 Palestinians leave their houses in the West Bank to go through the checkpoint process and work in Israel; 64,300 have permits, and the remaining 42,400 work in Israel illegally. The average daily wage in Israel for Palestinian workers is $66.20, more than double what they could make in the West Bank, and because of low wages and the lack of job opportunities, the checkpoints remain crowded except when the violence level is extreme, and then Palestinian workers are forbidden from entering. Since the end of the second Intifada there has been a diminution of bombings and Israeli peak of fatalities that were their main raison d'être. Nonetheless, between 2000 and 2007, there were thirty-five infant deaths and five maternal deaths at checkpoints. For the anthropologist and painter Ali Qleibo (whose family has lived in Jerusalem for eight centuries), writing in the locally distributed publication *This Week in Palestine*, the checkpoint experience is a relentless reminder of the Occupation. "At the checkpoint nothing moves. Along with the sense of entrapment, the feelings of aggravation and tension escalate. You are stuck going nowhere. Life feels like a traffic jam. . . . You cannot steer your car and you cannot steer your life."

The weekly grimness of Qalandia played such havoc with Niveen's nerves that she eventually decided the Ramallah job wasn't worth it. Her usual route to that job took her from her family's house on French Hill to the Israeli side of the checkpoint, and from there to Ramallah, on the Palestinian side. It was most convenient for her to drive, but her salary barely paid for the gas. She might have considered holding on to the job, Niveen told me, since like all young professionals she wanted to beef up her résumé, but her demoralizing experiences at the checkpoint had accumulated in her mind enough to convince her to quit. On the days she was scheduled to work in Ramallah, Niveen found herself waking up in the morning and dreading what was ahead. One encounter in particular haunted her. It happened during the second Intifada. Heading home from the West Bank, she had arrived at the checkpoint just as it was closing—there were five minutes to go before the six o'clock curfew. She hadn't driven that day and was planning to catch a cab ride home on the other side. To Niveen's dismay, the soldiers blocked her from the walkway and refused to let her pass. A sweet-faced young woman: why not relent? But soft compromise has no place here. Iron rules lock the soldiers' responses into predictable channels. Perhaps her abaya (long robe) was hiding a bomb. She pleaded with them in Hebrew to let her through. Her family, Niveen said, would be really worried if she didn't get home soon. And the (to her) authoritatively coupled words "family" and "worried" just bounced off the soldiers' helmets. Then the gruffest of the soldiers, using foul language, told her to hurry up and move on.

Darkness had already fallen, so she rushed along a temporary fence (this was before the far more impregnable "separation barrier" was built), hoping to find a hole she could crawl through or to run into someone who could help her get to another checkpoint that might stay open later. In the distance she saw several silhouettes, and soon a woman and a child and later a man materialized nearby. They had obviously run into the same problem. They nodded to one another but didn't speak. She heard shouting and what sounded like a gunshot not too far away. A light rain began to dampen her clothes. She thought she saw someone in the middle distance. Was it a figure falling to the ground? Had someone been shot? Would she be next? Her heart rattled against her chest. By then it had become so dark that she could barely see where she was going, and the temperature was dropping fast. A while later a car appeared out of nowhere, and the driver offered the little group a ride out of the West Bank—for a price. They all hastily agreed, and after she'd made it safely through another, smaller checkpoint, she ran along the road. Most of the little money she'd had in her wallet had gone to the driver, so a taxi wasn't a possibility, and she had to make her way to the nearest bus stop. When she finally arrived home, her family welcomed her with great relief—they *had* been worried. There was so much violence in that period, Zaineb told me, so many mass arrests, and so much use of administrative detention, that every Palestinian family worried when their children walked out the door.

———•———

Despite the obvious differences between twenty-first-century Israel and the twentieth-century, pre–civil rights movement, Jim Crow US South, the two are also similar, with one part of society moving along more or less successfully in its rigidly maintained "normal" way, the other under the boot of an unequal system codified by law and ratified by custom. When I first arrived in the country, I thought that a Jim Crow period comparison was more apt than the one the country's critics usually draw on, apartheid, because of the government's separate and unequal treatment of the Palestinians and the Bantustan-like refugee camps. Though they rarely mentioned them, the Abuleils had had to deal with the indignities of civil-rights-violating laws and customs all their lives. Even on the most visible level, municipal neglect, Palestinians are reminded daily of their low status by the inattention

paid to their environment. But in time, as the settler project became
more ferocious and was openly supported by a hard-right government,
the term "apartheid" began to seem more and more apt—though it
was challenged from the start by many Israelis as a misguided ap-
propriation of a state of affairs belonging to a specific place and time.
In recent years, a chorus of conservative voices, including that of the
prime minister of Britain, has even claimed that its usage was a form
of anti-Semitism.

———•———

A penetrating view of checkpoint reality was offered to me by Nazmi
Jubeh, a good-humored, urbane, German-educated professor of archaeology and history at Birzeit University. Jubeh is former codirec-
tor of RIWAQ, the Center for Architectural Conservation, which is
charged with protecting Palestinian architectural heritage sites, a task
that must have required nerves of steel in a place where nearly every grain of sand is contested. In 1991 Jubeh worked alongside Israeli
peace negotiators at the Madrid Conference, and in 2003 he labored
on the Geneva Initiative Peace Agreement, efforts that earned him
respect from leftists on both sides but angry reactions from certain
Palestinian quarters where he was accused of collaborating. Had he
been threatened physically? I asked. Such threats and actual attacks
are not uncommon. He laughed. "I am from a very, very large family.
Nobody will attack me. The Jubehs in Jerusalem and Hebron—and
this is just the men—number three thousand. I have an *army* behind
me, so, no, physically I was never attacked, but intellectually, in articles
and so on, yes."

In his youth, Jubeh was arrested several times—the first time,
when he was sixteen, for trying to establish a forbidden political organization, a student union; the second time for actually belonging
to another political organization; and the last time for reasons still
unknown to him. "I don't know [even] . . . now why. It was 1979. I was
released for a few weeks and then rearrested." Our conversation took
place in comfortable upholstered chairs over coffee in the lobby of the
popular Ambassador Hotel in Sheikh Jarrah. Christian tour groups,
in pastel and plaid, flocked in expectant clusters in and out of the entrance, and East Jerusalemites, mostly but not only men, chatted on a

terrace outside, many of them puffing contentedly away on narghiles, or, as they have been known in English since the seventeenth century, hubble-bubbles.

Of his confinement in prison, Jubeh told me, "We had a very tough time. I will not deny that sometimes I felt full of hatred for the Israelis. But even though surviving in prison was hard, it opened up important experiences in my life. The group of us who were young political prisoners, we were five tough young people; we were teaching the others to read and write. My character was shaped in there—those poor guys, with drug problems and all kinds of social problems—in some way my attachment to them shaped my future. And by the way, I was not an exception. According to Red Cross statistics, 70 percent of my generation has been arrested and jailed at least once.

"But," he added, "I lost my teenage years because, when I was released, everybody had to treat me like a national hero, a national leader, which I hated. I had to act like a mature, responsible adult, so I couldn't do any nonsense. I couldn't be a boy." When Jubeh told me a story later about one particular checkpoint experience he'd had with a young Israeli soldier, I was reminded of the toll the conflict exacted on the young. I was reminded of this again when he told me about his daughter, who was affected for years after she walked down her street to the local supermarket to buy candy after school one day when she was eleven, as she did every day, and was inside the store when a young Palestinian boy was shot and killed just outside the entrance. She saw everything. The boy had just come through a nearby checkpoint wearing a backpack, and the soldiers, speaking Hebrew, had told him to stop. But he couldn't understand them, so he'd kept on walking, and the soldiers shot him, and no one was allowed to offer him help until after the army had sent a robot to see what was inside the pack. By the time it was discovered that the backpack contained only schoolbooks and pencils, he was dead. Now, seven years later, her father said, his daughter still awakens with nightmares of the incident. "Really," he said, "we need a whole army of therapists to help our children."

One cold, rainy winter night some years before that incident, Jubeh was driving home late in the evening after a long day of work north of Ramallah, smoking and listening to a beautiful symphony on the car radio as he approached a checkpoint. He wasn't worried about trouble because he had the kind of VIP pass that smoothed his way through most official obstacles, including checkpoints. It was warm and comfortable inside the car, and it was around 10 p.m., the time that checkpoint closed. It was a small checkpoint with only one young soldier assigned to guard it. There was no line of cars approaching it, and, Jubeh told me, "I drove up to it slowly, slowly, and put off my lights—I am very well trained." When Jubeh rolled down his window he could see that the boy had obviously been standing out in the rain for some time, and he looked miserable. "He was very thin, perhaps eighteen or nineteen years old and totally soaked. Large raindrops trickled down his uniform." Jubeh showed him his permit and realized that the soldier was about the same age as his son Bashar. There was a beat of awkward silence between them as the boy examined the permit and glanced at the car. He carefully avoided eye contact with Jubeh.

"What are you doing here? Do you even know why you are doing this?" he was suddenly surprised to hear himself asking the boy in clear, good Hebrew. "Really," Jubeh said to me when he recalled that moment, "I was asking him which of us was more entrapped."

The young soldier didn't answer but gave Jubeh a hard, blank stare. "But I think he understood my question very well because there were tears in his eyes, and when he thrust my ID back at me he snapped, 'Sa! Sa!!' [Go, go]" Jubeh drove away and at first felt only anger. Then, about a third of a mile away from the checkpoint, he pulled over to the side of the road. "I also began to cry because, you know, this young man—I don't know from which family he comes, he has parents who probably can't sleep at night thinking about him. . . . The whole scene was a paradox. I am the Occupied, and I am sitting comfortably, and he is supposed to be my oppressor, standing with his M16 gun. He is supposed to be the hero, Rambo. . . . You could laugh at this scene, but to me it was a very killing moment. I am for sure the age of his father, and he's supposed to control me?"

Thus it was, he said, that he couldn't stop himself from weeping. No one other than Jubeh told me a story with quite the same elements, but it is all too comprehensible that someone would weep about the home truths of any conflict in which adversaries have come to think of the "other side"—as Simone Weil writes in her famous pacifist essay about *The Iliad*—solely as a *thing*: the enemy.

Whatever the Abuleils felt about the fact of the Occupation, it was always offering reminders of its presence. "It's like a low ceiling," one of their friends said to me. "You're always pressed up against it." In 1981, noxious gas was sprayed through the window of the Abuleils' first small house on French Hill. Niveen was only two at the time and has no recollection of the event, but Zaineb remembers it very well, and it still disturbs her, especially its seeming randomness. Zaineb's voice climbs northward whenever she gets excited or upset, and it rose nervously as she talked about the incident.

"This woman knocked on our door and, all smiles, asked if she could come in and see what kind of appliances we had and where everybody slept. She spoke Arabic and her Arabic was good. We thought she might have come from some other Arab country. We didn't want to be rude, so we invited her in. She looked around for quite a while and told us she was thinking about moving to the neighborhood. She examined our appliances but seemed to be particularly curious about the windows. Then she left. Whoever had been there agreed it had been a strange visit, but we didn't think too much about it until a few days later." Recalling the woman's odd way of completely ignoring the people in the room, Zaineb shook her head and continued. "Then, in the middle of the night, when the whole family was asleep, there was a lot of noise, and someone forced open a window and sprayed some horrible gas into the house. We were all coughing, and our eyes were tearing, and we had to run outside. There was a hideous smell, and we needed to get away from it. Sana was especially badly affected and had to be taken in an ambulance to the hospital." She had adjusted to many hard things, Zaineb went on to say—"This is life." But she had never before had the feeling that the inside of her own house was unsafe, and it unnerved her.

The *Jerusalem Post* ran a brief story about the incident, along with a picture of the family standing disconsolately in front of the house. An investigation, the article said, was being initiated, but the identity of the culprits was never discovered.

The family disapproved of violence and went about their everyday lives concentrating on living as rewardingly as they could, but the rumble of the conflict reached them in a thousand different ways. It seeped into their consciousness via newspaper reports, the internet, TV, and the conversation of friends and general word of mouth, making it impossible to ignore the fact that they continued to be unwilling combatants in an unevenly waged war.

I was directly introduced to a modest version of ordinary, day-to-day, Occupation-related violence on a visit to the ancient city of Hebron. In Hebron, perhaps the most afflicted of the occupied cities, there are twenty internal checkpoints in places where clashes have occurred between settlers and Palestinians. Its Shuhada Street was once a bustling thoroughfare, but after 1994 it was closed first to Palestinian vehicles and then to all Palestinians after the demented settler Baruch Goldstein walked into Hebron's Cave of the Patriarchs and killed twenty-nine Muslim worshippers and wounded another 125 before he himself was killed.

For the Jewish settlers, Hebron is the site of the Tomb of the Patriarchs, which is believed to contain three double tombs: of Abraham and Sarah, Isaac and Rebecca, and Jacob and Leah, though to my knowledge no one has ever called it the Tomb of the Patriarchs *and* Matriarchs. According to Islamic tradition, the Prophet paused in Hebron during his night journey from Mecca to Jerusalem, and its mosque is believed to hold one of his shoes. It is known by Muslims as the Ibrahimi Mosque. It is a Herodian era (37 BC–AD 70) structure, which over the centuries, as the site was alternately ruled by Christian and Muslim conquerors, was converted and reconverted between mosque, church, and subsequently synagogue after Hebron was occupied in the Six-Day War. It thus has so much spiritual significance that it was rather awkwardly split in two, with Jews worshiping in a synagogue on the southeastern side and Muslims worshiping in the rest of the mosque but entering on its northeastern side. Christians no longer makes any claims on its real estate.

On Shuhada Street, the main road leading to the Tomb of the Patriarchs, the Israeli army sealed Palestinian residents' doors and blocked their residences with razor wire. In order to walk to the market or do anything outside their houses, residents, including the elderly, must climb up to their roofs and traverse nearby rooftops. Once a vital shopping destination, Shuhada Street today is empty and shabby looking, its shops deserted, its businesses and municipal offices departed. Papers blow along the street. Settlers, protected by the army, move freely along it. The small Arab open-air market on another street in the Old City, a market that a handful of vendors struggles to keep going, had to be covered with mesh netting because the settlers who live above it in high-rise buildings have been known to throw garbage, dirty diapers, used sanitary napkins, and human waste down on it. Hebron is the largest of the West Bank cities, and 215,452 Palestinians live there. The settlers number only eight hundred, but their residence in the heart of the city and governance by an entirely separate municipal body, along with the 1,500 Israeli troops stationed in the streets and on rooftops to protect them, make the atmosphere in and around Hebron continuously tense.

I had successfully avoided going to Hebron until, several years into my research, I reluctantly drove there with my husband and two friends from Berlin who were keen on seeing the mosque. Walking along a street with a guide, we suddenly found ourselves squarely in the sight of a rifle pointed at us by a man on the rooftop of a nearby yeshiva. The rifleman continued to aim directly at us while we remained, somewhat frozen in alarm, beneath him. Our guide, an ebullient middle-aged Al-Quds law professor, had just been explaining that the yeshiva had once been a Palestinian school; in fact, it was the one he'd attended as a boy. The man pointing the rifle was dressed in the black coat and black hat of the ultra-orthodox. None of us had ever cast eyes on him before. One of our friends, a writer and former student of mine, clutched my shoulder, terrified. It was only her second day in the country. "Why is he pointing his gun at *us*?" she asked. There was, of course, no sane explanation. Was it merely because we were walking along an "Arab" street? A small boy stood next to Black Coat—perhaps his son.

Even after our little group, overcoming temporary paralysis, moved quickly on, the man eerily followed us as we strode along, changing his roof position to keep us steadily in his rifle sight until we disappeared around a corner. For the local Palestinians, our guide told us, attacks by the settlers in and around Hebron are depressingly frequent—smoke bombs thrown in windows, beatings by settler gangs, desecration of the Muslim cemetery, racist graffiti scrawled on homes—and so were middle-of-the-night military incursions into private homes. The Hebrew University scholar David Shulman works to defend Palestinians in the South Hebron Hills from set-tler violence. One incident Shulman wrote about epitomized for him what the Occupation had wrought in human terms. "On Feb. 2, 2015, the army destroyed twenty-three homes in Jimba and Halawa in the South Hebron Hills, leaving eighty-seven people, sixty of them chil-dren, without shelter in the depth of winter. The excuse: The army needs Jimba and the surrounding eleven villages for a firing zone—as if there were no empty spaces inside Israel for such exercises."

———•———

When I met Niveen she was thirty-one. She had already acquired her master's in speech pathology from the University of Jordan in Amman, where she'd lived in her own apartment, and she seemed in no hurry to find a husband. Some of Niveen's sisters dressed con-servatively, and some didn't. But I learned after a while to accept the limitations of my assumptions about the significance of traditional clothing. Niveen wears a hijab and abaya when she's outdoors, sweats when she's at home, but the former—her public wrappings that seem conservative to me—bear little apparent relation to the modern high-spirited woman within. The result of Niveen and her sisters' encour-agement by their father to seriously pursue their studies had been that all of them had thought quite a bit about what it means to be a modern Palestinian woman. And though Arab women tend to marry early, only the second-oldest Abuleil sister, Khawallah, did so.

Then one day a retired teacher at one of the schools Niveen works at encountered her on a school visit, took a strong liking to her, and decided she'd make an excellent wife for her only son, Mahmoud. Niveen was dubious—as was Mahmoud when his mother returned home trilling Niveen's praises and suggesting they meet.

Mahmoud Abu Rumeila, a gentle, likeable IT manager for the global humanitarian aid NGO Mercy Corps, was thirty-five and Niveen's match for independent-mindedness. At that point, though graduate school was behind her, Niveen was still living with her fam-ily and sharing one of the family's small bedrooms with her sister Ruqaya. Still ahead of her remained certificates she needed to acquire to move forward in her profession. It occurred to me that the many degrees and certificates that the Abuleil progeny so diligently collected were surely one way of establishing personal, rational order in a chaotic societal milieu. Mahmoud had attended college in the US, at the University of Kentucky (he'd been lured to Lexington by the offer of a large scholarship but had come to wish that he had attended one of the more competitive schools that had offered him less money but where there might have been more Arab students). His father, a journalist, and his mother had strongly encouraged him to study in the States. In fact, they had *pushed* him; it was the time of the second Intifada, and they feared for his safety—too many young Palestinian men were being jailed, wounded, or killed. Too many Palestinians in general were dying. In the short span of February through June 2002 alone there were 659 violent Palestinian deaths. By the time the intifada was over, 3,000 Palestinians and 1,000 Israelis had been killed. More than a few Arab parents I spoke with had also strongly encouraged their sons to study abroad. "We didn't like being separated, but that was better than having to bury him," one father said.

One result of Mahmoud's exposure to American ways was that he had become accustomed to living on his own. In Jerusalem he rented his own apartment, an unusual arrangement for an unmarried son in his society but one that he enjoyed. Reluctantly he agreed to meet Niveen, and, to their mutual surprise, they each liked what they saw. Their encounter was repeated—and repeated again. Reader, they fell in love.

They chose Istanbul for their honeymoon, and Niveen's nephew, also named Mahmoud, who was then a medical student in Istanbul and had come to Jerusalem for the wedding, accompanied them on their trip to Turkey. On the way to the airport, Niveen and the Mahmouds chatted amicably. But the closer they got to Tel Aviv, the quieter they became. Unless they remain in the embrace of their own neighborhoods or limit themselves to other Arab destinations, travel is tricky for Palestinians, particularly international travel. Since the summer of 2013, after a pilot period that began in 2010, the airport security people no longer pick passengers selectively to have their checked bags scanned. Everybody's bag is now scanned, but Palestinian travelers are still singled out for intense scrutiny.

When Niveen and her husband and nephew arrived at Ben-Gurion Airport, the elder Mahmoud wasn't too worried about himself. Because of his work at Mercy Corps, he carried a pass that, like Nazmi Jubeh's, sped him through checkpoints and across borders. And, indeed, though every corner of his baggage was scrutinized, he passed through with only the normal professionally brusque security-gate treatment we all have grown accustomed to. Niveen also negotiated the security line uneventfully. But her nephew, a bona fide Seeds of Peace–nik who had spent two complicated, more or less disappointing summers in Maine with Seeds of Peace—an international peace advocacy and leadership group—when he was sixteen and again when he was eighteen—was not so lucky. His suitcases were spirited off to security hell and would arrive in Istanbul neither the next day nor the following one, a Jewish religious holiday; they ended up taking ten days to reach him. In the recesses of the airport, he was strip-searched and subjected to a tattoo of accusatory questions and unable to join Niveen and her husband until just before the plane took off. This had happened to him more than once before.

Eventually, like Niveen and her workplace commute through a checkpoint, Niveen's nephew decided that his trips to and from Istanbul were too stressful. An awkward political and economic situation had also developed. Despite young Mahmoud's being a top student in his class at the university, the Palestinian Authority—the major channel of funds to Palestinian students—refused to recommend him for a scholarship. This was because his father, Khaled Masalha, was born in one of villages in the Galilee, Kfar Qari, and therefore carried an Israeli passport, as did his children. Kfar Qari is part of a concentration of Arab towns called the Triangle, which Soviet-born Avigdor Lieberman, then Israeli foreign minister, declared would be given to the Palestinian Authority in a land swap for the settlements in any final peace arrangement. Israeli Jews call that 21 percent of the state's population, some 1.9 million citizens, Israeli Arabs. The residents refer to themselves simply as Palestinians or as "Palestinians living in Israel" or sometimes "Palestinian Israelis." The Palestinian donor bureaucracy called them Israelis. Mahmoud called himself screwed, and, though he loved living in Istanbul, it galled him that students far lower on the academic totem pole were eligible for handsome support from the Palestinian Authority when he was not.

By the following year, Mahmoud had transferred to the University of Jordan in Amman and switched from medical to dental school. His father, a broad-shouldered, sociable man with a relaxed but commanding presence, told me that this was partly because he had a relative who was a dentist in Jerusalem who could fold young Mahmoud into his flourishing practice. After Mahmoud transferred, trips home, now via the nearby Allenby Bridge (still ruled by Israel but run in part with Palestinian personnel), became far less fraught with anxiety, and Mahmoud had enlisted the help of a Palestinian Knesset member to help him get some financial support, a strategy that was ultimately unsuccessful.

Khaled was married to Niveen's second-oldest sister Khawallah. Over many years he had put himself through law school and somehow completed his legal studies while working full-time as a nurse in the Israeli hospital system and managing to pay for private schools for his five children. When I'd first met them, the Masalhas were crowded into an apartment that barely contained them, but with the extra money Khaled earned from his law practice, they had been able to move to a larger, sunnier apartment.

The new apartment was across the street from a mysterious horse rental stable. There didn't seem to be any visible bridle paths in the neighborhood that could conceivably be viewed as suitable for riding—no park or even a small patch of open field. Nonetheless, the ramshackle stable, probably a holdover from earlier, more bucolic days in the city, did a brisk business, and wildly galloping horses, occasionally ridden bareback, were a somewhat hallucinogenic but not uncommon sight on the Masalhas' otherwise unremarkable potholed city street.

Mahmoud didn't feel good about adding to his father's financial burden and was crushed when the Knesset member couldn't do anything about his fellowship situation. The PA said to him, "You have an Israeli passport—go to Israel." So Khaled was still paying Mahmoud's school bills along with those of two of his other sons and daughter. A fourth son was working for the Orange phone company.

I asked Mahmoud why his Seeds of Peace experience hadn't been positive. He sighed, "The Israeli kids mostly kept to themselves, and so did we. We had some interesting discussions, and I agree with the group's goals, but I'd have to say there was very little change in anyone's attitude." Mahmoud's younger brother Muhammed belonged to Peace Now, the granddaddy of all Israeli peace activist groups. Both brothers were all for the groups' good intentions, but their capacity to effect change, they concurred, even among the group's youngest members, had been disappointingly weak. No great spirit of amity had devolved from their encounters with young Israelis. When I met him, Muhammed was about to enter his last year of high school. A dedicated soccer player, his skills had earned him the position of goalie on the municipal soccer team, rather touchingly called the Employees. Muhammed lived and breathed soccer, but he was not planning to continue playing in college because, he said, glancing at his father, he knew he had to concentrate more on his studies. A handsome boy, with his father's broad shoulders and energetic, alert demeanor and his mother's easy smile, Muhammed was sure about his plans to study law, but where he would study was at that point a matter of some family dispute. Muhammed wanted to study in Spain or Italy; his father thought both places would cost too much and wanted him to attend school in Amman. The Palestinian universities like Al-Quds and Birzeit are latecomers to the academic world. Al-Quds was founded in 1984, and Birzeit, which started as an elementary school for girls, was established as a university in 1975. While they and other Palestinian institutions are preferred by many Palestinians, they are unsurprisingly riddled with problems, brain drain being the foremost (after the Occupation itself), since so many academics have been wooed away by the greater financial remuneration and untrammeled situations of universities abroad. Al-Quds University, in East Jerusalem, suffers additionally from periods where salaries are not paid, sometimes for months. In times of violence the roads to universities may be closed—and so might the universities themselves—so exams are missed, lectures postponed, and passage from one level to another delayed.

Mahmoud's mother, Niveen's sister Khawallah, who often looks a bit surprised by the tumult in her household, works in Jerusalem as a therapist for children with autism problems, and when she comes home each night she somehow manages to cook copious meals for her family. If Renoir had painted Palestinian women, he would, I am sure, have enjoyed capturing her plump prettiness. In her home, a steady stream of fruit, pastries, cooling drinks, and thick Turkish coffee flowed toward the living room. There, as elsewhere, I did my best to fulfill my duties as a guest, but any unfinished offerings on my plate seemed to cause a bit of disappointment. Did I imagine it? My increasingly plaintive attempts to arrest the snack onslaught riddle my recordings of conversations that took place in the Masalha house, just as they did at the Abuleils' house. One evening Khaled and I were each brought a dish of what appeared to be most of a basketball-size honeydew melon, cubed, and I polished off all but two morsels of mine. I looked up at my hostess expecting to see approval for once. Instead, there was Khawallah eyeing the two stragglers left on my plate, saying, "Ah, perhaps you'd prefer something else?" In nearly each recording of conversations I had in Palestinian houses and listened to later there comes a moment when I say, "Thank you, thank you, but no more. . . . Yes, really!" I am trying to sound normal, but it is not hard to detect in my voice a note of hysteria.

Khaled, who would be remarkable in any culture for his open-mindedness, persistence, and focus on his family's needs, in many ways fits what I'd come to think of as the modern Palestinian survival mold. He grew up in a poor farming family and had to set aside his early dream of becoming a doctor (his town notably has the highest number of doctors in relation to the population in the country) to help put his older brother through medical school. Until 1966, Palestinian Israelis lived under a harsh military rule that limited their right to work and rights of speech and association and restricted their movements. Even when they were allowed to become labor federation members, they were (and are) thwarted by discriminatory practices, including exclusion from large swaths of Israeli industry. After military administrative rule ended in 1966, some members of the Arab business class prospered, but new laws came along that have continued to keep that slice of the population marginalized. Ninety-three percent of Israel's land is owned by the state and by quasi-governmental organizations such as the Jewish National Fund, and, as with house-building permits, Palestinian Arab citizens face a mountain of obstacles to acquiring land, whether for commercial development, residences, or farming. According to Adalah, the Legal Center for Arab Minority Rights in Israel, there are more than sixty Israeli laws today that discriminate against them, including one that authorizes Jewish-majority communities to reject Palestinians who fail to meet vague "social suitability" criteria. On the afternoon that we were discussing his son's troubles getting financial aid, Khaled also pointed out that proof of having served in the army was a require-ment for many good jobs, and since Palestinian Israelis did not serve in the military they were ineligible. Over the last years many Israelis, especially right-wing Knesset members, have come increasingly to view their fellow Arab citizens as at best a demographic threat, at worst a fifth column. Adding to the obstacles Palestinian Israelis face is hostility sometimes from other Palestinians. In 1991, Khaled told me, he and Khawallah and their children, who then numbered two, moved to the Palestinian village of Issawiya, not far from where the Abuleils lived on French Hill, and some of their neighbors set fire to their car one week after they moved there.

In Khaled's family, too, education was identified as the indispens-able ladder out of the demoralizing circumstances they found them-selves in. Thirteen of Khaled's sixteen siblings have graduated from college. And most of the members of his family, he told me, for all the stresses of the Occupation and general travail of belonging to a second-class part of the population, would never consider joining the more than six million Palestinians who live abroad. *That*, perhaps, was at the core of Palestinian resistance—staying put. The Arab word for it is *sumoud*—perseverance or steadfastness—enduring, as the Abuleils and Masalhas did, the trials of their political situation and trying to live a normal life, simply getting up every day to work or study. Sometimes the word has been translated as "static" and so making a distinction from more dynamic, activist forms of resistance, though *sumoud* doesn't exclude acts of protest. One story Khaled told me about his family seems to nicely weave together the modern and traditional threads that characterize many current Palestinian lives. A few years back he tried to help along the marital prospects of a thoroughly modern sister who considers herself a feminist and was studying for a postdoctoral degree in sociology at the London School of Economics. But she steadfastly resisted his efforts.

"I brought her more than fifty people who wanted to marry her," he said. "No deal. Then she found the man she's married to. He's British. We were against it. But then we met him, and I thought he was great. My brother Ahab has a law office here, and he came to it. After about thirty minutes, I said to myself, 'This is the man!' I said he'd have to become a Muslim—my condition—and he had already done it!"

His sister was longing to come back to her country, Khaled went on to say, and her husband was OK with that. They have a blue-eyed baby boy and many friends in London, he added, but she misses her family. It was difficult for me to imagine that a Palestinian woman with a good life in a city with less conflict would willingly come back to the stresses and anxieties of Jerusalem, and I'm sure I looked incredulous as I blurted out, "Really? She'd leave London for this?"

Muhammed, in his soccer uniform, had just come into the room and shot me an equally incredulous look. "If her husband became Muslim to make her happy, he'll move to where she wants to. Look, she's far now from her family," he said. And clearly, for him, that rang the definitive bell. Muhammed himself had no desire to live permanently anywhere else, though he was eager to visit his aunt in London. It was, he admitted, "kind of hard to live in Jerusalem where there is always some kind of trouble," but that's where his home was, he said, and his family, so that's where he wants to be. "I'm probably not like other teenagers in the world," he said, adding almost as an afterthought, as he laced up a sneaker, "because of the Occupation. I'll study law and I'll sometimes be able to help other Palestinians." Khaled nodded approvingly. Since for a long time I had only caught glimpses of Muhammed as a blur in a soccer uniform racing out the door, I gathered that the idea of giving up soccer had not come easily and was the result of a number of serious discussions he'd had with his father. Khaled had told him he could study anything he wanted, Muhammed added, "But why wouldn't I study something useful like law?" "And then," Khaled cut in with a sly smile, leaning back with his hands behind his head, "I can retire, and he can take over my clients and office."

Before Khaled was able to fully launch his law practice, which already involved some of the particularly complicated real estate problems of Jerusalem, including the touchy one of local Palestinians sometimes trying to take over the property of other Palestinians who have lived or are still living abroad, he continued to work as a nurse in the Israeli hospital system. He did this mostly on night shifts, and he saw new clients in his law practice in the daytime between those shifts. "And now," he added, "I am the unofficial hospital lawyer. They know I passed the law exam and they are coming to me for advice." Medical professionals occupy a unique place in the culture of the country. Palestinians and Israelis alike agree that hospitals are the sole place where everyone can expect to be treated equally. I heard this no matter who happened to mention the subject. Khaled had worked in many different hospitals, but it was the same, he said, everywhere. And the staff in the hospitals worked hard to keep it that way. Khaled had toiled for over twenty years side-by-side with settlers and, astonishingly, could not recall a single instance of politics coming up or racism surfacing. "We didn't speak of politics. We work together every day, do our jobs, that's it."

In his twenties Khaled traveled to London, and he enjoyed his two years there. He had an English girlfriend, and it was easy to find nursing work, so there was always money in his pocket. But then, toward the end of 1985, two years before the first Intifada, he decided to return. "It was not a political move. I just missed my family, my friends, the smell of Palestine." Muhammed, nodding, added, "There he felt he had no nationality." Khaled went on: "For me, it's something hard to name. It's easier to be under Occupation. But you know, if I think about politics I can't work, I can't study, I can't do anything." Khaled and Khawallah, their sons Mahmoud, Abdallah, and Muhammed, and daughter Lana, who was eleven when I first met her, seemed somehow to have succeeded in relegating their feelings toward Israelis to a back room of their lives, though Khaled said it didn't take a degree in law to understand "that there were two kinds of law, one for the Jews and one for the Palestinians." From my earliest conversations with the Abuleils and the Masalhas, I was startled to discover that most of the time neither they nor anyone around them actually called the Israelis "Israelis"—rather, they and Palestinians in general referred to them as "Jews" (*yahood*), an inheritance from the early, pre-Israel days of Jewish immigration and an ongoing, not-so-subtle act of non-recognition. In circumstances where Palestinians and Israelis were thrown together professionally or academically, however, this linguistic blanket of otherness ceased to be the norm.

The Masalhas' oldest son, Ahmad (whom I had met briefly at the Abuleils' on one of my first visits), is a graduate of Hebrew University, where he majored in accounting and law. He went on to acquire an accounting graduate degree at the University of Haifa. Ahmed was a lot less stoic than the rest of the family. At our accidental meeting at the Abuleils' apartment where I was chatting with Niveen, he was outspoken and voluble about the situation of his people. After that time he did not return calls or respond to messages, but at that encounter he spoke with some heat about the "situation," and "the so-called mantle of democracy of a country that refused to allow any commemoration of the Nakba, locked up people at will, keeps them in prison without charging them day after day, and humiliates us in a hundred ways." The Nakba commemoration issue Ahmad referred to was the official frowning on the Palestinian custom of marking Israel's Independence Day as a day of mourning and occasion for commemorative events, an official response that took a draconic turn in 2011 when the "Nakba Law" was passed. The law authorizes the government's finance minister to reduce state funding or support to an institution if it allows any activities that reject the existence of Israel as a Jewish and democratic state or commemorates Israel's Independence Day as a day of mourning. Several civil rights groups along with the parents of Palestinian schoolchildren and school alumni filed a petition with the Supreme Court protesting the law, but the court rejected the petition, ruling that the case was "premature" because the law had not yet been used against any specific institution, a response that the civil liberties groups said ignored the fact that the law had already had a chilling effect. Like his brother, Ahmad had once belonged to Seeds of Peace and remained in the group for two years but left because he felt it was ineffectual. "For Palestinians, there is no law really. Last week was the anniversary of the first Gaza War, and we students wanted to go on strike as a commemoration. As an alternative, he said, his voice dripping with sarcasm, "We were invited to the police station. We didn't go but didn't have our protest. Very democratic. This is the real situation—nothing's going on. We have dialogues about politics, but it's just talk. Really," he added, "I don't have hope anymore." At that point, Ahmad was twenty.

Over the last decade, other walls besides the Security Fence have been built in Israel—along its border with Jordan, along its border with Lebanon, and along its border with Egypt. If the "security fence" was basically built to keep Palestinians contained in their towns and villages, these walls were built to keep people out. There are naturally many thoughtful Israelis, including Ruth's husband, Yaron, who over the decades have written eloquently and critically about the country's ever-rightward movement. Foreigners are quick to notice that the press in Israel is far more robust and frank on the subject of the conflict than the US press. Two Israeli journalists, Amira Hass and Gideon Levy, have written more or less uninterruptedly about the ugly treatment of Palestinians. Hass, who writes a column for *Haaretz*, is said to be the only Jewish Israeli, or one of the few Israelis, who has actually lived among the Palestinians, formerly in Gaza and today in Ramallah. Levy, a member of the editorial board of *Haaretz*, also writes a column, "Twilight Zone," that week after week focuses on the travails of ordinary Palestinians, often children, who have run afoul of the army or one or another Israeli rule or law.

Though Hass and Levy have their fans for being among the rare observers who describe Palestinians as actual people rather than as abstractions like "the enemy" or "the other side," they are not widely admired by most of their compatriots. The British *Independent* began a 2010 article about Levy with the comment, "Gideon Levy is the most hated man in Israel—and perhaps the most heroic." Sometimes Levy finds the Occupation as absurd as it is tragic. He mentioned to the *Independent* reporter the 2009 detention of the famous Spanish clown, Ivan Prado, who was on his way to a clown festival in Ramallah and was detained at the Tel Aviv airport, then deported, for "security reasons." Levy asked his interviewer, "Was the clown considering transferring Spain's vast stockpile of laughter to hostile elements? Joke bombs to Jihadists? A devastating punch line to Hamas?"

The depressing truth is that for the most part each side remains ignorant about the other. Few Israelis I met encountered Palestinians, and the Palestinians rarely encountered Israelis. Even the young idealists who intermingle at the peace group summer camps do not appear to have had their minds profoundly altered about "the other side"—though miraculously some continue to *hope* for some avenue of change, and some even belong to human rights groups that do demonstrable good. Statistically, the vast majority of Israelis and Palestinians insist that they yearn for peace, but there has been little indication that the best efforts of diplomats can bring it about or that the desire for peace is as strong or as all-enveloping for the Israelis as the security demon.

The year after I first met the Abuleils, Abdallah died, and Niveen and Mahmoud had a beautiful baby boy, Muhammed. In 2015 they had a baby girl, Sarah. Abdallah's death left a big hole in the family's life. Zaineb suffered a stroke, but everybody, especially Sana, helped her recover. "Dug in" is probably the most accurate way to describe the Abuleils and the Masalhas—passionately devoted to their families, focused on their professional and private lives, weary of the indignities the far right has brought about as it has more and more set the tone of Israeli policies, but unwilling to tread the path of violent resistance. As Khaled put it, "Violence, no. Bombs, no—we don't approve of that way."

Travels with Fuad III

➤ Fuad's youngest sister-in-law, Renal, was getting married, and he and his wife, Kivo, invited me to the celebrations. Fuad's family and Kivo's were Fatah people; the young groom's family were loyal to Hamas. Part one of the bride's festivities, for women only, took place at the home of Fuad's mother-in-law, Mageda, an energetic, good-humored widow who had battled serious cancer but appeared to have recovered well. Mageda's house sits in a narrow ravine accessed via an extremely steep, uneven, and long stone staircase that the guests, in their ground-grazing abayas, descended slowly and with care. With their long robes billowing in the breeze and dark hijabs the women resembled a flock of cautious birds. Their daughters, ranging in age from eight to eighteen, were also on hand, which gave me a shred of hope for the coming party, which I'd feared might be a somber religious affair.

I needn't have worried. The moment they walked through the door, abayas were shed, the flock repaired to the bedroom, and a few minutes later they emerged as a dazzling array of glittering ladies with elaborately coiffed Big Hair, many short, short evening dresses, low necklines accommodating push-up bras, sparkly bling, and enough iridescent eye makeup to sink a battleship. For more than two hours there was steady dancing, more or less in the belly-dancing mode, in which everyone present, eight to eighty, enthusiastically participated. None of the Arab music on the playlist was familiar to me, with the exception of several plaintive songs that I was pretty sure were by the widely beloved Lebanese singer Fairuz, whom some friends had played for me on an earlier occasion.

I love to dance, but nothing in my repertoire of moves comes close to what was happening in front of me, so I sidled over to a wall, hoping to remain in the shadows. But this was not to be—

even though I saw plainly that the universal we-are-all-one-people principle definitely stopped at the door of belly dancing. Pulled good-naturedly into the melee, I did my best to imitate the dancers around me. The children found my efforts hilarious, and I observed with stoic resignation that my antics were being recorded on a video camera, doubtless to be replayed on some gloomy winter evening for those very same children as an alternative to an animated cartoon.

From time to time clusters of the family's menfolk could be glimpsed through a window, chatting outside, but the two groups never mingled. Afterward, for the second half of the evening's celebrations—the women rewrapped in their long robes—we drove to a large banquet hall where sweets and soda bottles and plastic cups had been placed on the tables, and bridal gifts were ceremoniously unwrapped on a stage and admired by the guests. There was much oohing and aahing, except from one group of unsmiling, rather severe-looking women who shared a table and were, I was told, from the groom's family. Chatting with Mageda, I learned that all the official formalities of the union had already been settled, as is the custom, and that this evening was simply celebratory. The men were having their own party a few doors down. In Jerusalem Palestinian society, I also learned, the bill for all of this is generally footed by the groom.

Compared to the pre-party party, the banquet hall celebration seemed pretty tame, and, unlike every other Palestinian social occasion I'd observed, it was absent a cornucopia of food. Fuad assured me the next day, as he was driving me to meet someone, that the men's event had been duller. It had been dominated, he said, "by endless political and religious lectures." It had struck me as a bit surprising that Fuad hadn't invited my husband, who had just arrived from New York, and like me had a warm relationship with him. But, Fuad told me, as we waited to get through a small checkpoint, because of Hamas's participation he'd had a fairly good idea in advance of how things would go and wanted to spare my husband the boredom of it.

Several weeks after the wedding, as it happened, I had a chance to hear some of those lectures myself from two of three senior Hamas politicians who had taken refuge in the Red Cross compound in East Jerusalem to avoid deportation. One of them was a relative of someone I knew. Not long after the 2006 Palestinian

Legislative Council elections, three Jerusalem deputies and the former minister of Jerusalem affairs—Muhammed Totah, Muhammed
Abu Tir, Ahmed Attoun, and Khaled Abu Arafeh, respectively—
were informed by Israeli authorities that they had to resign from
the Palestinian government or have their East Jerusalem permanent
residency status revoked. They refused, pointing out (irrelevantly
as far as the Israeli authorities were concerned) that they had been
democratically elected and that Jerusalem was where they were born
and where their homes and families were. Subsequently a military
court sentenced all four to two to four years in prison.

They were released in 2010, and again the government threatened to take away their Jerusalem residency rights. Despite promising—even fruitful—back-door negotiations between the Israelis
and Hamas over the years, the government still considered the
Palestinian organization illegal. The charge leveled against the four
was the legally fuzzy-sounding "breach of trust," with its odd echo of
divorce court. Muhammed Abu Tir, probably the best known of the
legislators because of his bright-orange, henna-dyed beard (hom-
age, he said, to the Prophet, who also dyed his beard with henna),
was rearrested on June 30, 2010, when he refused to leave the city
and was eventually expelled to the West Bank. The other three men,
fearing the same fate, fled to the International Committee of the Red
Cross compound. Officials at the Red Cross released a statement
saying that the three East Jerusalemites were considered protected
persons under the Fourth Geneva Convention, which forbids Israel
from forcibly transferring Palestinians out of the city. Outside the
Red Cross building, the street bristled with surveillance cameras
and bright lights. At the time of my visit, the men had been living
together in a dormitory-style arrangement for nearly a year. Subsequently, Israeli forces would enter the Red Cross headquarters and
arrest Attoun—and, later Abu Arafeh and Totah—and all three
would be expelled to the West Bank. By then Attoun had already
been imprisoned four times, and prison had played havoc with his
medical conditions, which included heart and kidney problems and
diabetes. But when I visited them at the Red Cross headquarters,
they still held out hope that they would be able to return to their
wives and children in their East Jerusalem homes. The Red Cross

told the press that against that hope was the reality that its power to shelter them was limited since they did not have diplomatic immunity and couldn't prevent the Israelis from arresting anyone.

Abu Arafeh was napping when I arrived, and, probably because of my connection with a relative, Attoun and Totah wanted only to talk about how much they missed their families. Their wives and children, like all other visitors, were received under a giant, Bedouin-style plastic tent where protests were also held. Chairs were arranged in a circle as always. When it came time for their families to leave, Attoun said, the children all began to cry because they couldn't understand why their fathers refused to leave with them.

When I managed to steer the conversation toward more political subjects, I was treated to a well-honed recitation of Hamas's mounting list of reasonable acts, including its agreement to a *tahadiyyeh*— a period of "calm." They also mentioned a declaration they clearly thought would be appreciated by an American: the announcement that, in light of international revulsion expressed after the events of September 11, 2001, Hamas would suspend all suicide attacks on the condition that Israel cease all attacks on them. Observers with an intimate knowledge of Hamas strategies have long pointed out the complexity of the organization's political approach, its internal battles between hardliners and more reform-minded members, and some of its generally underpublicized pragmatic moves toward moderation over the years. On the one hand, it had never at that point disavowed its fanatic, poisonously anti-Semitic fundamentalist charter that, among other things, lists the destruction of Israel as one of its goals, and it had never agreed to recognize Israel. On the other hand, its ideology hadn't stopped it from exercising a practical strategic flexibility that allowed it to respond to its constituency, sometimes in ways that appeared to contravene its charter. Inside the organization, voices questioned whether it was achieving its goals through violent resistance, and the same voices urged dialogue with Fatah rather than resisting merely for the sake of resisting.

In the spring of 2017, the organization publicly acknowledged what even its leader, Khaled Meshal, had earlier described as the charter's irrelevance, calling it "a piece of history." Hamas surprised the international community by issuing a new declaration of principles that some saw as for the first time distinguishing between the Israelis and the Jewish people as a whole. The new document also framed the Palestinian struggle in anticolonial rather than religious terms and set in writing what Hamas representatives had been hinting at for years: it was "willing to accept" a two-state solution along the pre-1967 borders (something countless Israelis and Palestinians seemed by then to have given up on) provided that the Palestinians received what one Hamas leader called "a true and genuine state." The new document did not, however, formally recognize Israel or renounce violence, and thus it was rejected out of hand by Prime Minister Netanyahu, who declared it insincere and an attempt "to fool the world."

On the day we spoke under the plastic tent, sipping scalding, thick Turkish coffee, the Palestinian legislators also mentioned the promising nature of an already discussed plan for a renewable ten-to-fifteen-year ceasefire. Our conversation took place well before ISIS gained international prominence, targeting Hamas, encouraging its extremists, and declaring that Hamas functionaries were responsible for all Gaza's troubles, which were an expression of God's displeasure with them. Just before I left, as Attoun and Totah took pains to remind me of the extreme hardship of life in Gaza and expressed hope that a way out of the decades-long impasse could be found, I found myself considering the possibility that even Hamas, with its infamous brutalities, attacks on civilians, and religious severity, might be mellowing into some form of elder statesmanship. As I was preparing to leave, however, we had one last exchange about Hamas leaders' unchanged view of the right of return:

> **Me:** "With so much political change and international shifting, including your own, what do you see as your final goal?"
>
> **Both men, taking turns speaking:** "Our people will be back— all of them—in their homes or in the places they came from."
>
> **Me:** "And the Israelis?"
>
> **Totah:** "They'll go back to where they came from."

Me: *"What 'back'? There is no 'back.'"*

Both men: *Inscrutable expressions.*

After their expulsion, all four men—Muhammed Totah, Muhammed Abu Tir, Ahmed Attoun, and Khaled Abu Arafeh—lived in Ramallah, where their families visited them when possible. In September 2017, the Supreme Court of Israel ruled that the original revocation of the Jerusalem residency status of the four was illegal. It gave the government six months, however, to pass *new* legislation to amend the law in a way that gave the interior minister the right to forcibly revoke residency for East Jerusalemites. In November 2018 Attoun was rearrested in Ramallah and placed in administrative detention, and when his lawyer, Fadi Qawasmi, asked to know the basis for the new arrest, he was told that there was "secret evidence" against Attoun that could not be disclosed. At this writing Qawasmi has brought another suit on Attoun's behalf, and Attoun remains in administrative detention.

CHAPTER 7

PERSPECTIVES

It would be only a slight exaggeration to say that in addition to her two older brothers and younger sister, Ruth HaCohen grew up alongside a fourth sibling, the state of Israel—a sibling sometimes well-behaved, sometimes out of control, but always contributing to her sense of who she was, an inescapable part of her life that rarely faded entirely away. And was not meant to. Since Ruth was born just a few years after the founding of Israel, the country was establishing its identity just as her own was unfurling. Whatever else it might entail, the process of growing up in Israel, even in an age of rampant consumerism and "me generation" self-absorption, still incorporates the idea that young people no less than adults are meant to play a significant role in shaping society. Are you apolitical? It doesn't matter. You will still have to serve in the army unless you are ultra-orthodox. (In recent years the exemption of that slice of the population from military service has been reconsidered, though in the right-wing-dominated Knesset there has been little enthusiasm for pushing through the necessary legislation.) The more I got to know Ruth and her family, the more I came to grasp the centrality of this phenomenon of expected service. Though there were many aspects of our lives that were similar, I felt how different her upbringing had been from my own and from any of the children I grew up with.

Ruth's sense of self, like her mother's, would be dual—as she expressed it, "bifurcated"—partly grounded in religion and religious custom, partly open to and enriched by the errant winds of secular culture. But unlike Esther's, Ruth's nonfamilial horizon offered far more opportunity for individual flight—and Ruth was an eager fledgling. The vistas opened by secular books she read—often supplied by her mother—piqued her curiosity enormously, as did the music she listened to and later joyfully played on her flute. The wider cultural world and its attractions were an embellishment to Esther's life, not its core. Ruth, on the other hand, grew up in a country defined by change and experiment. Not that she was a rebellious girl—that space was occupied by her younger sister, Nechama, for a time a high school dropout, who chafed openly against the religious constraints in her upbringing and grew up to be a well-known therapist who counsels trauma sufferers (Arab and Jewish), Holocaust survivors, and victims of sexual abuse. Ruth was the obedient one, at least when she was young. She felt warmed by the religious texts she absorbed and the rituals and holidays the family observed—"there were ... beautiful things about it," and she was happy to be part of it. By the time she was four she could read, and at seven, attending synagogue with her father on a religious holiday and sitting alone with only an old lady for company in the women's section, she took pride in her ability to read through the entire book of Lamentations.

But in contrast to the serious little girl solemnly absorbing the historic grief of the Jewish people there was also a playful, aesthetically alert one who reveled in rolling around on Jerusalem's many grassy lawns at that time, playing ball, swimming, or just lying around in the sun, letting her mind drift and feeling free to do whatever she felt like doing. As she got older, she continued to appreciate the richness of Jewish culture. (Her twenty-first-century work reflects this: she has received prestigious awards for her book *The Music Libel Against the Jews*, about the historic Christian hostility to Jewish liturgical music and the perception of Jewish "noise" in a world of Christian harmony.) Still, the grimness (or to use her word, "heaviness") of certain aspects of Ruth's religious life began to oppress her. Every year, in the middle of her summer vacation, for example, when she was eagerly looking forward to trips to the sea or hiking, came the somber holiday of Tisha B'Av (on the ninth of Av, the month of the Jewish calendar in which it is observed). And before the holiday came three weeks of privation ("in which you are forbidden to do all sorts of things—no swimming pool, no sea, no bikes!—and when the day finally arrives then you must fast and go to the synagogue").

Several years after her prodigious reading feat as a seven-year-old, Ruth joined a youth movement group, which proved to be life-changing. Hers was a religiously oriented one, Bnei Akiva (or "the children of Rabbi Akiva"), which, like all Israeli youth groups, stressed salutary activities like hiking and folk dancing and celebrated Zionist and general Jewish history. Though Bnei Akiva accommodated the upbringing of its religiously grounded members, its pleasures were mainly secular, and they lit up Ruth's life.

Israel's youth groups, which had their origins in eastern Europe and which a majority of young Israelis join, are a phenomenon with no exact counterpart elsewhere. You could compare them to scouting organizations (which also exist, independently, in Israel), but this analogy inadequately conveys their importance to the culture at large. Perhaps scouts plus therapy group, leadership-training incubators, plus nationalistic hootenanny, comes closest. Looking in from the outside, the society's progression from youth groups to the army and finally to army reserves (for men) seems to constitute an inescapable matrix for the country's cradle-to-grave social ethos, implacable in its focus on the Zionist project and encouragement of groupthink. Israelis tend to dismiss objections of this sort as frivolous or as not taking sufficiently into account the need for a formal sense of community in a small country in which citizens of so many different cultures—Ashkenazic, Sephardic, Ethiopian, Russian, and Druze—are thrown together and might at any moment be called up together to fight a war. But for Ruth, her years in the youth group meant something else entirely: a spiritually open flight path. At summer camp, Ruth's group slept in tents they set up themselves in groves, and they lived, as Ruth described it, in a young person's utopia of hiking, swimming, singing, and dancing, so it was wrenching when all such pleasurable activities had to be suspended to commemorate a sad religious holiday. The Jewish history as taught in her schoolrooms, discussed in her youth group, and honored in the synagogue, Ruth began to feel, was a heavy weight on her slim shoulders. As she grew older and music especially "worked its magic" on her, she began looking at the world with new eyes, and comparing aesthetics versus Zionism, individualism versus collectivism, and European versus Israeli ways of thinking.

Bit by bit, Israel's problematic relationship with its Arab population also began to slowly seep into her consciousness, but not at school. In her classrooms, the textbooks of that period were rife with anti-Palestinian ideology. As Nurit Peled-Elhanan points out in her 2012 exhaustive study of Israel's schoolbooks, "The cult of Jewish continuity in the land of Israel/Palestine also includes obliterating all signs of Palestinian continuous existence on the land." (Peled-Elhanan, the daughter of a famous general and peace activist, Matti Peled, lost her thirteen-year-old daughter in a Jerusalem suicide bombing in 1997 and is a member of the Parents Circle–Families Forum, a remarkable group of over six hundred bereaved Palestinians and Israelis who have lost children, parents, sisters, and brothers to the conflict's violence and preach reconciliation.)

The Palestinian "narrative" (as it has become irritatingly customary to call it) makes only cameo appearances in Israeli textbooks, just as the Israeli one (ditto) rarely surfaces in Palestinian classrooms. But in one respect the textbooks seem to have improved since Ruth's day. Somewhat surprisingly, a 2013 study of the textbooks of Palestinians and Israelis found that though both sides continued to distort the history of the conflict, the Palestinians only rarely demonized Jews in their textbooks. The study, conducted by a team of Palestinian, Israeli, American, and international education experts (without the cooperation of the Israeli government), discovered that instances of "extreme negative characterizations" were rare in Palestinian textbooks, and the number of cases of Israeli demonization of Palestinians that Peled-Elhanam had found a few years earlier had decreased too. Out of seventy-four books examined, there were just twenty "extreme negative characterizations" in Israeli secular books, and there were seven in books of the ultra-orthodox. It may be that textbook authors chose simply to ignore "the other side" instead of vilifying them. The same study revealed that in 58 percent of the post-1967 Palestinian schoolbook maps, Palestine is represented by an area encompassing everything between the Jordan River and the Mediterranean Sea, including what is now Israel; contrarily, 76 percent of the post-1967 Israeli schoolbook maps show Israel alone between the river and the sea, with no recognition of Palestinian areas, and no depiction of the Green Line that marks the supposedly separate entities of the West Bank and Gaza.

Much of what Israel's Jewish children are taught in school fosters and has always fostered a profound sense of national vulnerability. Ruth brought this up more than once in conversation with me. "We all grew up with it," Ruth said. "It was a kind of myth we came to know about later on. And with this went an unconscious fear—not really unconscious, it was more subconscious on the verge of consciousness—that one day all the Arabs can come and just slaughter all of us." Growing up, this seemed to Ruth to somehow be inextricably bound up with Jewish history. "It was on my shoulders all the time, something that a child accepts as a matter of fact, that the enemy, Arabs, were all around." Her parents did not subscribe to this view. "If the Arabs were presented to us in school as very hostile, even murderous, in our house there was never an expression of hatred or, on the other hand, fear." In her own family there hovered a "hope for peace, as an ideal or a utopia," Ruth said. "We could see from our windows and balcony Arab shepherds with their sheep grazing in their fields of Emek Hamatslevah [the Valley of the Cross]." These actual Arabs "looked friendly, though different and inaccessible. . . . The whole scene added to a pastoral feeling." Ruth's rosy if distanced and dreamlike picture of the shepherds couldn't have been more different, she added, from the one generally prevalent while she was growing up. In the press, on the radio, and in political speeches, Ruth told me, "They were definitely 'the other side.'"

Ruth's early years coincided with an incredibly optimistic time for Israelis. And, at least in the non-Arab world, the country was considered a success story. Most Israelis were still poor, but the country's economy was on the upswing—agriculture, particularly in the citrus orchards, was strong; the fledgling automotive industry (though it would prove to be short-lived) was thriving; new housing was springing up everywhere; and Tel Aviv, with its theaters, concert halls, museums, and sidewalk cafés, was working toward becoming the country's financial, technological, and cultural epicenter. After the 1948 war ended, the green line on the maps drawn at the 1949 Armistice Agreements became a shorthand term for the region's new boundaries, which would serve as the country's de facto borders until the 1967 Six-Day War. East Jerusalem and all land on the West Bank of the Jordan River were henceforth to be under the control of Jordan, as was the Mount of Olives, and the Egyptians were ceded the Gaza Strip. Ruth's family and everyone they knew, exhausted from the hostilities of the war, like many Israelis, considered their de facto borders more or less acceptable, although there were always those who only reluctantly—or never—gave up the religious Zionist dream of a nation on both sides of the Jordan. But among the country's generals there was a strong conviction, a certainty really, that the 1948 war would not be the country's last—a self-fulfilling prophecy since the military was known to consider the armistice lines incapable of being protected. As the always-trenchant Israeli writer Amos Elon—who decamped to Italy for the last years of his life—put it, "Sadly, almost from an inherent inclination, Israelis waited for the next war as for the predictable visit of a wearisome mother-in-law."

Though Ruth's family's economic situation began to improve in the late 1950s, Israel's postwar boom turned out to be ephemeral. By the mid-1960s, the economy and the morale of the country were both taking a downward turn. There was a bad recession and a marked drop in immigration along with a huge surge of people, many thousands, deciding to leave the country for good. What one observer characterized as "a psychology of decline" began to slow the economy even more. Even those who were committed to staying felt that the country was plummeting or at least that the old values of national unity and communal sacrifice had lost their burnish. Simultaneously, the political situation in the mid-1960s was again becoming highly charged. Various militant Palestinian groups launched a series of civilian and military attacks in the country. A number of the guerrilla groups involved came from Syria, Lebanon, and Jordan, which increased tensions, as did Egypt's assembling its troops in the Syrian desert and again closing the Straits of Tiran to Israeli vessels. At that point, 90 percent of Israel's oil was transported through the straits. Even though Nasser had not wanted war, his generals did, and he announced that his goal was the destruction of Israel. Nonetheless, Israel's foreign minister, Abba Eban, failed to interest Britain, France, the US, or the UN in coming to his country's defense, chiefly because none of their top officials believed that a war between Israel and its Arab neighbors was likely, considering Nasser's words as mere bluster. There were some who saw in all this an opportunity to change the face of the country's map and expand its borders. Ruth's parents had some sense of this and opposed it, but the military shunted aside all qualms about a new war, including those of the country's disapproving prime minister, Levi Eshkol, and struck its enemies rapidly and forcefully.

The 1967 Six-Day War that followed, from June 5 to June 10, has been extensively written about from various points of view, but few students of the region would disagree that its dramatic outcome transformed the geopolitics of the Middle East. Few would disagree that when the Israelis destroyed the Egyptian air forces on the ground in the first few hours, the war was already won. By the war's end Israel had captured the Sinai Peninsula and Gaza from Egypt, East Jerusalem and the West Bank from Jordan, and the Golan Heights from Syria. Despite Nasser's bellicosity, Yitzhak Rabin, who was Israel's chief of staff in 1967, told a *Le Monde* interviewer the following year, "I do not think Nasser wanted war. The two divisions he sent to the Sinai would not have been sufficient to launch an offensive war. He knew it and we knew it." But while Israel decisively won the war and exponentially enlarged its territories, it also now had (according to the Israeli state archive document of a census taken shortly after the war) more than one million more Palestinians from the occupied territories under its rule. And crucially, as Michael Oren, Israel's ambassador to the US from 2009 to 2013, points out in his book about the war, it did not bring the country closer to the peace so many Israelis hoped for, nor did it mitigate the Arabs' hostility to Israel—*au contraire*—or their desire for revenge. Ruth was only eleven that June, but two months before the war began, on an annual excursion to Mount Zion her youth group went on at Passover, she was startled to hear the children in another group singing about "next year in a whole, complete Jerusalem." This was a brand-new interpretation of the holiday phrase familiar to her, and she didn't know what to make of it. For the Palestinians, a measure of their attitude toward the Six-Day War can be gauged by their name for it: An-Naksah (the Setback). The war's impact on the affected populations was catastrophic—145,000 of the more than 250,000 Palestinians who immediately fled the country were already refugees from the 1948 war. On the other hand, the dismal failure of the Arab states and pan-Arab nationalism blew fresh energy into the Palestinians' own national movement and identity, and eventually the PLO would be acknowledged as the sole legitimate representative of the Palestinians. That the Israelis did not want the refugees back was clearly demonstrated by the UN-documented destruction of refugee camps and the scores of demolished villages, among them Surit, Yalo, al-Jiftlik, Beit Awwa, and Agarith. Most of the new refugees had nowhere to go but the already overcrowded, miserable refugee camps in the countries they fled to.

Approximately half of all Palestinians lived in what had once been Mandate Palestine before the 1967 war; after it the majority of Palestinians lived outside. At first, nearly all Israelis were in a state of euphoria about the victory. Jews throughout the world celebrated the capture of numerous holy sites, particularly the Temple Mount, as it is called by Jews (to Muslims it is Haram al-Sharif, or Noble Sanctuary), and its Western Wall, which over the years Jews had gazed at longingly from afar. The fact that the site with its al-Aqsa Mosque and Dome of the Rock was also considered sacred to Muslims was for the moment pushed aside, though as time went on competing claims about the site made it yet another pivot of contention. That history was accelerated three days after the Israelis took control of the Western Wall site, when the entire Moroccan Quarter with all its houses was bulldozed to make room for what is now the plaza facing the Western Wall.

But for the messianic-minded slice of the Israeli population that even before the war had been keeping the Greater Israel dream alive (roughly, the entirety of the state of Israel plus the Palestinian territories, though the implications of the term have varied at different times), the war's outcome acted like a giant vitamin pill. Even for those unconnected to fantasies of religious messianism, there was a shift in morale from gloom to giddy optimism. Money and tourists from abroad poured into the country. Immigration began to surge again. The pessimism of the preceding years, which had dogged Israelis, evaporated. Plans were quickly made to establish new Israeli communities on the occupied lands, although even according to one of the government's own legal advisors such settlements were against international law. With surprising speed, the official posture toward the newly occupied territories and the changed situation started the country down a slippery slope that would in time earn it the condemnation of most of the nations of the world. Beyond that, its continuing absolute control of the Palestinians and the occupied lands sent it further and further along a dangerous path that it appears to be unwilling to quit. Though Israeli officials have never ceased characterizing the nation as a victim, that description now seems ludicrously inapplicable. Israel has gradually become a major regional colonial force and, according to some estimates, is among the world's largest military powers.

Among the very few demurring voices raised at the time was that of the reliably clear-headed Amos Elon, who, as early as June 18, 1967, a little more than a week after the war ended, wrote in *Haaretz* that to the people who had been displaced, "We have a moral obligation because the road to Israel's independence was paved on the backs of these people, and they paid with their bodies, their property and their future, for the pogroms in the Ukraine and the Nazi death chambers." Yeshayahu Leibowitz, a professor of biochemistry, organic chemistry, and neurophysiology at Hebrew University, well known for his public forthrightness about ethical, religious, and political issues, also proclaimed soon after the war that if the occupation were to go on, it would inevitably lead to the country's moral decline. In "The Territories," an essay he published in 1968, remarkable for its prescience, he predicted a future in which

> the Arabs would be the working people and the Jews the administrators, inspectors, officials, and police—mainly secret police. A state ruling a hostile population of 1.5 to 2 million foreigners would necessarily become a secret-police state, with all that this implies for education, free speech and democratic institutions. The corruption characteristic of every colonial regime would also prevail in the State of Israel. The administration would suppress Arab insurgency on the one hand and acquire Arab Quislings on the other. There is also good reason to fear that the Israel Defense Force, which has been until now a people's army, would, as a result of being transformed into an army of occupation, degenerate, and its commanders, who will have become military governors, resemble their colleagues in other nations.

But at that time the vast majority of Israelis simply felt relieved—once more they had been spared from destruction. They were ecstatic that they could now enter the Old City, formerly under Jordanian control and off-limits, and pray at the Wall, and for many Jerusalemites there was a huge sense of relief that they were no longer encircled by hostile enemies. Even the sobering news of the angry retaliatory persecution of thousands of Jews in Arab countries, of mobs burning synagogues and assaulting the Jewish residents of Egypt, Yemen, Tunisia, Lebanon, and Morocco and the arrests, fining, and expulsion of more than seven thousand Jews from the venerable communities of Damascus and Baghdad, while inspiring sympathy, did not much alter the euphoric mood. In Tom Segev's book about the 1967 War, which, unlike Oren's, does not strive to always present Israeli motives in a favorable light, he recounts two well-known dark jokes that were popular just before and after the war that nicely illustrate the tenor of the societal turnabout. The first, which circulated at the time of national gloom and massive emigration, cites a sign hanging near a boarding gate at the airport, asking the last one in the country to turn out the lights. And the second, which circulated after the war, describes two army officers discussing how they will spend the day. "Let's conquer Cairo," one of them proposes. To which the other replies, "What will we do after lunch?"

One citizen who regarded the unbridled optimism and giddy jingoism of those days with increasing alarm was Ruth's father, Eliezar. For the duration of the 1967 hostilities, Ruth, her sister Nechama and brothers Rami and Yehuda, and some of their girl cousins, the children of their aunt Hannah (she of the heroic rescue of her father from Buchenwald), were stowed in the basement-shelter of the apartment building where both families lived, along with their paternal grandmother, then in her late seventies, who uncharacteristically could not stop weeping. In the days leading up to the war, Ruth admitted, the elaborate military preparations—the piling up of sandbags in her classroom, the taping of windows, and the drills for the shelters—were rather enlivening. Her parents for some reason opted to stay upstairs in their third-floor apartment during the day—they said long afterward, according to Nechama, "There have been much worse wars in the world and we survived them." But the family lived near a site that was subjected to a good deal of bombing, and their days became frightening when shooting actually began. During a brief lull in a pe-

riod of heavy fighting, Esther ran down the street to fetch Nechama
from nursery school, and, on the way back, with Nechama in tow, she
had to dodge bullets. Despite Ruth's parents' bravado in the face of
possible danger, Esther, half-fearing the worst, had stockpiled honey
and flour and other provisions, just in case the war proved to be as
prolonged as the 1948 one.

At night the boys remained in the basement, but the girls were
moved to their aunt and uncle's apartment in the same building,
where there was room for them because the family's three boys were
away in the army. From only 150 yards away, artillery soldiers kept up
a tattoo of countdowns, "2–2! 2–1!—Fire!," and a constant barrage of
ear-splitting booms shook the house. One night part of a shell arrived
on the balcony with a tremendous thud—perilously near where Ruth
and her sister were sleeping. In one way, it terrified her—of course—
but in another, Ruth remembers thinking appreciatively, "What a
great story to tell my friends!"

When it was all over, the talk among the Yeshiva boys and the
particularly pious girls in Ruth's youth group about fulfilling the ultimate Zionist mission took on a new, more determined cast and began
to seem more and more annoying to her. A rift began to open between
her, young as she was, and some of her friends in the youth group,
especially the older ones, who now spoke more fervently in nationalistic, messianic, and romantic or mystical ways about the occupied
lands, about the chosenness of the Jewish people, and about redemption. A more goal-directed version of the same kind of talk was blow-
ing in the wind in adult circles too. It would reach fruition in the
1970s after the brutal Yom Kippur War of October 1973 (in which the
Egyptian-Syrian alliance had at first scored some military successes),
in the creation of the messianic, radical right-wing activist movement,
Gush Emunim (Bloc of the Faithful), dedicated to establishing Jewish settlements in the West Bank, the Gaza Strip, and Golan Heights.
While the group no longer officially exists (it was slowly displaced
by other organizations over the course of the 1990s), its ideological
descendants have proliferated, and its project became a major shaper
of Israel's policies.

Immediately after the 1967 war ended, Eliezar sat his children
down on the sofa facing the valley where the artillery had been sta-

tioned just days before. Opening a large map, he showed them the lands that had just been conquered and said, "Of course we must give them back—it's the only way we'll have peace." "Land for Peace" was the oft-proclaimed desire of those who yearned for an end to the conflict, and if there were ever a moment for it to happen, this was it. But it didn't. In late June 1967, Israel's cabinet met secretly and, in a close vote, decided to give back the Golan and Sinai (though not the West Bank) in exchange for peace agreements with Syria and Egypt. But political and military obstacles prevented the plan from moving forward. One problem, archival documents show, is that the Israelis asked the US to represent them in their backchannel explorations about the plan, and the US may or may not have told the Arabs about it. The Arab League's Khartoum summit later that year resulted in what became known as "The Three No's": "no peace with Israel, no recognition of Israel and no negotiations with Israel," a declaration that is often cited as the crux of Arab intransigence. But archival research has shown that there were actually parallel results from the conference: a decision and a statement. The statement, for public consumption, was the source of the three no's. The decision left room for negotiation. Privately, both Nasser and Jordan's King Hussein had made known their willingness to work toward a just peace agreement. Moshe Dayan, then Israel's defense minister, at a certain point—through an emissary—offered Hussein all of the West Bank though not Jerusalem in exchange for peace, but, because of the omission of Jerusalem from the deal, Hussein said no. In contrast to the often repeated claim that Khartoum was a kind of rejectionist model for all peace attempts thereafter, Avi Shlaim has argued that the gravamen of Khartoum was something far more complex: "No formal peace *treaty*, but not a rejection of peace; no *direct* negotiations, but not a refusal to talk through third parties; and no *de jure* recognition of Israel, but acceptance of its existence as a state."

In time, Ruth herself began to feel a growing sense of discomfort about the new situation. "It was odd. Somehow, when Jerusalem was smaller and more vulnerable, we at least thought we had a definite idea of where things stood, but now I couldn't understand what was going to be with the new population. There was no feeling of relief, only unease."

Years later, when the low drumroll of the settler movement had become a loud din, Ruth remembered that moment when her father had spoken to them, because it had cut through so much of the rhetoric whirling around her. "My father's words and somber expression," she said, "became engraved in my heart." Not long after the war the Society for the Protection of Nature in Israel sponsored trips for young people to the Golan Heights, and Ruth very much wanted to go on one. Esther felt dubious about it—were snipers still around?— but she agreed to allow to Ruth go when her sister-in-law Hannah said she would accompany the children. From the bus window, Ruth saw one abandoned Arab village after another. The children passed them in silence. Neither she nor the others had a context for what they were looking at—doors left open, beds unmade, household objects strewn about. "Nobody explained the meaning of what we saw ... so it looked as if the people had left yesterday. We didn't get out ... but I saw very clearly, and it was a sort of dissonance. What was no less amazing to me was that a few years later, let's say about four to five years, when I again visited the area, I could not see any of these villages, only some ruins. That was confusing, but I didn't ask what really happened. Maybe I couldn't rely on my own memory? I thought I'd dreamed it. Only later when I'd learned the facts, this vision came back to me as a reconfirmed reality."

The goals and ferocity of the settlement movement had become far clearer by the time Ruth's sister, Nechama, was invited on similar tours, and she had a much more immediate reaction to what she considered propaganda trips to the occupied territory. I visited Nechama in her airy, uncluttered Tel Aviv apartment, and she told me that she had refused to go on these trips. In general, she said, she rebelled strongly against the drift of the religious milieu she was a part of and agreed to return to high school only after her parents allowed her to attend a far more open school than the one she'd been attending. Chafing against the numerous religious rules she had to follow, including those about "modest" apparel, she began to secretly change into jeans in the garden after she left the house, rolling up her skirt and hiding it in the bushes, then changing back when she returned home. It seems like a small enough rebellion, but in the realm of obedient orthodoxy it wasn't perceived that way. "It took me about two years before I was able to wear them in front of my family," she told me. "They were just not allowed for religious girls. The first time I wore jeans at home, my mother said, 'What's this?'"

"I said, 'This is jeans.'"

"And she said, 'What are you doing with them?'"

"I said, 'I wear them. I like them. I bought them.'"

"And she said, 'This is not what we're wearing here!'"

"And I said, 'Well, I like it.'"

For Ruth, the messianic chatter, among the orthodox girls she knew, was becoming unbearably high-pitched, and eventually it led her, too, to rebel in her more quiet way. She engaged in angry exchanges about the subject with her best friend, often on the way home from school, which eventually led to the end of their friendship. (The former friend now lives in a settlement in the Golan Heights.) For Ruth and her family, who, after all, were religious, it was for years a complicated time. One evening as Ruth and I ate dinner together outdoors under an umbrella at a quiet neighborhood restaurant in the fading light of a hot Jerusalem day, Ruth said, "Sixty-seven changed so much. The friend I told you about had really tried to draw me into her messianic circle. And when I refused to go along with them, a lot shifted for me. And for my family too." For one thing, in 1968 her beloved cousin Bami, just twenty-two and adored by everyone, was killed by friendly fire in an army accident. His father, Hannah's husband Ephraim, had lost his entire family in the Holocaust, and, though his adopted country had been born in war, Ephraim hoped he had finally left untimely death behind. They all did. Somehow, it was eleven-year-old Ruth who was dispatched to her father's school to deliver the terrible news to him. "The death of Bami," Ruth went on, "broke the family. I mean that it broke our spirit. Something changed." Along with familial change there came, incrementally, a shift in the family's view of their country. On the one hand, while many religious families took advantage of the legal exemption allowing them to decline to serve in the army, Ruth's family believed that those who lived in the country should serve. At Bami's funeral, his father severely criticized boys who hid behind their prayer books to escape serving.

On the other hand, her family was increasingly troubled by the country's new posture as an occupying force. Ruth described to me the confusion of feelings she grappled with in that era, comparing them with her mother's, especially when she had been a young girl in Munich: "I was old enough, like my mother, to understand ... that something took place that was awful." But whereas the new reality had eventually become clear to the young Esther in Munich, "Here things were not clear."

Ruth knew about the geography of the situation and that there were lots of places she was again not allowed to venture to. In time she was aware of the terrorist attacks of the late 1960s in a supermarket and at a university cafeteria and retaliatory Israeli attacks directed at Jordan. But Ruth had yet to grasp the full magnitude of what was transpiring—such matters were not discussed in detail at home except for worried conversations about the new rabid messianism. Nearly two years after the Six-Day War, Ruth attended a particularly heartfelt discussion with her youth group at a special study-group meeting about the occupied lands and the redemption of their people. Coming home a bit off-balance and momentarily open to what had been said, she asked her mother about it.

"Redemption?" Esther had said. "What are you talking about? What we need is peace. Peace—which the book of Judges tells about—'And the land was quiet for forty years.' That is what is desirable. That would allow the country to go forward in education, agriculture, and industry. *That* would be the wonderful thing." After that, Ruth continued to attend her youth group meetings and lead campers on hiking trips and summer holidays, but she quit its study group. Her days of listening to what she describes as "messianic blah blah blah" were over. "All those young women becoming so pious and speaking softly and wearing those special sorts of clothes ... with this sort of holiness that was hovering above them. I didn't like it, and I heard these things and said to myself, 'Enough. I'm never again going to the meetings where that sort of discussion will take place.'"

Over the next years, Ruth's pilgrimage to the wider world was accelerated by books, art, and especially music. But she never stopped her faithful attendance at the general gatherings of her youth group, which over time became more and more central in her life. When she served in the army she joined as part of a religious unit of conscripts and did community service among religious people. Her willingness to be part of religious formalities, however, had at that point far more to do with her respect for her parents and unwillingness to hurt or disappoint her mother than to her religious attachment. Nechama, though she had a complex relationship to her religious observance, was less conflicted and asked to join the regular army, where she could be among secular people. Her family was against it, but she went anyway. Part of the time Nechama served in the army she was sent to the West Bank, where she lived among settlers. "They were talking," she told me, "about the looks of those olive trees and beautiful gardens and fruit trees and orchards of the neighboring Arabs and said, 'All those are going to be ours one day.' I couldn't believe it. . . . They used to walk into the middle of those fields and destroy them. Just a sense of power and entitlement. It was unbearable." When she went home she described what she'd seen and heard. "Those people [the settlers] are going to kill us because we don't think the same," Nechama told her family. "They are very dangerous people. They don't believe in democracy." Though her parents were in principle against the settlements, they responded, "No, no. You are always so extreme." Nechama later remembered, "They didn't believe me. . . . They all thought I was a little crazy and exaggerating. . . . And then when Rabin was killed, I was in the States studying for my doctorate. My parents called and said, 'You said this would happen.'"

For Ruth, her long walks alone along the Jerusalem streets from her parents' apartment building in Rehavia to the old part of the city where her youth group meetings were held were increasingly moments of pure joy. Joyful too was the freedom of her trips to the group's summer camp. So satisfying was this part of her life that she didn't leave the youth group behind until she was twenty. Over the years she also learned to play the flute well, and music and musicians became a major part of her life. Just as the secular books Ruth devoured opened up the world—she was struck in particular by Hemingway's stories and novels and the way they alluded to "entirely different norms from a different universe existentially and sexually." Her free mind and the

bracing independence of her times at summer camp led her to eagerly anticipate the open possibilities of her future and her individual
choices. That and her reading, she believes, allowed her to make the
larger world her own. Schooled as she had been in religious reverence,
her widening field of vision brought her the perspectives of irrever-
ence and skepticism.

CHAPTER 8

THE 1,001 NIGHTS OF
WASIF JAWHARIYYEH AND
THE MINGLING OF CHRISTIANS,
JEWS, AND MUSLIMS

Late one afternoon a few months before Abdallah died, after we'd gorged ourselves on a delicious meal of *maqluba* (a traditional dish made with rice, meat, and vegetables and flipped upside-down onto a serving dish), in the middle of a conversation about his family's life in prewar Lifta, Abdallah mentioned the good relations that had once existed between local Arabs and Jews. Many of those he called the "native" Jews came from Arabic-speaking countries and had been in Palestine for as long as anyone could remember. Some even dressed like Arabs, he said, and wore caftans and spoke Arabic with their Muslim neighbors. In his father's time especially, there were relaxed, neighborly, interreligious friendships. And shared complaints about their Turkish and British rulers.

"But those friendships were rare?" I asked.

"Not so rare. Especially when there were common courtyards and people constantly ran into each other. There were even intermarriages—but those were rare."

"*Yani*, things changed," he added, with the huge flood of Zionists who mostly came from Europe and who were looked upon solely, and pretty much by everyone, as the latest wave of colonial threat.

I heard similar stories from an elderly relative who lived down the street from the Abuleils and from an older man in Amman I visited who had grown up in Lifta and belonged to a popular club of Lifta refugees and their descendants now living in Jordan, who met from time to time to share meals and memories.

I confess that for a long time I tended to regard these stories about the old days with a fair degree of skepticism. I suspected they sprang from some dewy version of a past that never was, viewed through the lens of nostalgia.

Over the years there have been, of course, some accounts of better relations between Jews and Arabs, but the majority of histories of the late Ottoman and Mandate years, the period Abdallah was referring to, rarely speak of amity between Arabs and Jews, though they sometimes mention commercial encounters between the two populations. Rather, they confirm the conventional view of mutual antagonism, bloody confrontation, and ongoing distrust—the three pillars of the conflict today.

So I was truly astounded when I came across *The Storyteller of Jerusalem: The Life and Times of Wasif Jawhariyyeh, 1904–1948*, a popular Jerusalem amateur musician's recollections of his social, cultural, and personal milieu that focus on the last years of the four-hundred-year span of Ottoman rule and the thirty-one years of the British Mandate. The book represents the effort of nearly a decade by its editors, Salim Tamari and Issam Nasser, and translator Nada Elzeer. Jawhariyyeh wrote his memoir in the late 1960s and early 1970s, partly from memory (his was rumored to be photographic) and partly from old diary notes, long after the events described took place. Some of the darker realities of the period, particularly the violent juggling for power of the city's leaders, go unmentioned. But if his is not an especially political work, as the narrative progresses from 1904 to 1948 his nationalistic feelings increasingly enter the picture.

From early childhood on, Jawhariyyeh's passion was music, though as an adult he earned his living as a civil servant. An Eastern Orthodox Christian whose father was trained as a lawyer and also served as the *mukhtar*, or leader of Jerusalem's Eastern Orthodox community, young Jawhariyyeh became widely admired for his mastery of the oud and other regional instruments and for his beautiful voice.

Music was the glue that held Jawhariyyeh's life together, and his memories too. Its joys elevated his days beyond the reach of Turkish occupation, British high-handedness, and Zionist incursions.

Describing one of innumerable arak-fueled Jerusalem gatherings he attended and was often at the center of in the 1920s, singing and playing his oud all evening, Jawhariyyeh writes, "I should mention that we were all extremely inebriated." He continues, "On a large table in the room, we placed a small table and a high wooden chair on top of it. I climbed up ... and stood on the chair, holding on with my left hand to the ceiling ring that hung high in the middle of the dome, at the highest point in the house. Then, I grabbed the oud from my friend and began to play and sing. ... We carried on like this until daybreak ... [then] set off on foot, with everyone who had been at the party walking around or behind me as I played." Jawhariyyeh goes on to say that he and his friends went on, with everyone cheering, winding their way along the brightening city streets. People awakened by the din stared at the revelers through their windows, with what reaction he does not say, mentioning only that his acquaintances and neighbors remembered the event decades later.

Had this scene taken place in Rome or New York or Paris or Berlin, it wouldn't be all that surprising, but it happened in the early part of the twentieth century in a Jerusalem that in this anecdote (and in Jawhariyyeh's memoir in general) bears as little resemblance to today's conservative modern city, with its modestly swaddled women on both sides of the religious divide and its ranting fundamentalist scolds, as Earth does to Saturn. One of the astonishments of the memoir, which only became available in English in 2013, is the clear picture it provides of the city's social fluidity—Christians mingling with Muslims and both mingling with Jews—at least among the middle and upper classes.

Jawhariyyeh's musical life was central to his identity, but his family's practical well-being was inextricably bound to its protectors, the Husseini family, thirteen of whom served as Jerusalem's mayors between 1864 and 1920. Jawhariyyeh provides an intimate overview of the tightly hierarchical but permissive mores of the Husseinis, who were among the powerful feudal landlords and patrician elites who ran the city and often jostled against one another at the top rung of its social ladder. The luxury and opulence of some of the houses Jawhariyyeh visits make them seem like Arab versions of Downton Abbey. Both Jawhariyyeh and his father helped the Husseinis look after their village estates, and over the years one or another Husseini provided them employment, financial support, and entrance to the homes and

social life of a wide swath of the city's well-to-do residents. Wasif's father was a successful merchant and silk farmer, but his relationship to
the Husseinis was crucial to his family's status. In *The Storyteller of Jerusalem* the full force of favor and patronage is portrayed straightforwardly and uncritically as the central reality of Arab public life that it
was (and to some extent is today). One conclusion becomes unavoid-
able—that it would take far more than the shibboleths of democratic
wishful thinking to unloosen the grip of such a deep-rooted system.
The prevalence of power-hoarding and the disconnection of leaders
with their constituency remains a central affliction of the Palestinian
political class today.

Jawhariyyeh's father served on Jerusalem's municipal council, a
job that came with a bit of extra money from the Greek Orthodox
Patriarchate and allowed him to serve as mediator between his patron, Hussein al-Husseini, and the powerful Archbishop Damianos.
Said to command any room he entered, Damianos was a tall, impos-
ing man with a long snowy beard who sometimes wore a tiara en-
crusted with bright gems. "On festive occasions," reports Jawhariyyeh
about his father, "he would join the archbishop and the patriarch's
head translator, and together they would visit the notables of Jerusalem ... and hand each high official their allocated share of gold,
packed in a small bag of pure white silk." "These allocations," he writes
without irony, "were given in view of the patriarch's status and power
in the country, and in this way, the ... Patriarchate in Jerusalem had
the sympathy of the entire government."

Young Wasif became a protégé of Hussein al-Husseini, who
served from 1909 to 1917 as Jerusalem's mayor, a job he inherited from
his father. Husseini was admired by Jews, Christians, and Muslims
alike for his efforts in the development of the city, including paving
many roads. Husseini trusted Wasif enough to assign him the task
of looking after his mistress when she fell ill. And when Wasif's
father died in 1914, Husseini became, Wasif tells us, like a second father. But privately Jawhariyyeh considered his mission in life to be
learning, playing, and composing music. So when he was young he
had no problem accepting, through patronage, civil service work that
required little, sometimes nothing, apart from collecting a salary. His
relation to his work changed when he married and began raising a

family, but it also changed when he lost his patron to pneumonia four years after the death of his father and several weeks after Husseini surrendered the city to the British.

At the picnics, festivals, and parties Jawhariyyeh attended, music played an important role. It also brought him together with well-known artists from Cairo and Beirut. He often mentions the Jewish families his own was friendly with, particularly the Elishars, Navons, Anteibis, and Manis. Schools were no less segregated then than they are today in Jerusalem, but Arab children sometimes attended Jewish schools and some Jewish children were enrolled at Arab schools. The Mani progeny, for example, along with several other Sephardic Jewish children, attended the progressive modern school—no corporal punishment, no rote memorization—founded in 1909 by the Palestinian educator Khalil Sakakini, who was anti-Zionist but far from anti-Semitic, a distinction that in the years to come would increasingly blur. Wasif, too, attended Sakakini's school for a while.

Arab and Jewish families often celebrated their holidays together, he tells us, eating, drinking and even sleeping together under their fig trees. And since the Jerusalem calendar then as now was replete with religious celebrations, there were numerous occasions for this sharing. Wasif's memoir provides an interesting take on these festivities. "Without these religion-based celebrations," he writes, "people would have succumbed to gloom, particularly in the days when they lived inside the wall and the gate was closed at sunset in order to prevent potential attacks by Bedouins."

It is common to read in histories of the city accounts of one of those celebrations, the infamous 1920 Nabi Musa (the Prophet Moses) event. Annually, then as today, Palestinians made a seven-day pilgrimage from Jerusalem to the site in the Judean Desert near Jericho where the body of Moses was said to have been buried. In 1920 this pilgrimage devolved into bloody riots resulting in the deaths of five Jews and four Arabs and the injury of hundreds. Three years earlier the English had made public the Balfour Declaration, and the riots were the culmination of subsequent long-simmering resentment and tensions in relation to Zionist land acquisition. The violence was incited by incendiary anti-Zionist speeches by Jerusalem leaders, particularly two of the Husseinis—Haj Amin, who was then only twenty-five, and Musa Kazem, sixty-seven, the heretofore moderate mayor at the time. Haj Amin was arrested for incitement, sentenced to ten years in prison, but escaped to Jordan and a year later was pardoned by the British and appointed Grand Mufti. British officials removed Musa Kazem from office and replaced him with Ragheb Nashashibi—about whom I had heard so much at my ill-fated visit with his nephew and biographer Nasser Eddin Nashashibi. Sakakini, who considered himself an Arab patriot, was among the seventy thousand present the day of the riot. After watching an Arab man from Hebron smash the head of a cowering Jewish shoeshine boy, he later commented, "I am disgusted and depressed by the madness of humankind."

Jawhariyyeh's recollections give us an enlarging picture of scores of festivals and processions that passed uneventfully and at which most people had a good time. When the Jews celebrated Purim, a holiday in which costumes and parades figure prominently, he and his brother dressed up in costumes and joined the festivities. The neighborhood of Sheikh Jarrah, better known in recent times for its settler takeover of Palestinian homes and attendant protests, was in Jawhariyyeh's era a place where an all-day celebration known as the Judea Festival took place. Those who attended included Muslim Arabs, Christians, and Jews. And he and his friends, Jawhariyyeh writes, "never wasted an opportunity to be among them."

Nowadays it's not unusual for some Palestinian Muslims to dismiss their Christian Arab kin as "not exactly Palestinians," as well as to disparage Palestinians who by a twist of history have Israeli citizenship. Jawhariyyeh believed that these depressing—and damaging—divisions began with the British. Though most people were happy to see the end of what he describes as the "tyrannical" Ottoman rule and especially Turkish conscription, which decimated the community in World War I, the various denominations and religions had more or less lived amicably together under it. But when the British occupied Jerusalem, Jawhariyyeh writes, they tried to sow trouble, particularly between Muslims and Christians. Christians were banned from al-Haram al-Sharif, the city's main mosque, and the Muslims from the Church of the Holy Sepulchre. But Jawhariyyeh's gaze is mainly on the daily life and culture of the circle he moved in. He mentions but doesn't focus on the degree to which the British consolidated their power by encouraging awareness of religious and ethnic difference. He also tells us that the lives of municipal workers like himself went on pretty much as usual under the British and that those who had worked for a long time at government jobs kept them.

If the long period of Ottoman rule was marked chiefly by continuity, the British Mandate era ushered in one of dramatic change, brought about by electricity and automobiles (among other innovations), the trend toward greater literacy, and the Zionist juggernaut. The British governor, Sir Ronald Storrs, who served from 1917 to 1926, was knowledgeable about Arab traditions (he had served previously as oriental secretary in Cairo) and frequently asked Jawhariyyeh to play at his parties. But Storrs seems to have been too besotted by the country to see the issues before him very clearly. T. E. Lawrence called Storrs "the most brilliant Englishman in the Near East" and "the great man among us," but in time he became a despised figure to both sides, particularly the Zionists. In his memoir (which was written without benefit of any of his papers from the period he served as governor, since all his books and papers were destroyed in a fire, relying instead on detailed weekly letters he wrote to his mother), Storrs sums up the core of his position: "Two hours of Arab grievances drive me into the synagogue, while after an intensive course of Zionist propaganda I am prepared to embrace Islam." In a sense his vacillating loyalties mirrored only too well the inconsistency of British policy toward Palestine. Storrs himself claimed godlike neutrality. "I am not wholly for either," he insisted, "but for both." Another time he described the political events transpiring over the period of his governance as a conflict "between right and right." But over the years, his anti-Zionist statements became more prevalent, and the most virulent attacks against him came from Zionist critics—probably justifiably.

Jawhariyyeh grew increasingly ambivalent about Storrs, but since his memoir offers no detailed political analysis of his policies, we are left with a picture of the governor as someone who, despite his flaws, transformed a weary, post–World War I city into one with a building boom and a bracing sense of progress. Jerusalemites had for a time faced starvation, as the Turks, in retreat, Jawhariyyeh writes, had not left "much that was eatable or moveable behind them." While his account shows more and more irritation caused by his sense of British favoritism toward the Jews, Jawhariyyeh is unable to shed his accustomed mantle of generosity and still warmly welcomes the governor's chumminess. As in most of his descriptions of everyday life, there is an almost fairy-tale quality in his portrayal of colonial municipal habits. In a café under pine trees near the municipal building where Jawhariyyeh worked at the registry office, he and his fellow employees would regularly enjoy a leisurely mid-morning break. "All the employees, heads, and subordinates alike would meet," he writes,

> and put their sense of humor and story-telling skills to the test. My colleagues still miss those days and speak of how good they were. . . . In winter . . . they would all have snowball fights. One morning I went to work to find that many of my colleagues had been waiting for me. As soon as I arrived they started throwing snowballs at me. I shouted, "Storrs, Storrs! Help me!" Storrs suddenly appeared and came to my rescue, frenetically pelting them with snowballs. Thanks to his strong build we won the battle and spent most of that day at the governate drinking whiskey and cognac. An atmosphere of friendship and understanding prevailed among all the civil servants.

"Storrs liked this way of life," Jawhariyyeh thought, because he had been for many years in Egypt and Sudan. "And having come to know the ways of the Orient. . . . He decided to adopt them."

As time passed, however, the governor's jolly parties and bonhomie began to pall and become less significant than his country's policies, and his actions were perceived as manipulative. In Storrs's memoir, Jawhariyyeh's name does not appear. Jawhariyyeh writes, "Our rejoicing about the British occupation that had ended the despotic Ottoman rule turned into bitter disappointment as we sensed Britain's bad intentions for the country and its people." Jawhariyyeh's characteristic satirical style, which he uses to great effect to create a vivid portrait of the follies of Jerusalem's upper class and Ottoman and British leaders, as well as the people he encountered in his everyday life, is cast aside when he writes about his own family, about whom we learn almost nothing. He was clearly devastated by the

death of his wife, Victoria, and, like half his fellow Palestinians, he
became a refugee in 1948 and spent his last days in exile in Beirut.

After reading Jawhariyyeh, I couldn't help but wonder how many
other voices have been lost to the West in the untranslated and un-
published private diaries and memoirs of the same period and what
those times looked like through Jewish eyes. A complicating factor
in this particular corner of history was that whatever good relations
existed between the inhabitants of various Arab towns and Jewish
communities, it became more or less unacceptable to mention them.
Palestinians didn't want to look like they had been collaborators in
their own tragic history, and Israelis wanted to maintain their picture
of an implacably hostile enemy, central to justifying Palestinian expulsion. Happily, as it turned out, a fresh wave of post–New Historians,
academics chiefly, wondered about the same thing, although the fruits
of their labors have yet to reach popular notice. The most interesting
of these excavations is the work of Menachem Klein, a political science professor at Bar-Ilan University who served as a member of the
team that drafted the 2003 Geneva Initiative. Klein's *Lives in Common: Arabs and Jews in Jerusalem, Jaffa, and Hebron* exponentially aug-
ments the *Storyteller of Jerusalem* revelations. Drawing on a multitude
of private papers, biographies, diaries, and interviews, Klein too re-
veals a complex world of intimate relations between Arabs and Jews
in Palestine at the end of the nineteenth and beginning of the twentieth centuries. He confirms from other Arabs Abdallah Abuleil's
distinction between native Jews and Zionists, most of whom in that
period were from Europe. "Whereas Arabs viewed the former as na-
tives of a somewhat inferior status," Klein writes, "the latter were seen
as European invaders who had to be repelled." He quotes the father
of the novelist A. B. Yehoshua as saying, "The residential courtyards
of the Jews and Muslims were common . . . we were all friends . . . Our
mothers poured out their hearts to Muslim women and they poured
out their hearts to our mothers . . . Our children played with their
children." The British journalist and former Middle East editor of
the *Guardian* Ian Black, in his excellent *Enemies and Neighbors: Arabs
and Jews in Palestine and Israel, 1917–2017*, published three years after
Klein's book, explores the underlying attitudes and societal structures
that worked to perpetuate violent events and to some extent corrects

the hopeful portrayal of the two groups' sometime recognition of each other's humanity. Black, as well as a few other modern historians such as Saleh Abdel Jawad, warns us not to look for some imaginary golden age of harmony between Jews and Arabs but to understand that, depending on the tone set by the rulers of past eras, Arabs and Jews in different periods could enjoy good relationships. Nonetheless, Jawhariyyeh and Klein challenge the persistent idea that relations between Jews and Arabs were solely defined, always and forever, by the conflict between two nationalistic movements and utterly separate communities. Rather, they portray a common native identity that bit by bit was undermined and in 1948 torn asunder. One thing is certain: the place they describe is no more.

Travels with Fuad IV

▶ A particularly fine, clear May day. The city seems lit from within, and in the distance, as Fuad and I are driving along, the dome of the al-Aqsa mosque, ubiquitous subject of the tourist postcard, glows as if it had magnetized the morning light. We were on our way to Nazareth. I was planning to have lunch with Amal Jamal, a Druze scholar and author of a recently published book about the development of political identity in Israel's Arab minority. I'd talked with Jamal before and admired his work. Fuad was telling me that most Palestinians only encountered the Druze in nasty clashes with the IDF. The Druze speak Arabic, and their religion originated as an offshoot of Islam, but they are not considered Muslims. Since the creation of Israel they have been part of the Israeli army, but their service has brought them neither equal treatment from the Israelis nor anything but scorn from their fellow Palestinians. In recent years, Fuad said, he'd heard that many Druze now refused to join the army, but many still did, and, because they are regularly assigned to the Israel Border Police, they are overrepresented in clashes at settlements and roadblocks. It was the considered opinion of many of the Palestinians involved in those clashes that the Druze acted even more meanly and aggressively than the other Israeli soldiers.

We were having this conversation, driving along one of the city's main streets the day preceding Independence Day, when a sudden piercingly loud siren sounded, traffic ground to a halt, and all around us people stepped out of their cars, drivers and passengers alike, and stood completely still. I had no idea of what was going on. Fuad, his hands remaining on the steering wheel, his gaze focused straight ahead, said quietly, "It's the country's Remembrance Day—for the ones who died."

In every direction cars, trucks, and buses had stopped. I later learned that this scene had been mirrored on highways and back roads all over the country and in city streets all across Israel to honor its fallen soldiers and victims of terrorist attacks—too many, though the estimated numbers are famously unreliable. The siren system was installed by the British to warn of enemy bombers and expanded afterward by the Israelis. National flags were also lowered to half-mast that day, and the event always takes place the day preceding Independence Day. On Holocaust Remembrance Day, in April, Israel similarly comes to a halt, and the sirens sound then too. An intake of national breath, it was an eerie and dramatic display of collective pain and sorrow, noisily summoned and quietly acknowledged in a gesture of one-big-family commemoration. Not standing were the Muslim cab drivers, many identifiable by their bushy mustaches. Like Fuad, they mostly stared straight ahead, hands resting on their steering wheels. Then everyone got back in their cars, and traffic started moving again. Fuad and I drove away in silence for a while.

The Palestinian dead were also honored in Nakba ceremonies organized by the PA in the West Bank, but in Israel no public acknowledgment of their mourning is anywhere on the national calendar. Of course it wouldn't be, since public recognition of the primary event that turned Palestinian life inside out is forbidden. The cumulative figures for Palestinian fatalities are similarly unreliable, but most sources agree that in recent wars the fatality ratio of Israeli Jews to Palestinians is approximately 1:10.

A joint alternative Israeli-Palestinian Remembrance Day ceremony organized by the indefatigable, nonviolent, and reconciliation-promoting Parents Circle–Families Forum, as well as Combatants for Peace, has been held in Tel Aviv for many years. Thousands show up for it along with numerous hard-right activists who curse and threaten the attendees and make every effort to disrupt the ceremony. In 2017, for the first time in twelve years, the West Bank Palestinians who set out to attend were refused permits by the Defense Ministry and barred from attending, though they spoke to those gathered in Tel Aviv via a prerecorded video.

Finally, as we left the city behind, Fuad broke the silence. "You know," he said, turning toward me, "you'd look good in a hijab."

I laughed. "*Never!*"

"Well, I'm just saying. Very nice. You would."

CHAPTER 9

THE EZRAHIS

The walk to Ruth and her husband Yaron's house from my short-term rental studio in Jerusalem's leafy German Colony—named after the evangelical German Templers, who settled there in the mid-nineteenth century—takes about ten minutes. Along the way I pass streets named after gentiles considered good for the Jews—Lloyd George, for one, and Émile Zola, for another; a phalanx of kosher restaurants that cater to the ever-burgeoning number of the religious who have moved into the neighborhood and edged out many mom-and-pop stores; and a small, popular supermarket where I often shop. From my very first visit to the market, I was amused and annoyed in equal measure by a singular aspect of the place: despite its extremely narrow aisles and general crowdedness, almost nobody makes room for you when you need to pass through. Even after you say "*Shlicha*" ("Excuse me"). Even after you politely repeat it. No movement. Nothing. At first I thought it was a fluke of that day, but I soon came to realize that, no, it was the Israeli way. There didn't appear to be any aggression in it. People more or less magnetized into a comfortable clump and saw no reason to budge. Recently I saw a photograph of an Israeli dance troupe performing, and there they were, in a graceful cluster, as if glued together. It was, as Yaron puts it in his lucid and most straightforwardly topical book *Rubber Bullets: Power and Conscience in Modern Israel*, "A pattern of interaction that derives from the lack of a Western sense of an impermeable, invisible circle [that] protected the private space of each individual." Reading that passage, I thought of rush hour in the New York subway and what I've always regarded as the incredible forbearance of most of its long-suffering passengers, packed into the cars, who nonetheless, even there, sensitive to the concept of "private space," are forever apologizing for sticking an elbow in your ear or a backpack in your face.

On the one hand, Yaron attributes this national phenomenon in part to the closer proximity of people living in the Middle East. On the other, it's a component of his larger portrait of his culture's preoccupation with collective liberation and cultural revival. "Once," he writes, "I found myself telling my students at the Hebrew University of Jerusalem that there is a very curious social phenomenon called a 'queue,' in which people spontaneously line up, standing one after another in a line without touching or shouting, for example in bus stations or banks; students who wanted to observe or study such curious behavior, I said with only slight exaggeration, would have to travel abroad."

On a more serious level, in *Rubber Bullets* and in much of his writing Yaron provides a persuasive analysis of his country's ongoing conflict between the collectivist national ethos that created and perpetuates the state and its capacity to embody the principles of a global democracy. He points out the ways the historical "need to fight a war of survival, to justify the ultimate sacrifice of lives, and later to cope with terror, coupled with a delayed reaction to the Holocaust, reinforced the tendency to idealize state power." But he also shows how that history badly weakened Israel's ability to nourish liberal democratic principles. *Rubber Bullets* was published in 1997, and since then Israeli society has been transformed in important ways. The cohesiveness that was once considered immutable has diminished and become far more complex. Groups with a strong sense of identity who do not often agree with each other—the ultra-orthodox, Russian immigrants, the Sephardim, Ethiopians, and Palestinian Israelis—have created a more fragmented society. A few years after *Rubber Bullets* appeared, at a time when a relatively dovish government was in power, Yaron wrote in an essay in *Foreign Affairs* that "the rise of Israeli individualism, which brings with it a spreading distrust of authority in almost all spheres of life," had caused notable shifts in the country. During the country's more recent rightward drift, I have failed to detect much evidence of this in the political realm, though it is certainly true that the getting-and-having culture seems to have pretty much obliterated the old kibbutz ethos. Yaron's other publications include *The Descent of Icarus: Science and the Transformation of Contemporary Democracy,* which examines the role of science as a political force in democratic societies; *Imagined Democracies: Necessary Political Fictions,* a brilliant reframing of the history of political thought from ancient Greece to modern times, which one reviewer called "a contemporary masterpiece"; and a book about music and politics that he cowrote in Hebrew with Ruth. A slew of his other works all circle around issues related to democratic and antidemocratic values.

Yaron and I first met at a low-key neighborhood café not far from his house. Like nearly all Israeli men, he was dressed in a relaxed way—a short-sleeve shirt and khakis, no tie, no jacket (the ubiquitous male national costume even in the Knesset). The top of his head was hidden that afternoon beneath a straw fedora, a precaution against the penetrating Mediterranean sun, which he and Ruth were leery of since both had struggled with bouts of cancer. The hat hid the fact that, like an amazing preponderance of his countrymen, he was balding. Some 30 percent of Israeli men experience balding by the time they are thirty, and 70 percent will lose more than half their hair by the time they reach sixty.

By then I had learned that the headgear of the men sitting around us at nearby tables provided clues to their identities. Normal-size *kippas* (or yarmulkes) meant religious. Colorful knitted ones indicated settlers or modern orthodox Jews (often Americans). Minute kippas, each precariously secured with a metal barrette, meant religious but not necessarily enthusiastically so, often worn by young men). Not seated at the café (not kosher enough) but peppily bounding by in the broiling midday sun, were black-garbed men wearing the *shtreimels* or heavy fur hats of married Hasidic men and sometimes non-Hasidic religious men called Perushim (from the Hebrew meaning "to separate"), who first settled in the country at the beginning of the nineteenth century. But Yaron's hat was just a hat. The clothing of the women was more varied, but there was a recognizable religious-woman costume consisting of a long tunic or blouse over slacks or long skirt and some kind of headgear (often in the form of what in my mother's generation was called a snood), an outfit I came to think of, incorrectly, as "kibbutz girl."

Yaron, who was born in 1940, grew up in Tel Aviv in an artistic milieu that acted as a strong countercurrent to the prevailing cultural winds. The era of utopian Zionism still powerfully influenced his family, but universalist, humanistic modern values were his daily nourishment. Yaron came of age in an Israel that ignored serious injuries to the native population, but compared to today, it was a less racist, fairly moderate society that still bore some resemblance to European social democracies. But whatever forces shaped him, the man who emerged radiated intellectual confidence the same way great athletes radiate superb fitness. Yaron credits his father with giving him an extraordinary sense of the largeness of the world and the beauty of art and music. His father, who died in 2003 at ninety-nine, was a violinist and composer who served as one of the directors of Israel's first music conservatory (and spoke eight languages, including Arabic). "His playing," Yaron writes in *Rubber Bullets*

> opened up gates to the self which I could appreciate only years later . . . but it may have struck me so forcefully because I was growing up in a society obsessed with collective liberation and cultural revival. The Zionist leaders and educators of our time, focused so intently on the monumental implications of our ancient tribe's return to its land, were not concerned with cultivating the solitary self, the lyrical personal voice of the individual. The modern Hebrew prose and poetry that we read in our elementary and high schools were immersed, in both style and content, in the collective political and cultural agenda of the Israeli revolution; they offered few examples of personal expression.

Yaron's father was of an altogether different mind-set. "He was just an incredible person. This is the greatest gift I've received next to Ruth . . . to have a person like this as your father—totally poetical, full of incredible imagination, and always, whether you are two years old or—he died when I was sixty-three—creating expansive space where growth is possible."

"And your mother?"

"Well, my father taught me how to fly, my Polish mother how to land. It was she who persuaded me when I was doing a lot of painting that making a living as a painter would be impossible—and she was probably right."

Whether he could have succeeded as an artist we'll never know. Yaron neglected to tell me many biographical details, preferring to

discuss his country's history. ("Talk to Ruth," he advised regarding
personal information. "She has more interesting things to say.") One
thing he failed to tell me was that one of his paintings had been included in a group show of young Israeli painters at New York's Museum of Modern Art.

Yaron's paternal grandfather, Mordechai Krichevsky, who was
imprisoned for a while for socialist-Zionist agitation, emigrated
from Ukraine to Palestine in 1894 and eventually became a leading
Jewish education reformer, president of the first union of Hebrew
teachers, and among the first authors of textbooks in Hebrew. It was
he who changed the family name to Ezrahi, which means "citizen."
Yaron proudly mentioned that his grandfather was one of the vanguard intellectuals in the scholarly circle of the lexicographer and editor Eliezer Ben-Yehuda, who is credited with being among those who
revived the Hebrew language, and of the poet Chaim Nahman Bialik,
a pioneer of modern Hebrew poetry. But there was a wealth of other
biographical details that he apparently didn't think worth mentioning,
things I would later learn about not from Ruth but from Yaron's son,
Ariel, or Yaron's sister, Ofra. An accomplished pianist who headed a
Jerusalem branch of the same conservatory her father directed, Ofra
told me that she was taken out of school for a year when she was ten
to take care of her baby brother, because her parents both worked and
couldn't afford help. She insisted, somewhat unconvincingly, that she
hadn't minded doing it. Ofra also mentioned that Yaron, whose gaze
was particularly direct (and in weighty discussions permanently set
on "Stun"), had been severely cross-eyed until an operation corrected
the condition.

Ariel is an international lawyer. Now forty-six, he is married to
a German writer and dance scholar. Until a few years before I met
them, the couple had made London their home, but they had since
temporarily anchored in Tel Aviv. Ariel told me that several ancestors
in a branch of his father's family, the de Lattes, served as physicians
to two popes, including Leo X, the Medici pope, and another relative,
Ezer Weizman, became Israel's seventh president. One afternoon, after I'd been trying and failing to extract from Yaron something about
his family's pre-Israel lives and instead hearing more about the country's sociopolitical history, I pointed this out—that a good many of

his answers to my questions about his personal history floated swiftly away into the currents of political ideology.

"Well," he said, grinning, "you can't ask a spider not to spin his web." But Ariel believes that that sort of sidestepping is more complicated and that his father—like many Israelis—doesn't talk much about his European history because "he looks at Zionism, and everything starts in 1948, and the history is not important." Ariel is slim and has finely chiseled features and pale blue eyes. He and his two sisters have dual citizenship because his mother, Yaron's first wife (who is also an academic), was born in the United States and has dual citizenship. For a long time, Ariel told me, he hadn't been particularly interested in his family's early history either—though he was proud of his father's nineteenth-century roots in the country—until he married. It fascinated him that his wife, Christina, who is a member of an old, powerful, German Protestant industrial family, could trace her ancestors back to the fourteenth century, and he became curious about his own.

There were, to put it mildly, adjustments for both families to make when the couple announced their intention to marry. Ariel said, "Marrying a German is breaking a big taboo. However, I was fortunate enough to have grown up in a family where ultimately liberalism trumped tribalism, if I can put it that way. . . . People preach liberalism . . . but when it comes to their front door . . . they don't want to hear about it . . . 'Let's keep things separate.'"

On his wife's side, he learned, the men who married into her family were sometimes dukes or princes. "One of the funniest things ever said to me was what my wife's father said, 'Thank God you're not a Catholic prince!' In the end, both our families offered us warm acceptance. The major problem for Christina's family was not [in] getting a Jew but [in getting] an Israeli. The fact that we're living in a war zone, we're living in the Middle East—in some ways that's been more of a stressful factor. I wouldn't say it's been stressful in our marriage but stressful for the grandparents on Christina's side."

Ariel and his sisters, Talya and Tehila, moved around a lot when they were young because both their parents taught as visiting scholars at various US universities, including Stanford, Harvard, Duke, and Princeton. Talya didn't have a strong opinion about those travels,

Tehila didn't like them, and Ariel believes he benefited from all that moving around and the other complexities of his upbringing—his father a Sabra, his mother American; his father secular, his mother religious; adjustments to the different customs in the places where they settled temporarily.

"Maybe that's why I ended up in a mixed marriage as well," Ariel offered as we sipped coffee on a Saturday afternoon in the café of an old, beloved movie theater, Lev Smadar, across the street from where I lived. The theater is perpetually threatened with extinction and is the lone establishment in the tightly shut down neighborhood that remained open on the Sabbath. Even though his parents were both Jews, Ariel said, their marriage was in effect mixed because "there was always the outside Israel, the external, foreign element. . . . But I think I've benefited from it, especially linguistically, because we had both Hebrew and English at home." Like his father, who did his graduate work at Harvard, Ariel ventured abroad for his schooling, attending Manchester University in the north of England for his undergraduate degree just after he completed his military service. Also like both his parents, he marched unswervingly forward in his schooling. Swarms of young Israelis check out for a while after they've finished their army time. They "sort of go and get smashed on some beach in Thailand after they've served in the military, but within months I was at Manchester for pre-law." After Manchester he went to law school at Georgetown in DC, where he also worked for the State Department at a job that required high-security clearance. Before being hired, he was subjected to tough questioning from an FBI interrogator who was suspicious about where his loyalty ultimately lay. In Israel? In America? The FBI knew that he had already served in the Israeli military as a medic with naval special forces. (Like his father's, Ariel's military service proved to be a relatively uneventful experience that didn't involve battle.) Ariel was asked, "How do you serve in the military of one country and yet be trusted by another?" His answer—that just as he didn't choose between his mother and father, he didn't choose between the US and Israel—apparently satisfied his interrogator because he got the job. But much as Ariel enjoyed his time in Washington, he began think-ing that he ought to be doing something useful back in Israel. "I didn't want to be one of those lawyers who just did business contracts. I

wanted to do something interesting with my life and make a difference of sorts, which led me to my next degree, a master of philosophy
in modern Middle Eastern studies at Oxford." Oxford was where he
met Christina and learned Arabic.

For a while Ariel worked extensively with Palestinian entrepre-
neurs, sometimes pro bono, and he took a break from his law firm to
do more work of that kind. Today he works as the director of energy
for the Quartet—the group of national, international, and suprana-
tional bodies committed to mediating or trying to forward the peace
process in the conflict. Ariel and Christina kept their London apartment when they moved to Tel Aviv, initially to be nearer his father
after Yaron had some serious health problems, but increasingly they
began thinking of Tel Aviv as their home, as did their two children, a
girl and a boy, who seemed happy there.

Ariel and his sisters grew up accompanying their parents on
protest marches and hearing passionate critiques at home of government policies, especially of government involvement in settler incursions into Palestinian areas. Yaron mentioned that the older of his
two daughters, Talya, who is married to a British storyboard artist,
was the most left-wing of the family members. I visited her in her
small, brightly decorated apartment in Jerusalem not far from Yaron's
house. Dark-haired and easy to talk with, Talya is not religious, but
because her mother was, she grew up attending religious schools—
with strong fish-out-of-water feelings. On the other hand, when she
was very young she was also half-embarrassed by her non-religious
father's lack of a yarmulke when he showed up at school in a sea of
yarmulke-wearing dads. But she also recalled with pride her father
coming to her class after a right-wing fanatic threw a grenade into a
Peace Now demonstration in 1983 and killed one of the demonstra-
tors, who, they later found out, had been one of her father's students.
Her parents had been heading out to the demonstration themselves
when they heard about the grenade, so everybody stayed home and
watched the TV news footage. I wasn't in the country when that happened, but I was when several other major events—the 2005 withdrawal from Gaza, the 2006 war in Lebanon, the killing of several
Israeli hostages—were taking place. Each time as the family watched
the news I was impressed by the heavy silence in the room, the total

attention those sitting around the TV gave the screen, and the intense discussions that followed and continued over the next days. After the grenade-throwing event, Talya recalled, her father came to her class the next day to give the children a lesson in democratic values, and she felt proud of him, though for her fellow students there was more than a little ambivalence about peace groups. The Peace Now cadre, then as now, were regarded by many Israelis as troublemakers. "My closest friend at the time actually said, 'Oh, you deserve to die!'" At that point, she was only ten, but today she thinks of the event and her family's attitude toward it as the origin of her political awakening.

I was more than a little surprised to learn from Yaron that it was not until he attended graduate school at Harvard that he actually had meaningful conversations with Palestinians. I might have been mistaken, but it seemed as if it had taken that long for the reality of the Palestinians' experience to pierce the armor of his Zionism. It took that long, too, for him to experience anti-Semitism. "I was exactly thirty. And I was invited to a conference in Cambridge, England. In the train station, I met another Israeli invitee, who later on became a professor at Cambridge . . . and we were so happy to meet each other because we knew each other as students from Hebrew University. And as we were sitting in the train, I remember, we spoke at length about our experiences and what we were doing. The train was not very full. Before us there was a person who was sitting with his back to us, reading a newspaper. When we reached Cambridge, we all got out, and he turned to us and said, 'Thank you so much for polluting the train with your Hebrew language.' 'Not at all,' I said. 'We want to thank you for polluting the entire Middle East with your English colonialism.'"

Ariel had an awakening similar to his father's. St. Anthony's at Oxford, where he studied, is an Arab center. "It's not like studying religious studies at Brandeis. . . . It's extremely Arab-focused. For me it was such an eye-opener, even though I grew up in a liberal environment and my parents were taking us to meet Palestinians, even when you weren't allowed to. But [there at St. Anthony's] was a conversation with people who were not from there, and [I saw] how they viewed things."

Over time I had come to think of Israel's hard-right drift, the erosion of its principles of liberal democracy, and its hidebound attitude toward the Occupation mainly as tragic. Perhaps when the current generation of leaders fighting old battles dies off, I thought, things might have a chance of improving. But Yaron's perspective, expressed during our very first meeting at the café and on other occasions over the years, differed. He said that accepting the situation as tragic was not useful as it left no room for change. "Responsibility comes through distrust of your government," he said, and, for him, so did calling attention to its hypocrisies—such as "hiding from the people the many attempts of the other side to negotiate." If it had taken me a while to accept the aptness of the word "apartheid" to describe the current state of the country, Yaron had no such qualms. Years ago, when former president Jimmy Carter used it in the subtitle of his book about Israel, the Israeli government and US Jewish leaders brought out their heavy guns to attack him. But in an interview at the time, Yaron said that Carter was right, and he reiterated that view to me. "Israel today is an apartheid state induced by the Occupation and embodied in the practices ... of settlers and endorsed by the current right-wing government." The content of his critiques, however forceful, never left room for doubt about his concern and love for his country, and perhaps partly because of that Israeli TV and print media reporters could often be found on his doorstep whenever a large-scale military event, diplomatic move, or significant Knesset brawl took place. Interviews with him have appeared frequently in the international media (including the *New York Times*, *60 Minutes*, the BBC, and CNN), and his comments have often been laced with humor. When the Education Ministry issued a directive that flag-raising and the singing of "Hatikvah" would henceforth be mandatory for nursery and kindergarten children, Yaron told an interviewer, "They are doing an injustice to the state of Israel and to Jewish identity by starting this only in kindergarten," he said. "They should start in the maternity wards.... Instead of wrapping babies in a white sheet, they should wrap them in an Israeli flag, and hang Israeli flags over every bassinet, and make sure that in the delivery room they play 'Hatikvah' in the background."

One difference between Yaron's point of view and his daughter Talya's, which is also a major dividing line on Israel's left flank, is between those who believe the country's antidemocratic downward slide began in 1967 with the Occupation, and those who believe that the

events of 1948 were no less unjust than those of '67. Yaron belonged to
the former camp, Talya the latter. Those who share Talya's perspective,
many of whom belong to her generation, believe that Zionism was
"born in sin," as Yaron put it, and what was done to the Palestinians
was unacceptable and since then has only festered. Full stop. "People
like me," Yaron said, "believe the creation of the Jewish state in blood
and fire under incredibly difficult circumstances was necessary, which
does not diminish the injustice and suffering of the native Palestinians." But there's a moral difference, he said to me, between "the Jews
looking for a refuge in the place they were born and the '67 country,
already a homeland and a state, trying to annex more territory by ap-
plying messianic visions to the rest of the land. There was no excuse
for sending thousands of immigrants who were misled by offers of
cheap land in order to change the demographic composition of the
West Bank—'67 was an explosion of Israeli colonialism." Once when
Yaron and I were discussing the latest depressing legislative sortie
from Prime Minister Netanyahu's cabinet ministers (whom Yaron
had taken to referring to as the "seven dwarves"), I asked him point-
blank how he thought it was possible that the country could ever be
truly democratic *and* Jewish, considering the millions of non-Jews
who lived in Israel. He sighed but answered straight away, "It's a goal."

The divisions in Israeli society were a subject we returned to repeatedly. Yaron believed that the "extreme right and the extreme left
both look at a similar continuum of endless war." The "extreme right,"
which has been in ascendance, believes that '48 was a continuation of
the Holocaust and '67 was a continuation of '48—an ongoing battle
against the Jews' implacable enemies. On the "extreme left," he said,
"what is seen as the racist colonialist behavior of '48 was merely given
a new iteration in '67."

Israel has fought eight wars since 1948, but, for the most part, the
official fighting of more recent engagements has taken place far away
from the younger members of the Ezrahi family. While this cannot
be said for the period of the intifadas and the 2015 violence, this distance has shaped their world and their worldview, which are different
from those of the previous generation who felt war's icy breath close
by. When Yaron was eight, before the British left the country, his parents told him he needed to sleep on the floor away from windows,

because the Irgun was fighting, and heavy clashes were taking place near the family's Tel Aviv apartment. "One night we heard the sound of bullets smashing the plates in the kitchen; another time an artillery shell went right through our house. And the engines of the planes overhead made a *huge* noise. But even before all that, in 1944 on their way back from Africa, when the Italian fascists bombarded Tel Aviv, two hundred people were killed."

"How did that affect you?"

"It was frightening, yes."

Yaron also remembered wandering into an orange grove when he was a boy, after '48, where he had previously often seen an Arab farmer. The farmer was gone, and Yaron ate an orange, he said, without really knowing why he felt uneasy there. Talya was too young to remember much about the 1973 Yom Kippur War, but like Ruth in '67 she remembers a sense of excitement watching her family cover the windows with black paper. The '73 war, which some Israelis consider a continuation of the Six-Day War, was instigated by Egypt and Syria and a coalition of Arab states against an initially unprepared Israel. Egypt wanted to regain the Sinai and Syria the Golan Heights, which they had lost to Israel in 1967. The Soviet Union and the US both weighed in, sometimes fanning the war flames, sometimes cooling them. At one point US-Soviet diplomacy had so degraded around the conflict that the US put its nuclear weapons stations on worldwide alert. Despite some military victories for Egypt and Syria over the three-week period of the war and Egyptian president Anwar Sadat's vow to willingly "sacrifice a million Egyptian soldiers" to regain Egypt's lost territory, in the end—especially after the US agreed to help Israel with an airlift of fresh weapons—there were no clear winners. Nonetheless Egypt had gained enough face with its military victories to enable Sadat to sign a peace treaty with Israel six years later and to regain the Sinai for his country. The war, had a high body count—12,000 Egyptian fatalities, 3,000 Syrian, and 2,650 Israeli— and many atrocities were committed, especially against Israeli prisoners of war, many of whom were summarily executed. The Syrian defense minister at the time, Mustafa Tlass, liked to present himself as a worldly man of culture—he would later direct Syria-backed Lebanese soldiers fighting multinational peacekeeping forces in Lebanon

in 1983 not to attack Italian soldiers because "I don't want a single tear
falling from the eyes of Gina Lollobrigida, who I have loved ever since
my youth." But, notoriously, he boasted in a December 1973 address
to his country's national assembly that he had awarded one Syrian
soldier the Medal of the Republic for killing twenty-eight Israeli prisoners with an axe and committing other barbarities.

Talya remembered the fact of the Yom Kippur War and the
heightened atmosphere that came along with it but not its dangers.
"I don't think I felt scared. I felt excitement that something different
was happening." She paused, then added, "But probably my parents
protected me from the sense of possible death, because I don't have
that." Talya's sense of safety couldn't have been more different from
the feelings of Ruth and Yaron. One morning we were sipping tea
again in Ruth's kitchen (which had recently been painted a sort of
Scandinavian shade of blue), discussing what it had been like growing up in a war zone. The discussion took place at the time of the
2006 Lebanese war, on a day I had planned to drive up north but
changed my plans when I learned that Hezbollah rockets were raining down on that part of the country. (My landlady, a can-do sort of
woman whose officers must have blessed the day the brass decided
that female citizens ought to serve in the military, on hearing about
my change of plans gave me a look that said, "What? You're afraid of
a little Katyusha rocket?")

Like many Israelis, Ruth grew up in an era when people were
expecting the next war to be just around the corner. "At some point
in '62–'63," she told me, "there was on the news the report that said
Nasser was preparing for World War III, and I started crying; all the
grownups were just laughing, but I took it seriously. And after 1969,
when the terrorist bombings began, I remember going to bed and
thinking to myself, 'Am I hearing a bomb pulsing or a clock?'"

———•———

Talya's tall, affable British husband, Lewis Kerr, grew up in an activist family like his wife's and frequently took part in London protests
against South African apartheid, which he knew a lot about, having
grown up in Southern Africa, where his parents worked as teachers.
While he agreed with the criticisms of Israel's undemocratic policies

and had often marched alongside Talya at protests against the Occupation, he'd become convinced that the international Left's "obsession" with Israel was "distorted." "It seems bizarre," he said, "to focus so entirely on it when the situations and poverty in other places [are] so much worse." He paused and was silent for a moment. "This is an argument many Israelis make, which in this case I can't say I disagree with. There are so many other horrors going on right now in other places, aren't there?" He went on: "Living with my family for many years in Malawi and Zambia, there was an entirely different level of horrors taking place there. The same could be said of the Congolese villages and Darfur. I mean, there are full-scale holocausts and jungle wars. Where's the indignation about all that?"

As a young British activist, he said, he'd had only the most simplistic view of the situation in Israel. "A place for one race? Fascistic. Antithetical to everything I believed in. But I had no firsthand knowledge. Talya was only the second Israeli I knew, and the first that I got to know well." He went on to say that the undemocratic structure of the place still appalled him, but there was another way his take on things had shifted. "In England, as a citizen I feel entitled to leave and return to the country, but that doesn't mean it's only a place for white Christians. Lots of other people are entitled to have the same feeling. I think something like that has to happen here. It should be a modern state for all its citizens, but one where Jews, because of the reality of their special history, have a right to expedited citizenry. Not a state for the Jews but one with a special provision for them."

Something struck me as unusual about the way Lewie hesitated as he formulated his thoughts, but I couldn't quite identify it until after I'd left the apartment and was heading down the stairs. Then I realized that he had been speaking hesitatingly because some self-interrogation was happening as he went along—a phenomenon I had rarely observed among Israelis, at least the ones I encountered, who tended to present their opinions in a more signed, sealed, and delivered way. Of course, Lewie had been thinking about these issues for only a matter of years, whereas the Israelis have been scratching at them for decade after decade. Perhaps centuries of fervent Yeshiva disputation play some role in this as well.

Lewie had come to Israel with Talya partly because the technically advanced company he worked for as a storyboard artist when I first met him looked attractive. But in a major company downsizing, most of the foreigners (who tended to be liberal) had been let go, and although the men who owned the company were also liberal, the Israeli staff that remained tended to be more right-wing. It was becoming, Lewie said, "a bit of a closed shop"—which seemed all too familiar to him. More and more he had taken to working at home because the atmosphere at the office was beginning to remind him of his growing-up years in Africa, when his family was surrounded by tea plantations, sites of colonial rigidity. A few years later the Israeli company closed, and he now works for the London-based company Locksmith Animation.

Shortly before I was about to end one of my visits to Israel, in a clamorous coffee shop on the German Colony's main artery, Talya and I spoke about the 2008–2009 conflict in Gaza, also known as Operation Cast Lead, in which 1,166 Palestinians and 13 Israelis had died. She brought up the rockets that Hamas had fired at southern Israel, the destruction of Gaza's civilian targets, and the ongoing misery of the place—with Israel controlling its airspace and territorial waters and restricting the movement of goods in and out.

Talya was haunted by the helplessness she felt about her capacity to affect the war, a feeling she said she'd had repeatedly over the years. Almost no international aid got to Gaza, and, according to a Doctors Without Borders organizer who brought a mobile medical unit to Gaza, the Arab states were "not really trying to help." Ten years after the siege, she noted, the factories were still destroyed, miles of houses were still rubble, and sewage flowed in the streets. Around us the chatter of café patrons, the clatter of cutlery, the hiss of the milk-steaming machine, and the occasional burst of laughter led me to think of Auden's great poem "Musée des Beaux Arts," which describes the way suffering is absorbed heedlessly in the everyday world.

Talya sipped her coffee quietly for a minute or two and then went on to say more about her political beliefs. "I'm not anti-Zionist, but I would welcome a one-state solution to the conflict." This is a possibility being discussed, argued over, by more and more people of every political stripe in the country. "I don't feel the need for the country to be a Jewish state." Only gradually, she added, had she arrived at this position. "I wasn't brought up questioning 1948. I was brought up questioning 1967." But the atmosphere of national fragility and fear of Arabs so ubiquitous in the religious and nationalistic school she attended were no part of her upbringing. "I didn't drink it with my mother's milk (a phrase of my dad's); my parents didn't bequeath that to me, even though my mother's field was, or used to be, Holocaust literature. It's true, however, that we weren't allowed to buy *anything* from Germany, even a pencil sharpener. Out of bounds. We'd have to return it to the shop." In our earlier talk, Lewie had wondered aloud if Zionists could accept his idea of a state that admitted as citizens anyone who wanted to come even if they weren't Jewish but somehow had a "fast track" for Jews that would address their age-old need for a place of refuge. He wasn't confident that they would.

In the event, far from moving toward inclusiveness, the country's steady march in the opposite direction culminated in July 2018 in the Knesset's passage of the Nation-State Bill, which unequivocally established Israel as the home of the Jewish people, with a "united" Jerusalem as its capital, and specified that the Jewish people had an exclusive right to national self-determination. The new law downgraded Arabic from an "official" language to one with "special status" and—unlike the Israeli Declaration of Independence, which ensured "complete equality of social and political rights to all its inhabitants irrespective of race, religion or sex"—made no mention of equal or minority rights.

From an immediate, practical point of view, the law didn't change the way its Palestinian citizens—one-fifth of the population—are treated, but it enshrined their second-class status in stone. Since Israel does not have a formal written constitution, its Basic Laws, including the new Nation-State Law, serve as a de facto constitution and are understood to be underlying principles of governance that might one day be drawn upon for a formal constitution, in which case, the omission of the words "democratic" and "equality" takes on a greater and depressing significance.

Like her brother, Talya returned to Israel—in her case with Lewie from England, where they had been living—intending to remain for only a short while, but somehow she and Lewie, too, have stayed put. As parents of two little girls, they have appreciated the country's child-friendliness and the warm family circle they are part of. Until 2014, Talya worked as an editor at the human rights nonprofit Search for Common Ground, where the staff is both Israeli and Palestinian. It was a good job, but she yearned to get back to filmmaking, the profession she trained for in England. She and Lewie both have degrees from the London College of Printing and Graphic Arts (now called the London College of Communication), and in 1999 they made a documentary together in collaboration with a Palestinian friend, Kamal Jafari. The film, *The Jahalin*, depicts the plight of the Jahalin Bedouins, who traditionally lived in the Negev until they were evicted in 1952 and moved to the valleys between Jericho and Jerusalem, where they again struggled with eviction and demolition orders, trying to keep their tents and tin shacks from being bulldozed to facilitate expansion of Ma'ale Adumim, the fastest-growing settlement in the West Bank. Over the years since then there have been high court petitions against plans to move Bedouins out of their villages to "permanent settlements," and some have succeeded, while some have not. Since 2016 Talya has worked for an Israeli NGO called Emek Shaveh (a place name from the Bible signifying a common meeting ground). The organization focuses on the role of archaeology in the Palestinian-Israeli conflict and in particular strives to prevent the politicization of archaeological sites.

For a while, 2009–2013, Jerusalem Israeli activists—mostly young people but also a handful of well-known writers, academics, and artists—attended a weekly Friday demonstration in the East Jerusalem neighborhood of Sheikh Jarrah, following the eviction of two Palestinian families from their homes and later eviction of others, all of whom had been living in them for many decades. The evictions by settlers were made possible by the 1970 law that permits Israelis to reclaim properties that had been owned by Jews and then abandoned after the city was divided in 1948. In 2008 and 2009, Palestinian residents began receiving eviction notices from settler groups with Ottoman-era or other deeds that the government had put its stamp of approval on. I don't know what documents the evicted families possessed, but settler documents generally trump any *kawasheen* (certificates of ownership) held by Palestinian families despite the efforts of lawyers to defend their legitimacy. The numbers of protesters varied from week to week, but at one point there were hundreds of people standing around on the Sheikh Jarrah streets (there were few sidewalks) near walls covered with graffiti.

It was the most modest section of an otherwise fancy neighborhood known for its handsome villas and consulates. Two mangy dogs sniffed around suspiciously. There were drummers, banners (emblazoned with the word "Solidarity" in Arabic), a mixture of mostly Israeli and some Palestinian students, and a general upbeat sense of righteousness. Alas, despite the good feeling all around and the wonder of the Palestinian families involved that Israelis would make this effort for them, the protests didn't get the evicted families anywhere. On one of several occasions when I went to the Sheikh Jarrah demonstration, the police had made several arrests and then moved everyone some distance away from the disputed houses. At another, I bumped into Ruth and Yaron, heads and bodies covered to protect them from the sun. They were nodding and smiling at so many of the people around them that for a moment I had the wild thought that the small crowd, two hundred or so that day, might constitute all that remained of the Israeli Left. It didn't, of course. The Left comprises an estimated 8 percent of the Israeli population "on a good day," as an Israeli friend of mine likes to say. And there are scores of indefatigable human rights groups—among them B'Tselem, Ir Amin, the Association for Civil Rights in Israel, Molad (Center for Renewal of Israeli Democracy), Adalah (Legal Center for Arab Minority Rights in Israel), the Association for Civil Rights in Israel, Physicians for Human Rights, Yesh Din, Rabbis for Human Rights, MachsomWatch—that toil ceaselessly in challenging the government's antidemocratic moves and laws and are part of an endless legal battle to protect Palestinian lands, residency rights, and security. In the light of the ongoing frustration the Left was constantly experiencing and its poor showing in recent elections, however, you might be forgiven for thinking that two hundred people comprised its entirety.

Tehila, nine years younger than her sister Talya, is a talented painter who, at the time I met her, regularly toiled with the grassroots, Palestinian-Israeli activist group Ta'ayush. Members of Ta'ayush dig out Palestinian farmers' wells that have been filled in by settlers, plant olive saplings where they have been uprooted (in 2012 settlers damaged or destroyed more than 7,500 olive trees of West Bank Palestinians, according to the UN), strive to protect Palestinian civilians from attacks by Israeli settlers and soldiers, and generally show up wherever they are needed to counteract settler assaults.

Yaron's good friend David Shulman has been associated with Ta'ayush for nineteen years and revealed in the *New York Review of Books* that it was one of the human rights groups targeted by right-wing spies. In the same essay Shulman also reported on a bill then making its way through the Knesset, the so-called Transparency Bill, that, if passed, would force all Israeli human rights NGOs receiving more than 50 percent of their funding from foreign governments (as many do) to disclose their foreign sources of support each time they appear in public. Originally the bill also required that representatives of all organizations receiving funding from foreign sources wear identity badges when they entered the Knesset or other public places, but, as Shulman wrote, "Netanyahu, still apparently capable of seeing the invidious analogy to the badges the Nazis forced Jews to wear in public, squashed this clause." In view of my earlier errant thoughts at the Sheikh Jarrah protest, I was unnerved to read in the same article that Shulman estimated the number of boots-on-the-ground human rights and peace activists "in the field in Israel" to be "no more than a few hundred . . . a few hundred too many in the eyes of the far right and, I guess, of large parts of the political center as well."

On July 12, 2016, in the early morning hours, the Transparency Bill was passed into law. Relevant Israeli nonprofits must note their foreign funding in all their communications with the public, including their Internet communications, TV, newspaper communications, advertisements and letters, and "government messages." The law is written in such a way that it exempts groups that have received funding mostly from individual rich donors, as most conservative and ultranationalist groups do. More than twenty-five groups affected by the law announced they would challenge it in the courts.

Like the biblical Rachel, Tehila, the youngest of the Ezrahi progeny, met her husband, Sam Thrope, an American journalist and Iranian studies scholar, at the wells—in her case when they were both volunteering for Ta'ayush. Tehila did not feel especially enlarged by the academic migrations of her family, as her brother did, or by its dual national identities, or its intense scholarly focus. (Ariel provided a good sense of the high-powered engine that drove the family's academic ambitions when he mentioned in passing that he "ended up with three degrees—two law degrees and then a Middle Eastern studies degree . . . because clearly I couldn't show my face to my family without a degree in addition to law because law is not considered an intellectual pursuit." He was smiling when he said this, but still. When I came across the information that Israel ranks third among member countries of the OECD [Organisation for Economic Co-Operation and Development], after Canada and Japan, for citizens with tertiary degrees, I was unsurprised.) For Tehila, who has a bright, quicksilver manner, the family's peregrinations were unsettling. When she was a young girl, she confessed, she felt more confused than enlivened by the family's to-ings-and-fro-ings, and it took her longer than her brother and sister to find her footing.

Tehila's early work history sounds similar to that of many young Americans who struggle to find themselves. But in addition to the common challenges growing up presents to all young people in the modern world, young Israelis also must contend with the unique conflict that surrounds them. After serving in the army, Tehila traveled to Nepal, and then, back home, worked at various odd jobs—waitressing, boutique sales—until she landed one she really liked as an assistant to an art therapist, a lovely woman who happened to be Ruth's sister-in-law, Edna, working with children in a hospital. She remained at that job for two years, and then went to India for a year. When she came back she was twenty-six, and though she continued to work at odd jobs for a couple of months, she eventually decided to join the rest of her clan—*et tu*, Tehila?—and study for a degree in art therapy from a teachers college, the David Yellin College of Education—the same school her grandfather Eliezar had studied at in the thirties. She and Sam have a young son. Just before she became a mother, Tehila had been working as a guide for Arab and Jewish students at Jerusalem's Museum for Islamic Art. Currently she works as a teacher in a Jerusalem primary school.

———•———

In the 2006 war between Hezbollah and Israel, an estimated 1,300 Lebanese died, the vast majority civilians, and one million were displaced after their homes were destroyed. During the thirty-four-day war, Yaron and Ruth together wrote a closely argued letter, which they sent to their friends, many of whom, they thought, did not see the need for Israel to fight yet another war. By the war's end, 119 Israeli soldiers and 43 Israeli civilians would also die in the conflict. Wars like this one, not between two states but between a state and a militant, secretive, fundamentalist group, would become all too familiar in the years to come. Yaron and Ruth's letter took pains to try to clarify what they believed was the war's background: "Because we agree with part of the decisions and actions taken on our behalf and not with others, our letter to you necessarily reflects our fears, concerns, confusions, and hopes. We do not enjoy the comforts of emotional coherence and moral clarity manifest in the attitudes of the enthusiastic supporters of the Israeli and Western right, nor the self-assurance and patronizing attitudes of the automatic and unqualified critiques of Israeli policies and actions on the left."

The specific Left group the letter focused on was represented at that time by the linguist Noam Chomsky (who in 2010 was barred from entering Israel). Chomsky, along with other signatories, wrote a declaration of protest against the Lebanese war. "Professor Chomsky," Ruth and Yaron wrote,

> stated many things with which we agree. But when he falsely claims that the ultimate aim of "Israel" is to exterminate the Palestinian nation, he provides Ahmadinejad with the precise pretext for [his] stated aim to eliminate the Jews in Israel. . . . The "Israel" Chomsky accuses of a conspiracy of extermination can only exist in a mind which in the name of human values can dehumanize millions of Israelis who as living human beings have millions of contradictory opinions, ambivalences, and aspirations. . . . To lump these Israelis together and describe a largely fragmented coalition government in a multi-party parliamentary system as a unified single-minded agent is a monstrous abstraction, a fantastic invention of a coherent demonic collectively conspiring

entity, a fantasy which is, of course, very common not only among contemporary Middle Eastern fundamentalists but also among last century's leaders of fascist Europe.

The long letter—five pages single-spaced—carefully enumerated many of the wrongs done to the Palestinians "during nearly forty years of repressive occupation and state support for the Jewish settlers in the occupied territories. While this doesn't justify the random killing of our citizens by suicide bombers or the landing of Kassam missiles on Israeli towns, it justifies the utmost restraint on our part in the use of arms against the Palestinians. We object to all attempts to see Hamas as an arm of Hezbollah or Iran and the call of the Israeli right that we should treat them alike." The letter embodies many of the qualities I had come to admire in Ruth and Yaron—especially intellectual passion and a nuanced historical grasp of the issues dogging their country. History has confirmed much of what they wrote in the letter, and some observers have even suggested that nowadays militant Hezbollah ideologues still have fewer doubts about the Iranian theocratic revolution's original goals than most Iranians, especially the young.

The 2006 war ended inconclusively, though both sides claimed victory. In the end, Israel declared the war a success though it hadn't succeeded in getting back its two soldiers abducted in the cross-border raid that precipitated the war. They were already dead, and their bodies would finally be returned in a 2008 prisoner exchange. But Hezbollah, which had far better control over the propaganda war, emerged as more successful in both its military and political operations and, most importantly, foiled Israel's effort to degrade its future military capabilities. Half a million Israelis were forced to leave their homes during the war. The world was shocked most, however, by the war's high number of civilian casualties, as it would be after the devastating third Gaza War in 2014. Israel's claim that the number was high because Hezbollah hid among the country's civilians was found to be true only to a small degree. (Before the war, Hezbollah's leader, Hassan Nasrallah, had publicly admitted that his soldiers hid among civilians "in their homes, in their schools, in their churches, in their fields, in their farms and in their factories.") The Israeli government insisted that many of the Lebanese casualties were actually Hezbollah fighters, but it was pointed out that their gravestones did not identify them as martyrs, as is customary when fighters die, but merely ordinary citizens, many of whom were women and children. Since that time we've also learned that Hezbollah has reportedly amassed one hundred thousand missiles and rockets, all pointed in Israel's direction, and that during the war many of their rockets were placed in crowded population areas, to guarantee maximum civilian casualties if Israel tried to destroy them.

To underscore the concerns behind his and Ruth's explanation of Israel's need to fight the war in Lebanon, Yaron took pains to point something out to me a few months after he and Ruth sent out the letter. Namely, the missiles in Cuba to which President Kennedy reacted in 1962 were nuclear but few. But when Hezbollah fired an estimated 3,970 Katyusha rockets and longer-range missiles onto Haifa and other northern civilian sites, forcing much of the population to live in bunkers for months, it was barely criticized by the international community. Nor, he observed, has the same community seemed particularly disturbed by Hezbollah's refusal to disarm, a condition of the ceasefire, nor by its boast just after the war that it still held twenty thousand rockets and missiles in its hidden arsenals. Of course, in the inflamed ongoing debate about who poses the greatest threat to whom in the region, the debate-stopper, tending to bring all argument to a standstill, is the unignorable reality of Israel's nuclear capability.

Over the years, as I spent long periods in Israel, any hope for an end to the conflict looked increasingly unlikely partly because both sides had the wrong leadership—politicians incapable of steering their people toward peace. Then, in 2015, a small, bright light illuminated the Stygian political landscape thanks to a remarkable Palestinian Israeli member of the Knesset, Ayman Odeh, head of a coalition of Arab parties called the Joint List. The humanistic platform of the Joint List included approval of the two-state solution based on the 1967 boundaries (which all too few people still believed to be a viable possibility), complete equality for women, and recognition of the Arab population as a "national minority with cultural, religious and educational autonomy." Perhaps more radically, Odeh (who is not related to Niveen's mother) also announced in his first speech in the

Knesset, that "pride and national identity do not negate the desire to be part of the broad community and the state." The statement astonished many of his fellow Knesset members and predictably drew disapproving jibes from many Palestinians, as well as from former Israeli foreign minister Avigdor Lieberman, who characterized the new coalition as representatives of "the [new] terror organizations." Writing about Odeh in *Haaretz* the journalist David Green described Odeh as "inclusionary," a word seldom applied to Palestinian nationalists by Israelis, and went on to note the suggestion made by Odeh in a TV debate that the ever-feeble Israeli Left ought to join forces with his coalition. "The left cannot bring about peace and democracy without the Arab population," he said. "What unifies our united list, which is for social justice, but not only, is that we are for national justice for two peoples."

Whether Odeh's example can have a meaningful effect on the lethal antagonisms of the Knesset remains to be seen. So far he has remained largely unknown outside the country, and many, even among his own constituents, have doubts about his pragmatism. And the bloc that would seem the most obvious to join ranks with him—Meretz, the social-democratic party—has shown no interest in doing so. An event that cast doubt on the possibility of Odeh succeeding was vividly provided at a plenary session of the Knesset on June 29, 2016, specifically in a discussion about an agreement recently consummated between Israel and Turkey. The agreement ended a six-year period of strained relations after Israeli commandos killed nine Turkish citizens (and an American) aboard a 2010 aid flotilla bound for Gaza with construction materials. Three of the vessels were flying Turkish flags. (The convoy was in international waters along Gaza's Mediterranean coast, but Israel, which controls all maritime entry into Gaza, contended that it was attempting illegal entry into its territorial waters.) Among the Knesset speakers that day was Hanin Zoabi, from one of the Joint List's factions. Zoabi, who had been a passenger on one of the aid vessels in the convoy, declared, "Israel did not disengage from Gaza, Israel cut off Gaza from the world and life." Zoabi demanded an apology for another Knesset session, in 2010, in which she had been vilified and drowned out by insults about her comments regarding the incident and after which she had even received death threats. At the June 2016 session, the Knesset's members again shouted "Terrorist!" and "Filth!" and other ugly insults at Zoabi, a large contingent of the members jumped out of their seats and menacingly approached the podium at which she was speaking, and the entire meeting devolved into bedlam. Four Knesset members were escorted out of the hall, and the security staff could barely control the chaos. Afterward, insults continued to rain down on Zoabi on social media. Refusing to be drawn into the fight, an official of the Joint List confined himself to saying to a reporter, "The easiest way to get some love from your right-wing base is to stage a fight with an Arab MK." Subsequently, the right's hostility to Zoabi and its uncompromising posture toward Palestinian factions in the Knesset was formalized when Zoabi was suspended from her Knesset duties after she criticized Israel's role in its assault on Gaza. Then, in the last months of 2016, the government's coalition chairman, David Bitan, when asked how he'd felt about Prime Minister Netanyahu's 2015 election day plea to the electorate to not fail to vote because "the Arabs are flocking to the polls," doubled down by responding that he would prefer that Arabs "not come to the polls at all." Ninety-five percent of them, he said "vote for the Joint List, which doesn't represent Israeli Arabs but Palestinian interests."

Just after reading about Bitan, the ruling coalition's whip, challenging the right of his country's many Arab citizens' to vote, I came upon an old email from Yaron reflecting on some of the more egregious laws his government was trying to pass at the time, including one that would have taken away the salaries of citizens who neglected to vote. "A lethal coalition of fanatic right-wing politicians who currently rule our country," he wrote, "cause great damage to the fabric of our society and particularly to Jewish/Arab relations. Still, I think in politics unexpected reversals can always happen."

CHAPTER 10

AUNT RASMEA

Niveen and I were driving to her family's house one afternoon, chatting about this and that, when she said tentatively, "You know about my aunt Rasmea?" I said I didn't. She volunteered that her aunt had been living in Chicago for many years and had earned a law degree at Al-Quds before she emigrated. She seemed hesitant about saying more, but I pressed her, and she added, "She spent many years in jail." I was surprised, considering the non-aggressive beliefs of the family and the fact that I'd been talking to the Abuleils for over a year and nobody had mentioned Rasmea, but though it was a revelation it was far from world-shattering. By then I'd met many Palestinians who had spent time in Israeli jails.

"Why?" I asked. "Google her," Niveen, staring straight ahead, replied. The conversation was closed.

And thus I learned from my laptop that her aunt had been convicted in 1970 by an Israeli military court for her alleged involvement in an infamous 1969 supermarket bombing, severely tortured in violation of the Geneva Convention, given three life sentences, and incarcerated for ten years before being released in a prisoner exchange. I also discovered that a special UN report and five-month investigation by the London *Times* described the torture her interrogators subjected her to preceding her confession. Since that time she had steadfastly maintained that the confession had been a false one, obtained by torture. In 1995, her father, who had in the 1960s moved back to Jerusalem, returned to the States, where he had become a citizen, to work. After he became sick with prostate cancer, Rasmea came to the US to help her brother care for him. In time her father moved back again to Jerusalem, where he died. Not long afterward her brother also died after fighting a losing battle with cancer of the spine. After that, Rasmea had moved to Chicago and worked as a social activist, organizer, and supporter of Arab women's rights ever since. In 2004 she became a US citizen. By the time I was inquiring about her, she had become the highly praised associate director of the Arab American Action Network (AAAN), a thriving nonprofit organization founded in 1995 by a group of prominent Arab activists, organizers, academics, and intellectuals with the goal of strengthening and supporting the Arab immigrant and Arab American community.

———•———

To be born in the middle of a war on the losing side wouldn't necessarily doom you to a life of upheaval, but Niveen's aunt Rasmea did seem destined from an early age to tread a tumultuous path. She arrived in the world in early 1948, one month before the Odehs were forced to flee Lifta for Ramallah. Tears and what seemed to be a nearly incomprehensible form of loss accompanied the family; they hadn't been remotely prepared for what was happening, or imagined (despite clear warning signs) that they'd ever have to undergo an upheaval of such magnitude.

After their chaotic departure from Lifta, they and their neighbors, farmers of varying degrees of prosperity, tumbled out of the dusty trucks that had driven them away from their homes and wondered how they would survive, *if* they would survive. Zaineb, who was thirteen at the time, remembers very well the palpable fear of the adults around her. And hunger. They were saved by the early 1950s migration to the United States of their father, a farmer now without land to farm. It hadn't taken him long to land a bakery factory job in Detroit. Though he missed his family and virtually every other familiar marker of his life, he was grateful to be able to regularly send money back home. Eventually, because of that money, his family was able to leave the overcrowded refugee camp where eighteen of them were crammed together in a tent—grandparents, aunts, uncles, cousins—and move to two rented rooms. But things took a turn for the worse when the father was hospitalized after a work accident that broke his leg. He returned to Ramallah to have one doctor, then another, reset the fracture, without great success. Like more than half of the Palestinian refugees in the world, the family's finances became unstable. The insurance money he received because of the accident helped but was insufficient. They were forced to turn for support to the United Nations Relief and Works Agency, the institution that over the years has provided crucial schooling, food, and health services for Palestinians in the West Bank and Gaza—and in Lebanon, Jordan and Syria, from which the Trump administration cut off funding in the summer of 2018. A few relatives tried to return to Lifta to retrieve household items but were prevented by soldiers from doing so, and they didn't pursue their quest after learning about others who'd ran into ugly situations while attempting to do the same elsewhere.

Rasmea, galled by the stern rule of her grandfather and uncle in their role of running the family, very early earned a reputation for being a one-person resistance force. At four she ran away from home, and it took a day to find her, which the family says afforded her much childish delight. Her three sisters had chosen not to challenge their grandfather's authority, nor had her brother Mustapha before he'd been plucked away by their father to be educated in the US—possibly because he was a boy and had been allowed greater freedom. Her grandfather believed that only her brother and male cousins needed to attend school, since the girls' lives were headed, as he saw it, inexorably and solely toward marriage, and they would always remain at home. Openly rebellious, to circumvent his argument that they couldn't afford the money for the bus that transported the girls to school, Rasmea walked a mile and a half or more to get there. Her sisters remembered that throughout her childhood she continued to wander around asking strangers where America was and repeatedly asking their mother where their father was.

"The point is," Rasmea said when I finally met her in the winter of 2011, at a café not far from the Art Institute in Chicago, a city she had come to consider her home, "we didn't have a father." She was then in her mid-sixties, an intense woman with a focused, assessing gaze, the kind of hair that has learned not to be fussed over, and the intensity and quickness of manner I associate with the moral surety of the universal activist tribe. She wore relaxed woolens—no hijab and no makeup. She looked exhausted but at first spoke readily about her past.

As it had with her sister Zaineb, the family's post-1948 sorrows and the virtual collapse of their mother's spirit left an indelible mark.

"My mother was *always* in tears. She cried all the time," Rasmea said, sighing. "I used to ask her 'Why are you crying? Where's Papa?' And she'd say that our father would return when we could go back to our old home—which actually the Israelis had already destroyed. When he came back to us for a while after he'd had the accident, before returning to the US, and my sisters called him Baba ("Father"), I couldn't understand it. But I had made that link, in my child's understanding of his full return, with *everyone's* return to their family homes. All around us were people reduced to the same condition we were, so I thought we should all solve our problems together." Secretly, when she was twelve, she began to attend communist meetings, and the next year she joined a nationalist group because it seemed to be focused on the very issues that she was dimly aware had a larger context.

"I think my life pushed me to be political. All the injustices of my life as a private person along with the injustices of our political circumstance pushed me to it." When I brought up the subject of the bombing and her torture, a raw look of panic crossed her face, something deadening, which was followed by an awkward silence. The animated woman I'd been talking with had left. After one of those moments that seem endless but actually last only a few seconds, she said, "I'm sorry, it's hard, too hard for me to talk about. Perhaps some other time."

Her father never fully recovered from his factory accident. Other medical problems followed. He moved from hospital to hospital. Somehow the family scraped together enough to buy a small house. When the Six-Day War came, Rasmea had just finished sitting for her *tawjihiyah* (high school certificate), and her father was away at a family house in Jericho—alone—as the climate there was supposed to be beneficial for his health. Frightened by what she was hearing about the heavy bombing and shooting of the war, though they had no car or other form of transportation, her mother nonetheless decided that she and her children needed to be with their father and should walk together from Ramallah to Jericho—a distance of some fifteen miles. "We've always been separated in life," she told her daughters, "at least let's die together."

I'd already heard about her family's dangerous Six-Day War trek from Zaineb, who was Rasmea's eldest sister. Zaineb didn't like to talk much about her past history (she often cut off her own musings about it with a sigh and a "This is life"), but one afternoon on French Hill she told me that that journey had been one of the most frightening moments of that frightening time. "On the road we saw corpses, many of them burned by napalm. There was a horrible stench in the air. We tried to keep looking down at the ground, but Rasmea didn't. We begged our mother to go back, but Rasmea didn't." In front of one building they passed, the entrance was piled high with charred bodies. It was impossible to tell, Rasmea recalled, "if they were civilian or military and this affected me terribly."

They arrived safely in Jericho, with its beautiful orange and lemon trees, and then, after twenty days, worried about their house, they walked back to Ramallah, again without their father. His bad leg made the walk impossible for him. When they finally arrived home, they discovered that one of their rooms had been destroyed by a shell, the other looted, and everything they owned of value—jewelry, some furniture, the little there was after 1948—was gone. In an interview with the Jerusalem-born novelist and journalist Soraya Antonius published in 1980 in the *Journal of Palestine Studies*, Rasmea described her dark feelings at the time: "The streets of Ramallah were filled with Israelis.... They were elated and happy and we were so wretched; they were free and we were kept under curfew, restricted, and I kept on asking myself how I could take part in the struggle. Everything was confusion and chaos, and political activity was largely confined to the students. We used to demonstrate and throw stones at the Israelis to protest against the desecration of mosques and against the looting."

A few months later, as it began to be apparent that the Israelis weren't going to be giving back the newly conquered lands any time soon, more organized activity began. The Palestinian students were given "theoretical visual training" about how to use firearms if they were fired on at their demonstrations. Rasmea's family didn't support any of this. "They didn't even like me to leave the house [at that point] ... because ... they were afraid of rape and insults.... Even before the war my family was very conservative.... It was accepted that the struggle and imprisonment were men's preserves. We were not to be involved in demonstrations in which Israelis might manhandle us."

Over the next few years, Rasmea told Antonius, her political

views solidified. As Antonius pointed out in an earlier article in the
same journal, a "characteristic of the women's movement in Palestine
and in exile has been its identification [since the early part of the
twentieth century] with the national movement against Zionism." "I
had always rejected this oppression of women," Rasmea went on to
say, "and my family didn't or couldn't forbid my commitment." Eventually she made her way to Beirut Arab University in Lebanon, which
her uncle and grandfather didn't oppose because they thought, erroneously, that being in Beirut would cool her politics. Her studies in
Beirut were precipitously cut short when the Israelis, possibly because
of her increased activism, didn't allow her to return to Lebanon after
a family visit to Ramallah. More and more frustrated by what she
perceived as the passivity of her fellow Palestinians, she joined the
Popular Front for the Liberation of Palestine (PFLP), a secular, revolutionary Marxist-Leninist group.

Rasmea's journey may have taken her to extremes, but she had
plenty of company on her path. Before the Six-Day War it was rare
to see women at the prison in Ramla, where Rasmea served ten years
of her sentence. But after the 1967 war, the increased participation
of women in demonstrations and political meetings did not go unnoticed by Israeli security operatives. Before 1967, the total number
of women imprisoned for political reasons was minuscule, probably
fewer than a dozen—in large part because their role in resistance activities was insignificant. Even in the immediate aftermath of the war,
few women were arrested, and those few were mostly given fines and
released. A few were deported to Amman. But over the next years, as
women's political activism increased, so did the incidents of clamping
down on them. A few of the women were involved with bombings
and would have been arrested and imprisoned by any nation trying to
protect its citizens, but the vast majority, according to Israeli human
rights groups, were political activists caught in overbroad dragnets.
In 1968 some one hundred Palestinian women were arrested; in 1969,
two hundred; and over the next decade, an estimated two thousand.
All told, since the Six-Day War, according to a special report published by the UN General Assembly on April 20, 2015, "The overall number of prisoners and detainees held captive in Israeli prisons
has exceeded 850,000 Palestinian civilians, including 15,000 women

and tens of thousands of children, in grave violation of the relevant provisions of the Geneva Convention." The increased incarceration of women imprisoned in Israeli prisons was a far cry from the gender equality shift that the young Rasmea had yearned for, but it was the one she got.

In certain ways, then, the conflict with the Israelis was instrumental in jump-starting the push for Palestinian women's independence. Rasmea couldn't fail to notice, she said, that

> the Israeli didn't differentiate between the sexes when he shot at demonstrators or when he searched the house or when he made an arrest, so danger changed the girls. Then the economic situation—inflation, unemployment—affected everyone ... men were no longer the only breadwinners. At first men opposed the state of affairs, but then they were forced to accept it. There has been an enormous change in women's situation, social and economic, in the occupied territories. And there was daily danger, and this also changed the women: they stopped thinking of how to please men and began to think of building social structures, of fighting the occupier, of the future.

A darker side of this optimistic picture has been pointed out by the Israeli-Palestinian sociologist Honaida Ghanim (who was herself involved in a well-known case of overweening airport security treatment). Ghanim has suggested that while activist women who have been brutalized and end up in prison may be admired for their sacrifice, because Palestinian society is still extremely traditional and for the most part conservative they may find themselves ostracized and unacceptable, even to young activist men, as candidates for marriage.

The PFLP was, after Fatah, the largest of the coalition of groups that at that time made up the Palestine Liberation Organization (PLO), which it sometimes was allied with. Its military wing was infamous for its airplane hijackings in the late 1960s and early 1970s, and in general the group opposed the more conciliatory of Fatah's political postures. Some thirty countries, including the United States, Canada, and members of the European Union, still consider the PFLP to be a terrorist organization. The PLO, of course, devolved into the recognized government of the Palestinian people, though it, too, was formerly considered a terrorist organization. The organization the PFLP grew out of, the Arab Nationalist Movement (the group Rasmea joined when she was twelve), was founded in the early fifties by Dr. George Habash, a Palestinian Christian and lifelong militant nationalist whose family came from Lydda (the site of the 1948 expulsions the former army commander couldn't remember), now called Lod and incorporated into Greater Tel Aviv.

Habash viewed the Palestinian fight for independence as part of a wider pan-Arab resistance to Western imperialism. He masterminded numerous hijackings and bombings in the late sixties and early seventies, but the group, like so many Arab political institutions, was riddled with internal conflicts, and in time it split into three separate bodies. Habash's nationalism was closely aligned with that of Gamal Abdel Nasser, who he believed could serve as the key to Arab unity and through it the liberation of his people. Trained as a pediatrician and often referred to as Al-Hakeem—Arabic for "Doctor" or "Wise Man"—Habash attributed the Palestinians' loss of the 1948 war to the hard reality of the "scientific society of Israel as against our own backwardness in the Arab world." Like a mirror image of the early Zionists, he called for the development of "a new breed of man" single-mindedly dedicated to the cause of Palestinian liberation. In time, Habash's star was eclipsed by Yasser Arafat and later Hamas, but until the late sixties he was a leading member of the PLO. He died in 2008. Currently, the PFLP, which renounced suicide bombings in particular as a viable form of resistance, is boycotting participation in the PLO's executive committee. It considers both the Hamas government in Gaza and the Fatah-led one in the West Bank illegal, since there have been no elections since 2006. The number of its current members is unknown, but in general it appears to have fallen into fossilized irrelevance.

Rasmea returned home to Ramallah from Beirut in early 1969, and on February 28, she, along with hundreds of others, was arrested and brought to the notorious Moscobiya Interrogation Center, also known as the Russian Compound (for its origins as a center for Russian pilgrimage). Palestinians call it "the torture factory." She was accused of participating in the bombing of the SuperSol supermarket on Jerusalem's King George Street on February 21, for which the PFLP claimed responsibility, along with a bomb placed at the British consulate that was successfully disarmed by the Israelis twenty seconds before it was timed to explode. The SuperSol bomb killed two young Hebrew University students who were in the store to buy food for a botany camping trip.

Forty-five days later a military court found Rasmea guilty, and she was given three separate life sentences. Israel is far from the only country to resort to what is euphemistically referred to as "enhanced interrogation," a term that originated with the Nazis, and she had been subjected to severe torture, she told Antonius, for over twenty-five days. "Without asking any questions they began beating and poking me. There were several secret police (*Mukhabarat*) in civilian clothes, ten or twelve, not less and perhaps more, and the uniformed military guard at the door. After about half an hour I started screaming; they beat me and I tried to beat them back and they put handcuffs on me again and cursed me in Arabic. Even those who don't speak Arabic at all had learned all the obscene words."

The ensuing treatment Rasmea endured can be written down but is unspeakable. The details of her torture and that of many of her fellow suspects were later corroborated by others at the interrogation center and by a special report published by London's Sunday *Times* on June 19, 1977, and also established by the *Report of the Special Committee to Investigate Israeli Practices Affecting the Human Rights of the Population of the Occupied Territories* of the thirty-third session of the UN General Assembly of November 1978. In addition, the torture and general brutal Israeli treatment of detainees has been noted by the US National Lawyers Guild, the International Committee of the Red Cross, Amnesty International, the Swiss League for Human Rights, and a number of Israeli lawyers, including Felicia Langer and Lea Tsemel. Long after the time of Rasmea's interrogation, in 1999, Israel's High Court issued a decision to prohibit torture of Palestinian detainees suspected of being involved in terrorism. It was widely acknowledged that previously Palestinians arrested by Shin Bet were tortured. As a result of the decision, torture has become far less prevalent over the last decades, though because of a loophole in the court's decision that stated that on moral grounds torture was illegal under "most" circumstances, the practice has not disappeared. In October 2018, Human Rights Watch, the New York–based advocacy group, released a report that also accused both Hamas and the Palestinian Authority of frequently using arbitrary arrest and torture to suppress dissent. Representatives of both denied the charges in the report, but the lead Human Rights Watch researcher insists that the evidence supports the claim.

Rasmea's interrogators continued to beat and abuse her to force a confession, leaving vision and hearing damage that continue today. At some point, they also brought in her father and two of her sisters to witness the abuse. When her father begged them to stop, they only responded, "To save your house from destruction let your daughter tell what she knows." In fact, the family's house had already been destroyed in advance of any court determination or sentence, as was and is today once again the custom in cases of suspected terrorists, to give any would-be terrorists second thoughts—or so the much-criticized theory goes. (After a Defense Ministry commission in 2005 concluded that house demolition did *not* act as a deterrent to future terrorist activity, the implementation of the policy was reduced significantly. But during the "Intifada of the individuals" in 2015, it was reinstated.) Rasmea resisted a forced confession until her father screamed and fainted on being told that he had to have sexual relations with her in front of her family.

At that point she decided that the limit had come and that her father was at risk and would not survive any further torture, so she told her interrogator that she would confess to whatever they wanted and signed a confession written in Hebrew, a language she did not understand (though she would learn it later, in prison).

Her interrogators also tried to get her to become an informer. They played tapes of people confessing and implicating her—all of which she later learned had been fabricated. Her father and her youngest sister Fatima were released after eighteen days because he was in seriously bad condition, a release aided by his green card and the help of the US consulate. But her second-youngest sister, Layla, was kept in administrative detention without being charged for nearly a year and a half. Theoretically, administrative detainees cannot legally be held in prison for more than six months, but a magistrate merely has to visit the prison and renew the detention period for another six months, and another, ad infinitum—all without a trial. Today nearly five hundred Palestinians are being held in administrative detention.

Rasmea spent twenty-five of her forty-five days at the Moscobiya in solitary confinement. After that she was transported to a Nablus prison and then came back to the Moscobiya to, as she later reported, "a room they called the court." Despite her earlier confession, she told a panel of judges that she renounced it—she did not admit to what she'd been accused of, but her renunciation was ignored. The court "ruled that I was to be imprisoned [for life]. I was sent to prison on a bus ... with the border guards who amused themselves by catching beetles or cockroaches (we were all blindfolded as well as handcuffed) and forcing them into our mouths."

When she was twenty-one, Rasmea arrived at the Ramla prison, where she would remain for ten years. At one point she tried to escape, adding another ten years to her sentence. She engaged in hunger strikes as protests against the prison's conditions and endured force-feeding and temporary blindness, which still occasionally returns. Then, in March 1979, she and seventy-five other political prisoners were loaded onto buses and released as part of a prisoner exchange for one Israeli soldier captured in the 1978 invasion of southern Lebanon. Henceforth she would be forbidden from entering Israel.

The torture of prisoners, long established as a breach of international law, is unfortunately all too frequently resorted to. Of the 141 countries (including, for a time, the US) in violation of the UN anti-torture convention they signed, most found ways to slide around the prohibition. "Since 2001, over 1,000 complaints of torture and mal-treatment at the hands of Shin Bet investigations have been filed," a lawyer with the Public Committee Against Torture in Israel told a *Haaretz* reporter in the fall of 2016, but "up to this day, not a single criminal investigation has been opened." The Justice Ministry, responding to the reporter's inquiries, said that they had no figures for torture complaints, though the torture of detainees in the country has been confirmed by many outside observers, as noted earlier. Rasmea's father, the family says, never got over the events at the Moscobiya, and whether from his old injury or the beatings in prison or a combination of both, he had a permanent limp and remained in poor health until illness defeated him.

While Rasmea was in prison, her fiancé, another political prisoner who was himself incarcerated for seventeen years, broke off their engagement. The two were widely regarded as a true love match. In the years since, she has never married, and I was warned by the family not to bring the subject up with her. What the Abuleils and Odehs may say privately about her past I do not know, since they prefer not to discuss it. Khaled Masalha, the frankest of the family members (Khawallah, his wife, is Rasmea's niece) claims that in the twenty-five years he has been part of the family he has never discussed Rasmea's history, and no one has ever broached the subject. It's impossible to know if this is mainly a circling of the wagons and the way they've decided to treat the subject with outsiders or whether that part of the family's history is simply too painful to revisit.

Rasmea's past has given her a certain intense, watchful alertness, but it has also sharpened her sense of social justice. She told Antonius, "From the time I was a child I had always rejected the oppression of women." She was furious when her grandfather demanded that her beloved eldest sister Zaineb, who was an excellent student ("she was *perfect* in school"), leave school so that she could help more around the house. "I challenged my grandfather about it, but it was useless. I fought him on everything. But they were only interested in the boys. That was why my father . . . brought my brother to the US. But I was determined to get training. To do something. I had the will to achieve." Even after she became interested in nationalistic matters, Rasmea remained focused on women's problems. "I couldn't accept the way I was treated. Forbidden to come and go, to act freely, to marry as I pleased. Just an armchair for men."

In the period I was initially in touch with her off and on, 2011–2012, Rasmea told me she was particularly gratified by the institution she founded at AAAN, in Chicago, the Arab Women's Committee— a group that encourages Arab American women to explore civil and human rights issues and social justice and to learn about community organizing and focus on education reform. "There are now six hundred women in the group, and many of them have themselves become community leaders. I'm really proud of them," she said as we watched the bundled-up weekend shoppers hurrying by outside a downtown café on that snowy Chicago afternoon. Rasmea obviously loved her work, and I learned from my daughter-in-law, a longtime Chicago union organizer, that her colleagues, the people she's helped, and the activist community in general held her in high esteem.

All in all, her life has been full, and her past, as much as it could be, seemed put to rest. That was until 2013, the same year, ironically, that she had been given the Outstanding Community Leader Award for her long service to the Arab community, presented by the Chicago Cultural Alliance—a consortium of community-based ethnic museums, cultural centers, and institutions. She had also recently completed a master's degree in criminal justice from Governors State University. But on October 22 of that year, she was charged with immigration fraud for failing to disclose her Israeli conviction and the time spent in prison, both on her 1995 immigration application and later, in 2004, on her citizenship application. Homeland Security agents in Chicago arrested her at her modest Evergreen Park apartment after her indictment was unsealed at a federal court in Detroit, where she had initially lived when she came to the country. The charge and subsequent legal actions threatened her with revocation of her citizenship, a possible ten-year jail sentence, a fine of $250,000, and deportation.

When I first met her in Chicago in 2011, few people in the US had ever heard her name, but several years later, after her arrest, she became the focus of intense public scrutiny. As soon as her arrest was announced, hundreds of Arab American activists and others who had worked with her for years immediately jumped on the case and organized a defense campaign, and leading Arab Americans in the region and across the country charged that the case was politically motivated because of the work she did. Zaineb couldn't believe that her sister's life trials were not yet finished. Few of Rasmea's supporters mention the old Israeli allegations against her. But the misstating of facts on her applications, as copies of them clearly reveal, is beyond dispute. Her lawyers took pains to say publicly, since the press tended to focus on her past, that Rasmea has always denied—except after torture and the threat to her father's life—participating in the 1969 bombing. They suggested that the possibility of Palestinians finding justice in an Israeli military court is itself open to challenge (as is well known, nearly all cases involving Palestinians tried in Israeli military courts result in a guilty verdict).

Rasmea's US trial was held in the US District Court for the Eastern District of Michigan in November 2014, but the defense's case was weakened considerably when the judge, an Obama appointee, Gershwin Drain, refused to admit as relevant any testimony about Rasmea's torture (though the government was allowed to present more than one hundred damning Israeli court documents that it had obtained with the help of a Koch-supported legal group, Shurat HaDin, with close ties to the Israeli government). Nor did Drain allow the defense's expert witness Dr. Mary R. Fabri, a clinical psychologist with an extensive background in treating victims of trauma and torture, to testify. Fabri, formerly on the staff of the Chicago-based Marjorie Kovler Center for the Treatment of Survivors of Torture, met with Rasmea six times over four weeks, for three hours each time. In her fifteen-page affidavit, Fabri wrote that she was convinced that because of her experience and severe PTSD, Rasmea could well have misunderstood the application and thought that it had referred solely to crimes committed and prison time served in the United States. Fabri believed there was a "strong possibility" that Rasmea's PTSD would have protected her from reliving her past memories of torture by cognitively reinterpreting the question on the application. But Judge Drain ruled that the jury was not to hear a word about Rasmea's torture or PTSD. He said it would be "very one-sided" and "unfair to the government" if she were allowed to testify about her experience.

Without either the torture history or Fabri's testimony it was an all but forgone conclusion that a jury would find her guilty, and one did. Four months later, on March 12, 2015, she was sentenced to eighteen months in prison (a far shorter time than the ten years the government was asking for), a $1,000 fine, and deportation. A torrent of letters to the editor and blog responses to Rasmea's continuing ordeal followed (including one from a rabbi who was the Midwest regional director of the American Friends Service Committee, who had worked alongside her for years). Though some expressed satisfaction that a terrorist had been brought to justice, most of the comments expressed outrage on her behalf and were supportive.

The judge admitted in his summation that he had struggled with the case, since it had "spun off in so many directions." He insisted that it wasn't a political case, despite the many references by both the prosecution and defense attorneys to the question of Palestine. "It was," he said, "only about being truthful to get in the country . . . not about the Israeli-Palestinian conflict and freedom fighters and all that." But as her supporters pointed out, if the case were solely about lying on an immigration application, it would have been sent to an immigration court and disposed of in a few hours.

An appeal was initiated, and on February 25, 2016, the Sixth Circuit of the US Court of Appeals unanimously vacated the earlier conviction, paving the way for the possibility of a retrial. The three-judge panel of the circuit court ruled that the judge, by excluding Rasmea's torture history and the testimony of the PTSD expert, had denied her right to a full defense. Not long after the announcement of the appellate court's decision, and a short time after I'd heard from her relieved family in Jerusalem, I joined Rasmea and a scattering of activists from around Chicago who had gathered together to celebrate International Women's Day and the presentation of the first Rasmea Odeh Awards to "women fighters." The setting was Chicago's spare Trinity Episcopal Church, whose sole decorations were its stained glass windows and organ pipes.

I almost didn't recognize Rasmea, who arrived a bit late. Transformation! Gone was the too-busy-to-fuss-with-my-hair and well-worn-clothes figure I'd met a few years earlier, and in her place was . . . glam Rasmea, with long, beautifully coiffed tresses, makeup, a richly embroidered Palestinian dress, and the demeanor of someone who knows she is not fighting her battles alone and possibly that from time to time she will find herself in front of news photographers. The months-long outpouring of support from all over the country (her advocates included the actor Danny Glover) and organized protests on her behalf, despite the strain of the ongoing legal ordeal, she told me, had energized and comforted her.

The date for a new trial was set for January 2017, but before it could take place the government prosecutors asked for and were granted a chance to have their *own* PTSD expert interview Rasmea, a move anyone who watches TV courtroom procedurals will recognize as an attempt to intimidate and discredit a defendant. To the government's dismay, however, their own expert agreed with Fabri's PTSD assessment of Rasmea and testified along with Fabri accordingly at a special hearing in open court. But Rasmea's legal team couldn't savor this promising turn of events for long. A few weeks later, defeated in their attempts to discredit her PTSD defense, the government prosecutors, now under the leadership of President Trump and Attorney General Jeff Sessions, reframed a new, superseding indictment in terms of terrorism rather than immigration matters.

Faced with an entirely new framing of the prosecutorial strategy and cognizant of the politically motivated tone of the new charges, Rasmea and her lawyers reluctantly decided to accept a plea agreement with no prison time. Deportation now awaited her, and the date of departure was set for September 19, 2017. At her final Detroit court appearance on August 17, 2017, where the prosecution and defense attorneys agreed on the already settled terms of her sentence, Rasmea's lawyer said, "This case should never have been brought." But when Rasmea herself was invited to speak and attempted to present her version of why she had been on trial, in which the context of Palestinian grievance played a large part, Judge Drain interrupted her, pointing out, as he had during the trial, that the case was about making false statements on applications, not about the Israeli-Palestinian conflict. After one of these interjections from the judge—there were three altogether—Rasmea declared, "I am not a terrorist. My people are not terrorists. I want to prove that we are not terrorists." With the threat of contempt of court hanging in the air, the judge again interrupted her, repeated his earlier admonishment and said, "I don't want to hear any more about this Israel–Paki . . . Palestine." More than 150 of Rasmea's supporters had showed up in a driving rain and were present in the courtroom and an adjourning overflow chamber where they watched the proceedings on monitors. When Rasmea finished speaking, they cheered and clapped. Afterward, outside the courtroom, Rasmea expressed her frustration with the judge ("[he] did not let me tell my story") and reiterated her lawyers' claim that the case was not about lying on a form but rather about "being Palestinian and our work in the community. It is political." As she concluded her statement, she added, "The US is a partner in the crimes of Israel. We will continue to struggle for our cause."

It's the charge of legal systems to discover truth, apportion blame, and administer punishment. But if in the course of doing so the state's authority becomes embroiled in a crime like torture, the prosecution has compromised its moral foundation, relinquished its legitimacy and its right to proceed. How can the legal process not be invalid when punishment precedes trial and sentencing? If such a case were nevertheless to be pursued, it should not be prosecuted by a surrogate political ally, as the US is to Israel. Rather, in an ideal world, a venue would be sought in, say, the International Court of Justice, which, lacking the moral burden of Rasmea's case, might follow facts wherever they might lead and apportion blame with a claim to objectivity.

———•———

If many Israelis will always consider Rasmea a terrorist, in human rights circles she has long been celebrated as an activist icon. A bit lost in the urgency about the unfairness and implications of her US case, because it would not have served her cause, was any sense of the youthful, political Rasmea who resented the Occupation and was stirred to resist it. A window into the thinking of that Rasmea, who then as now was a committed political being, is afforded by a 2005 documentary made by Buthina Canaan Khoury, called *Women in Struggle*, about Palestinian women imprisoned in Israel. The film, which was briefly cited by the prosecutors—erroneously, in my opinion, as confirmation of the defendant's guilt—focuses on Aisha Odeh (no relation), an artist, former teacher, and onetime political comrade of Rasmea's and by then the very picture of middle-class placidity. But the film also features Rasmea in several short segments. Aisha, like Rasmea, was a victim of torture and was also released in a prisoner exchange. She speaks proudly, as does Rasmea, of their work when they were fervent young nationalists. Several other women are interviewed in the film, and all concur that at a certain point it became clear to them that the Occupation's end would not be brought about by petitions or by being "gentle." They had concluded as well, in the familiar words of passionate militants for all causes, sane or insane, that freedom was something they would give their lives for. While continuing to maintain she played no role in the supermarket bombing for which her confession was extracted under torture, Rasmea, in her 1980 interview with the author Soraya Antonius, did admit to PFLP's collective responsibility for placing the bombs at the British Consulate: "We placed two bombs, the first was found before it went off, so we placed another. The intention then was not to hurt people but to remind the world that the Palestinians existed."

If the Khoury film proves nothing about Rasmea's alleged specific involvement in the supermarket bombing, neither does it disprove anything. It reminds the viewer of the violent ongoing toll that the strategies of militant groups take on civilians. A complicating and as yet unresolvable element in Rasmea's history was introduced when a strange and, if real, more damaging film of questionable authenticity surfaced on the Internet around the time of the second indictment. It was provided by an unapologetically anti-Palestinian NGO, Palestinian Media Watch, whose credibility received scathing criticism from at least one Israeli judge, and it purports to be another interview by an unnamed interviewer with a blurry Aisha Odeh, some years later, in which she says that she and Rasmea carried out the bombing. But the more fundamental issue both films bring to the fore is what Walter Benjamin, in his difficult essay "Critique of Violence," calls the "distinction between historically acknowledged so-called sanctioned violence and unsanctioned violence." It also uncomfortably reminds us of the complex truths involved in assessing the relation of violence to issues of justice. Was Nelson Mandela, whom we honor as a man of peace, someone else when he was called a terrorist?

If the women in the film were terrorists, what were the members of the paramilitary Stern Gang, and the Irgun, who planted bombs and over the years killed hundreds of innocent civilians? The Irgun was responsible for the bombing of the King David Hotel, and the Stern Gang, or Lehi, twice offered to form an alliance with the Nazis against the British and assassinated Count Folke Bernadotte, the UN mediator responsible for saving more than twenty thousand Jews in Europe. Nevertheless, Israel granted a general amnesty to their members, one of whom, Menachem Begin, became the country's sixth prime minister, and another of whom, Yitzhak Shamir, became its seventh. In 1980 the government established the Lehi Ribbon, a military decoration for "activity in the struggle for the establishment of Israel."

Of course the pre-state Jewish fighters were on the side of the winners, the Palestinians the losers. And in the wake of ongoing bloodshed, especially in times of global insecurity, unleashed barbarism, acts of militancy, and retribution take on what appears to be an unstoppable life of their own. By now, the disappointment over missed opportunities for peace is so entrenched that it is tempting to consider the possibility that all of the conflict's deep-seated oppositions, embedded in history, land, and blood, might be inalterable and the cycle of violence, revenge, and retaliation without end. But then I am reminded again of the Parents Circle–Families Forum, some of whose members I got to know over the years, who have miraculously managed to move beyond them. True, they are not heads of state and cannot sign any peace agreement, but somehow these Israelis and Palestinians who have lost daughters, sons, sisters, brothers, mothers, and fathers to violence from "the other side" continue to preach reconciliation, even at the settlements, even at the refugee camps, where no one really wants to hear them.

CHAPTER 11

YOTAM'S VISION

Before I met Yotam, Ruth's son from her first marriage, everyone I encountered in her orbit—her mother, her secular sister Nechama, her religious brothers Rami and Yehuda, her stepchildren, parents, aunts and uncles, cousins, and friends—all occupied a place somewhere on the spectrum of the Left. But Yotam's intellectual and spiritual development launched him on a different path—and one that at first took everyone aback. He had become ultra-orthodox and seemed to be swimming in right-wing waters. I use the word "seemed" because his description of his worldview when I first met him (he was twenty-three) was so difficult to pin down and complicated that I decided it would be best to present them largely in his own words.

Like his stepsisters and stepbrother, Yotam grew up in a liberal household. His parents divorced when he was six, and most of his day-to-day upbringing afterward was overseen by his mother. His father was a corps commander and commander of the IDF military colleges. As a child, even though both sets of his grandparents were religious, religion held no particular attraction for Yotam. He developed a bit more interest after his bar mitzvah, but it had little effect on the way he lived. After he turned sixteen, however, things changed, and he became more religious and politically conservative. I spoke to him in Ruth and Yaron's living room. At first, he freely admits, it was a form of teenage rebellion (how delightful a way to vex your secular and progressive stepfather!), as was his nonparticipation in his friends' rituals of drinking and drug use. His year at a religious *mechina*— a time of intense self-scrutiny, examination of personal ideals, and Torah study—deepened his religious feeling even more. (A *mechina* is a post–high school preparatory school for the army—more state cradle-to-grave-ism.) "A lot of my friends took a *wanderjahr* at that point," he told me. "I have a kind of nomadic urge, but I traveled that year in an interior way."

Yotam still went to parties, still played jazz on his guitar, but more and more he became attracted to the idea of a full religious life. "I felt it was a better way to live, a way to be more good," he offered as an explanation for his decision. We were meeting on a weekend when he was on leave from the army, where he was serving as an intelligence officer, so he couldn't talk about his duties. Yotam was then (2006) unmarried and unsure of where he might be heading professionally. Today he is married, with three small children, and his views, his mother told me, had continued to evolve.

Over the next few years he acquired two academic degrees, one in philosophy, the other in sociology-anthropology (continuing the family tradition of collecting academic degrees as if they were nesting materials). He now co-runs a successful consulting firm, DoAlogue, a "Strategic Consultancy and System-Thinking Training Group," that advises municipalities, NGOs, and the civil service department of the government about ways to better achieve their goals and identify why they might be stuck in some way from developing them. Yotam's wife, Nehami, who was then acquiring a degree in clinical psychology with an emphasis on research and is now working on her postdoc, shares Yotam's religious beliefs and wears the conventional modest clothes of the religious. But Yotam's views about society when I first spoke with him were far from conventional and often spilled over the standard categories of Left and Right, religious and secular. Over a long afternoon he described an unusual amalgam of conservative and idealistic beliefs that I could only sometimes follow. A core problem in his country, from Yotam's vantage point, was that people his age "didn't believe in politics" because politicians were too corrupt. "But I have my own vision of the way things should be in a Jewish country. Today it's nothing like it. We should be taking care of the poor instead of focusing on money and power. We need as a society to live in a more moral way. To be better and have a completely different discourse."

Somewhat surprisingly, in the ideal country he imagined that the two strands of Judaism and Islam would be able to coexist.

"Of course there would be a struggle between this vision and reality, but I believe it will happen."

"In your lifetime?"

"I'm not sure. . . . Before we build the third temple, we have to know what to sing. When Muslims go to the hajj more than once, they are supposed to take a different route the second time. The way you're getting there is the most important thing. It's the same in Judaism."

According to Yotam, the biggest obstacle to a saner society and country—currently a kind of dragon devouring its children—is the West and Western ideas of statehood and governance that have been imposed on a Middle Eastern world. "The whole discourse about borders is Western. Britain created ours, and we are fighting because of the borders they drew. Let's take out the discourse about border involvement. I really believe that the Palestinians have been right to object to the way the key issues have been unresolved in peace negotiations. I understand why they wouldn't want this little piece of land that we wanted to give them. They say, we would like to have a state in the West Bank and Gaza, but we would also like to go to Haifa. I have a similar dream about going to Nablus and Hebron. And I want to keep that dream, and I don't want to sign a paper saying I will give up on that dream. The point is: neither of us wants to give up on our dream, but we will have to find a way to live together."

"But how does your vision address the conflicting needs of the two peoples?" I asked Yotam. I was surprised to hear in his response, which described a new political system based on Jewish morality, echoes of Ahad Ha'am, the Zionist thinker and critic of Herzl.

"In this chaotic situation, the nation-state won't resolve anything. We need to be sharing. We are such a small land. There's too much that has to be shared—water, electricity, bridges. We are together. . . . The Arabs see a colonial state in the heart of the Middle East. They want 'the Jewish entity,' as they call it, to vanish. And I want it to be a Jewish entity! But there's no way for us to separate." I asked Yotam if he had ever seen the 2005 RAND report, *The Arc: A Formal Structure for a Palestinian State*, which offered a blueprint for an imagined independent Palestinian state, complete with detailed plans for infrastructure. He shook his head. When I pressed him again about his vision's practical workability, which was definitively different from most people's idea of the one-state solution, he answered somewhat obliquely and began treading down a more familiar-sounding path. "We are here because it is *our* land and our fathers' country. But we aren't meant to go back to the nineteenth century. Judaism always adjusts to the time. Jewish thinking contains modernity and postmodernity." Yotam's eyes shone as he warmed to his subject, but I squirmed in my seat because of its familiar echoes of right-wing dogma. Because of their love for him, the family had accommodated the "new" Yotam with respectful open-mindedness, but this part of the package, I thought, far more than the traditional religious part, must have been hard for some members of his family to accept.

Still unsure that I understood the gravamen of his argument, I pressed him a bit more, and he continued. "Even speaking about Judaism only as a religion is wrong. When I see Sephardic Jews, they are not split between religious and secular. Fatah people, too, are religious *and* secular. You can't really say, as people do, that those who belong to Fatah as opposed to Hamas are not religious—some are, some aren't. When they drink alcoholic beverages they don't say now I'm not religious. . . . The same for me. It is part of my religion being in the army, because I love my people, and I love my country, and this is part of what I have to do for my country. For me, army and study are the same thing."

"Well, a lot of religious Muslims and Jews would disagree with you about the importance of standard obligations of religious observance."

"I don't believe in making people do things they don't want to. But my vision of how I see my life—it's not a Western life."

"If the nation-state is such a terrible idea here, what would replace it?"

"The Jews and the Palestinians would be living together. The Western Jews who came here brought this [nation-state] idea with them. The Palestinians learned from us what it was to be a nation, and there was in it an illusion of classlessness. But in my vision the Palestinians will be part of a country not based on democratic ideas but based on Jewish morality."

"But that would ignore *their* dreams."

"No. To quote Rabbi Nachman of Bratslav, 'Everywhere I go, I'm on the path to Jerusalem.' We as a nation will have to come forward and see a lot of ideas coming up and going down. The nation-state will be put aside."

If I had momentarily thought I had gotten hold of the general tenor of his argument, I had lost it again, but I offered a question that seemed to me obfuscation-proof. "So you are against the two-state solution?"

This had mixed results.

"It's a different way of looking at the world and governance. The nomadic culture of Islam I to some extent admire and feel part of, but in that two-state division, the Qassam rockets will still fall on Tel Aviv."

In the borderless state that Yotam envisaged, the two populations would mingle, as they did somewhat in the late Ottoman and early Mandate periods, though it was far from clear how the wheels of government would turn.

I said something about the settlers and how their presence was costing too many lives on both sides. Yotam believed that they should stay put but not in the same places they now lived. "They are too Western in my opinion. The idea of building the settlements high on a hill as they do is wrong. They should leave the hills and move down and live together with the Palestinians among the olive trees." I mentioned how difficult this would be because of the deep anger that the conflict had bred and the legions of the dead that were a testimony to it, but he wouldn't engage with that subject and more or less brushed it off. As I listened to Yotam I was struck again, as I so often was, by Israel's incredibly complex stew of belief and political conviction.

"People have to fight for the things they believe in. They always have. If I were to put aside my dream of living in the land of Judea and only living in Tel Aviv—then I am living in a Western fantasy. . . . As long as we are not connected with those areas, we are still a colony. . . . I know the vast majority of people wouldn't agree with me, but I'm convinced there has to be first a cultural change to being more Jewish, which has nothing to do with being more religious. Being in the army is Jewish. Building a more moral society is Jewish." When I told him that I couldn't see how the country I saw around me could remotely shift in the ways he envisaged, he shrugged. "Maybe it will take fifty years," he said, "maybe a hundred, but we will get there."

Not long before, I remembered, a remark in the same vein had been made by Saeb Erekat, the chief Palestinian negotiator, at a talk he gave at Jerusalem's Notre Dame Center. Questioned about how disappointed and frustrated he must repeatedly feel coming away empty-handed from the many "peace" conferences he'd attended, he responded, "Well, I come from Jericho, which archaeologists believe is the oldest continuously settled city on earth. It dates from the tenth century BC. So it's been there a long time. We've been here a long time. Will we have to wait another ten centuries for things to work out? I hope not. But if we have to, we will."

"I believe we will get there," Yotam repeated. "I live my life in the belief that things take a long time. My great grandparents dreamed of coming to the land of Israel and never imagined that their dream would be fulfilled within a hundred years." The conversation with Yotam, which took place more than ten years ago, left me wondering where in the world Yotam would land when he grew older. But now he seemed to be thriving as a specialist in fixing the problems of large institutions—an outcome I couldn't possibly have predicted.

In January 2016 Esther, Yotam's grandmother, died peacefully. In the days afterward I came to half-believe that, right or wrong, in his heartfelt probing of his beliefs, Yotam could in certain ways be seen as the flower of her hope for the perpetuation of Jewish consciousness.

CHAPTER 12

SOLDIERS

Ruth's older brother, Rami, dreamt of tanks, as boys will, but in his case a tank was not merely a conduit for military valor but a fascinating object of mechanical complexity. I met him for the first time at his home in Nataf, an exuberantly verdant community twelve miles west of Jerusalem in the Judean Mountains, parts of which were devastated in the 2016 wildfires. Ruth drove me there, and when we pulled into the driveway, Rami came out to greet us, and on the way to his front door he introduced us to every plant, bush, and tree we passed and with evident satisfaction gave us its horticultural history, year of planting, and several reasons to appreciate it. A graduate of the Technion, Israel's MIT, where his brother Yehuda eventually became a professor of mathematics, Rami's degree was in mechanical engineering, and over the years he has helped build solar stations in the Mojave Desert that produce electricity for Los Angeles, designed bioengineering instruments for Israeli hospitals, and continues to work for hospitals as a technical project manager. He is four years older than Ruth. His wife, Edna, the principal of the Department of Pediatrics school at Hadassah Medical Center, welcomed us and showed us into their comfortable living room.

A soft-spoken, thoughtful man with the familiar balding pate common to Israeli men and what I had come to think of as the family lips (full and sensual, like those of Esther and Ruth), Rami was happy to talk about his life growing up in Israel, but when we got around to the subject of his soldiering days, he became several degrees more animated. Like most boys in his country, Rami had been captivated by the stories he heard about the army's heroic soldiers, and because of his aptitude for understanding the way things worked, he was particularly fascinated by tanks.

"When he was fourteen, he made a whole tank out of paper, thick paper, with all the details. Right, Rami?" Ruth said.

Rami nodded. "Yes, I liked all the business about tanks from the mechanical point of view—a big machine."

Tank-fixated though he may have been, Rami seemed like such a gentle, inward man, and Nataf itself such a peaceful place, that I wondered out loud if it hadn't been overwhelming to serve in battle, as he'd mentioned he had, beginning with his first tour in 1970–74—a longer than usual enlistment because he was called to serve an extra six months in the Yom Kippur War.

"No, because I dreamt about it. And I liked it—at first—because there were a lot of machines, tanks, and I'd dreamt about being a soldier in a tank. When they asked me if I wanted to join the paratroopers or the tank command, I immediately chose the tanks. It was after the 1967 war, and the soldiers of the armored brigade were its heroes. You know how the journalists created this myth. There was euphoria. . . . There was this sort of brainwashing about our army's invincibility and overconfidence about the war. But my understanding about the myths I'd been told about our great empire in the Middle East didn't really change until years later during the first Lebanon war. So I liked it . . . I didn't like the people very much—the officers and the guys—who were with me. My brother Yehuda's experience was different because he fought alongside people he knew and cared about. But I was fighting alongside strangers. . . . There was boredom, of course. We had a lot of hours doing nothing and lots of hours when you had to scrub the tank with a small brush."

Rami's boyhood fantasies of glorious, heroic soldiering came up against hard reality at his very first battle, where nothing was as he had imagined. He was stationed near Eilat when, he said, "someone took my tank"—and those of his entire unit, twenty in all. Apparently they had been reassigned without their crews to another sector in the war, and nobody had any idea where that was. But tanks also serve as homes for their men, and more or less "belong" to particular soldiers. Nonetheless, try as they might, they couldn't be found. Rami shrugged. "This is war; this happens." He was still searching for his tank when he was moved to the Syrian border, but after a week he found and retrieved it, just in time for one of the biggest and bloodiest battles of the war. Still caught in the grip of the military successes of 1967, his commanders were convinced that they could easily triumph. "The Arabs, we were taught, would just run away at the beginning. . . . We didn't have to do anything." Instead, Rami said, "At my first battle I ran away!"

"You ran away?"

"We went to an area where it was difficult to find our way, and the officer who led us couldn't find a way either. So we got to where the Egyptians were, and then a lot of missiles began raining down on us, and we had to move back. But then my tank had a problem—it just sank into the dunes in an area that had already been bombed by the enemy—so I had to leave it and run."

"Were you frightened?"

"No."

"Why not?"

Ruth: "We are Pinczowers." (In Rami's and his brother's case, the surname is spelled with a "ch" because when they both worked in the US, no one could spell or pronounce it the other way.)

"Pinczowers don't get frightened?"

Edna, half-smiling and echoing Esther's characterization of the deep-rooted family stoicism she'd described to me several years earlier, remarked, "Feeling is outside."

During the Yom Kippur War, Rami had finished that day, which had begun at six in the morning, at two in the afternoon—again without a tank. "So I was homeless. And it was my first experience of war, to run away. It was unbelievable to me."

This time his tank was recovered and returned to him in a day. Subsequently, in another battle, Rami and his fellow soldiers were on the Egyptian side of the Suez Canal, and then the Egyptians pushed them back to their side of the canal, and then, once again, after ten days the Israelis pushed definitively through to the Egyptian side and were about sixty miles from Cairo. The last battle had gone well but had by no means been the rout they had been told to expect. It was a nice morning, and for the moment he and his fellow soldiers felt reasonably secure about their position. Rami was pleased to get all his belongings back in the tank—"I got my home again." So he pulled off his shoes—something he'd been unable to do for many days. With-out his tank, he'd been sleeping on the sand, and now, using his water can, he began an impromptu washup, enjoying the quiet interlude. For the moment things seemed pretty calm. All around him most of the soldiers were napping—because they could. ("If you have a free period, immediately you sleep.") It was midday. Suddenly, from behind a small mountain, came two MIGs, fast, shattering the silence and shooting directly at the place where Rami and his comrades were taking their break. No one had heard the planes approach because they were flying against the wind.

"When I first heard the guns shooting, it was totally—I was in a war, I know what the noise of war is, but it was totally shock-ing. . . . They came *very* close to us. They were perhaps twenty meters away. But before they arrived we didn't hear them. I jumped into the tank headfirst without my shoes. Then ten seconds later those two planes crashed. Two Israeli planes also came out of nowhere and shot them down."

You might conclude from the country's focus on military strength and Sparta-like recruitment of citizens to fill its military ranks that this ethos would effect an almost total transformation of the popula-tion—which, in a way, was the original Zionist goal. But I was still having a difficult time imagining the soft-spoken Rami shooting any-one. Though tank warfare, I learned from him, had an unanticipated dimension, in truth a somewhat chilling one. However horrible the killing is, he explained, the tank itself doesn't permit close connec-tion with the "enemy," which hugely depersonalizes the act. "Nobody is right next to you. You see everyone from the tank with binoculars, and you don't have the same connection you would if you had a per-sonal contact. It's not the same."

In his first tour, he was twenty-one. How did he feel about the war he was called to fight in, the Yom Kippur War? "I didn't have enough time to think about it . . . though I saw that one important officer made a lot of mistakes, and everyone knew that the battle un-der him had been a failure. They put me in the tank with him, and I saw clearly that he didn't know anything about tanks. It was upset-ting because he was putting his soldiers in danger." After the battle, Rami chewed on what he'd seen so plainly and decided he had to speak to the officer's superior, who was the brigade deputy. And he did. "Don't worry, don't worry," he was told. "OK, I'll take care of that." But the matter wasn't dealt with immediately, and that same day they were called to fight in another bloody battle, and theirs was the first tank to go forward. Rami saw that the officer was in total shock. "He didn't know where he was." After the battle the officer was summoned to a meeting. Rami had just stepped outside the tank when intense bombing from the Egyptians began. "Nothing happened to me—I got some metal in my leg, that's all." They all heard that officer shout, "Sa! Sa!" to his men, and everyone dove for whatever cover they could find. And that was the last they heard from him—he had been killed in the attack. Since the officer had no friends in the battalion, when the commander asked who was going to visit the officer's family to say something about him, "nobody wants to go for this guy, because nobody knows him, just me, so the story ends that I had to go to the family. Anyway, by then I knew that from the outside the army looks exotic—but when you're inside, you don't feel that."

As Rami talked about his war experiences, I could see that Ruth was eager to say something, and at that point she jumped in to remind me that all that I'd heard so far was from the point of view of a twenty-one-year-old boy, and that her other brother, Yehuda, was even younger when he first served in the army. "After that time we all went through a process of realizing what kind of a country we were." She urged Rami to say more about his coming to terms with that shift in his perspective and with "the meaning of the army, all the unjust wars, all the mythologies we were fed."

Like Ruth, it took a while for Rami to slowly begin to understand that so much of what he'd learned about his country in school and from politicians was untrue. The big shift in his perspective came about nine years later, when he was thirty and serving as a reservist in the first Lebanon war. Officially called Operation Peace for Galilee, it involved a siege of Beirut and the shameful Sabra and Shatila massacre of Palestinian civilians by Christian militiamen allied with Israel. It also involved a confrontation with the Syrians and by the war's end saw (although estimates vary) between four thousand and five thousand civilian deaths and the deaths of some twelve hundred Israeli soldiers.

"I understood after two days that Sharon was a liar. He was lying to the soldiers and to the government. He said we were only going forty kilometers into the country; we were not going into Beirut. And then we'll go back to Israel." Ariel Sharon, who would go on to serve as prime minister from 2001 to 2006, was then the defense minister. And while the soldiers supported the stated goal of the war, to push Palestinian guerrillas back from artillery range of Israel's northern cities and villages, which they had been attacking, they couldn't understand Sharon's decision to press on to Beirut. But they did press on, with the well-known catastrophic result. Large-scale civilian protests followed—Edna remembered being at a protest and shouting against the war while she held her baby. Soldiers in reserve units like Rami's, when they were finished with their tours of duty, were openly expressing lack of confidence in Sharon and opposition to the war. Rami joined his brother Yehuda and other reservist veterans to form a group called Soldiers Against Silence, which demanded an immediate halt to the war. When the group met, they talked about their battle experiences—some of which have stayed with Rami, he said, for the rest of his life—and decided to try to talk to politicians, hoping to enlist their support. Although they gained the ear many of them, they got nowhere.

Among those they met with were Moshe Katsav and Ehud Olmert. (Katsav eventually became Israel's eighth president and in 2010 was convicted of rape and obstruction of justice and sent to prison.) At the time of their visit, Katsav appeared to be uninterested, even bored, with what the soldiers had to say. Olmert at that time served on the Knesset's Foreign Affairs and Defense Committee and went on to become the country's twelfth prime minister, after Sharon became incapacitated by a stroke. In 2012, convicted of bribery, Olmert, too, went to prison. Rami and the others were told they didn't understand the situation. Rami thought Olmert was entirely unmoved by their attempts to describe the toll the expanded battle was taking on their comrades and on the civilian population. And this was *before* Sabra and Shatila. He wasn't certain, but the sole politician he felt they reached was Yosef Burg, a religious member of the Knesset who, over a long career, held many ministerial positions and knew Rami's family. He too reacted negatively to the delegation of soldiers, but Rami had the impression that he might nonetheless have talked afterward with Prime Minister Begin, who grew increasingly depressed and isolated over the months that followed, and after the death of his wife gradually withdrew from public activities and a year later resigned his office.

Before Rami finished his time serving in Lebanon, he and many of his fellow soldiers had come to realize that Sharon's true goal was to rearrange the political geography of the Middle East, just as earlier colonial powers had. The fact that so many Israeli soldiers and so many Lebanese civilians were dying did not alter the plan. One day the army brass, an important colonel, paid a visit to Rami's unit. The colonel spoke chummily to the men and invited them to chat. Instead of responding with the customary foot-soldier hat doffing, Rami found himself telling the colonel that the war was a disaster and tried to persuade him that it was totally unnecessary. "If you ask me about my willingness to be in a battle with a Syrian soldier," he said, "I have no reason to." The colonel's face turned red, Rami said. "'I can't believe a soldier can speak like this! In all my years in the army I've never heard a soldier say such a thing,' and he left in anger." Rami's battalion commander, who heard about the exchange, angrily confronted him. But over the next few days, many soldiers came up to him and said, "You were right."

Yehuda, born between Rami and Ruth, seemed to me to be an even more unlikely candidate for martial enthusiasm than his brother. He and his wife, Iris, live in a book-lined, sunny apartment in the Haifa hills, and Iris's bright abstract paintings adorn their walls. Like Rami, Yehuda has a long face, a receding hairline and the family lips, but he also has something of his father Eliezar's alert lightness in his expression and a passing resemblance to the French actor Jean-Louis Barrault. He too said that he couldn't help but be affected growing up in a society that continuously lavished praise on the heroics of soldiers. He was thirteen during the Six-Day War. "We thought it was a miracle and read all the literature about it, and it became a kind of model for us. We all knew the stories about famous battles and so on." Somewhat balancing this was the special group that Yehuda—as well as Rami and Ruth—served with in the army. It was called the Nahal Brigade ("Nahal" being an acronym for the Hebrew words for Fighting Pioneer Youth) and allowed its soldiers to serve one-third to half their time in civil service jobs, chiefly agricultural, at kibbutzim, and half the time (for men) in combat service. Yehuda wasn't all that keen on kibbutz life generally, but he loved driving a tractor and working in the fields. "Of course we preferred the work on the kibbutz, but I wanted to be a good soldier. I didn't want to be an officer or to make a career in the army, but I wanted to do my duty and to be, let's say, not an excellent soldier, but a good one. I joined the paratroopers and parachuted around twenty times, but only in my initial training and in the time of my reserve training—it was like extreme sport in the middle of everyday life." He continued, "I liked it. The atmosphere of friendship among our group of soldiers was amazing, and I really appreciated it. Of course, they are very clever in arranging things so that the unit looks like a family. It's all very—I only know the German word, *heimisch*, or the Yiddish one, *haimish* [homey]." I mentioned that Rami's experience hadn't been all that *heimisch*.

"That's because in the tank unit things are much more formal and far more rigid—they follow the rules. Fighting in the war, things are, of course, very tense, but the rest of the time, as a group we were pretty relaxed."

Before the Yom Kippur War began, on October 6, 1973, Yehuda and his fellow draftees had been fed a steady diet of stirring words—"'We're the best army in the world' and 'You are the best unit in the IDF,' et cetera"—so they naturally believed that they would experience an easy repeat of the Six-Day War. In fact it lasted about three weeks, though his unit somehow didn't engage in any battles for quite a while, despite being in the Sinai. "There was a lot of chaos. We were supposed to be in front, but they just kept moving us around." After two weeks he, too, crossed the Suez, and the fighting was intense; a lot of people were killed in heavy bombing. "The dead Egyptian soldiers were somehow left on the ground for a very long time, and that added a macabre element to the battle scene."

Yehuda admitted to sometimes being quite frightened, especially when his commander, whom he liked and was standing close to, was killed. (Yehuda's first son, Avner, is named after him.)

"They were shooting Katyusha rockets, and when they shoot one, they shoot thirty. And you can hear them being fired, and you know that in one or two minutes it will hit you because it became clear that they knew where we were. There was nothing to do but put your head down and see what will happen and hope you won't get killed. I didn't experience all that happened on the battlefield as traumatic, but some of it was." When I told him what Rami had said about Yehuda having a worse war than he had because he was fighting alongside people he knew and because he saw death up close, he smiled.

"You know, it seems to be a phenomenon that many soldiers end up saying, 'My war was not so bad; my brother'—or 'friend' or 'schoolmate'—'had a far worse time.' Rami has told me lots of terrible stories about his experience. I think the truth is it's traumatic for anyone to have the experience of fighting in a war and then to keep repeating that experience in other wars. The question is, How do you feel after, and how do you function? Many, many veterans suffer from PTSD—for years." One man he knew could only sleep *under* a bed for the rest of his life.

Yehuda's wife, Iris, had been due to give birth to their second child in the middle of the Lebanon War, and the June week she was due he was given a leave so that he could be present for the birth. But the days came and went, and the baby did not oblige them. So Yehuda returned to his unit, which at that point was engaging in heavy fighting as it marched along the shore, driving toward Beirut. This was before cell phones, so Yehuda had no way of knowing what was happening with the baby. But his brother did. An excited soldier who had gotten word of Iris's delivery ran up to Rami and said, "Pinchover! Congratulations! You have a new son—your wife has given birth!" At first Rami just stared at the messenger. Edna hadn't been pregnant when he left home. Then he realized what had happened and laughed— but it was midnight and he was near the Syrian border of Lebanon, and Yehuda was somewhere across the mountains near Beirut. Even though Rami told the authorities who the right Pinchover was, getting in touch was impossible. So Yehuda didn't learn about the birth of his son until days later.

Yehuda, too, was told at the outset of the war that the army's mission was to move only twenty-five miles into the country. But his unit was sent first by coast road and next by sea to a place seventy-five miles into the country. The soldiers were also ordered to continue their maneuvers during a cease-fire, and all this prompted him to afterward join Soldiers Against Silence, further participating after his discharge in protests outside the prime minister's house and visits to politicians, though his reaction to Olmert and Burg, whom he visited at another time, differed from Rami's. Olmert argued with him, tried to persuade Yehuda that he was wrong, but in the end told him he would talk to the prime minister, and one of the biographies of Olmert confirms that this did happen. But unlike Rami, Yehuda felt that his visit to Burg had been useless and that the politician didn't take the soldiers seriously. Neither brother believes that their protests or those of the general population had the least effect in ending the war.

Yehuda occasionally still joins a protest, at which, he's observed, his fellow protesters are usually from his generation (not so at the ones I witnessed), but he has lost all faith in their efficacy. "The political dynamic is so complicated that a small person can't do much. Iris still goes to more of them, but I no longer believe they can be game changers." He counts Palestinian colleagues among his friends, however, and their friendships manage to survive the trying times their respective peoples are in violent confrontation. He, too, remembered his father sitting his children down at the time of the Six-Day War and telling them that the Occupation had to end quickly. But he credits a melodramatic speech given by a fanatic to his youth group when he was a teenager with opening his eyes to the dangerousness of the settler vision. The speaker believed in what he referred to as "the Kingdom of Israel," which encompassed all the land between the Euphrates and the Nile. In the question-and-answer session afterward someone asked him what he proposed to do with all the Arabs who lived there, Yehuda said. "And he made a gesture with his hand and arm across his neck and said, 'We will throw them out.' I was only thirteen, but I believe that it was at that point that I became a leftist. I could see that all he stood for was wrong."

Nowadays probably the best-known military group bearing witness to the realities of daily life in the occupied territories is Breaking the Silence, an organization of Israeli military veterans, founded in June 2004. Members of the group provide testimony about their on-the-ground experiences in the West Bank, Gaza, and East Jerusalem, and some of this testimony has been published in a revealing anthology. The book, *Occupation of the Territories: Israeli Soldiers' Testimonies 2000–2010*, details what the soldiers considered the army's disproportionate degree of violence and the brutalities of everyday army missions in the occupied territories. The testimonies were cross-checked for accuracy with additional eyewitnesses, along with material drawn from the archives of human rights groups, and in its early days even underwent scrutiny by Israeli military censors before publication. They document a substantial level of abuses, including the use of young children as human shields when soldiers were about to enter the house of a wanted Palestinian or to protect themselves from booby traps or stone throwers. The testimonies include numerous examples of intimidation, beatings, and night raids and arrests. The detailed revelations in the Breaking the Silence report echo S. Yizhar's seminal 1949 novella *Khirbet Khizeh*, one of the very few works of fiction focused on the 1948 war to emerge soon after it (though the anthology is a more direct work of political protest). In the novella, a soldier describes what it was like to remove Palestinians from their homes and roughly pack them off by the truckload, an act that stands in stark contrast to the official line on the IDF's activities. Despite cries of "Traitors!" from official and unofficial critics, most vocally in 2016 from Moshe Ya'alon, then Israel's defense minister, who characterized the soldiers' revelations as "treason," it did not go unnoticed that the soldiers' publication was not a screed from some fringe group but rather a cri de coeur from loyal sons of the country.

The Breaking the Silence veterans were young men who had reported for duty in good faith and like all soldiers entering zones of contention were prepared to encounter hostile villagers and combat situations. What they were not prepared for, they say, was the devastating "moral price paid for in a reality in which young soldiers face a civilian population on a daily basis and are engaged in the control of that population's everyday life," as the soldiers write in the book's foreword. They were also not prepared to discover that when dealing with the depredations of the settlers they had no authority to stop them. About settler-instigated incidents of violence one soldier reported, "Bottom line, if he does something? There's nothing you can do about it." A second Breaking the Silence report published in 2012 recorded the prevalence of humiliations, beatings, intimidation, and nighttime arrests to frighten young people into phony confessions and persuade them to reveal the names of activist relatives.

The Breaking the Silence revelations, which continued, were by then well known in the country's human rights circles, and the group itself has increasingly become the object of the government's scorn and legislative targeting. In 2010, more than one hundred complaints of IDF and police abuse of minors were filed with Israel's legal authorities and the United Nations. One of the cases cited involved a fifteen-year-old from the village of Beit Ummar, northwest of Hebron, who was used as a human shield when security troops entered his village to quell a protest organized to mark Palestinian Prisoner Day. According to several human rights groups, including the Palestine branch of Defense for Children International and the Association for Civil Rights in Israel, soldiers made the boy march in front of them so they would not be targeted by stone throwers and later on demanded that he himself confess to the throwing of stones, beat him, and forced him to drink foul water that made him vomit.

More recently, and a decade after the original Breaking the Silence publication, in mid-September 2014, forty-three veterans and reservists of an elite and heretofore secretive military intelligence unit known as Unit 8200 lodged a protest with their community officers, the prime minister, and the chief of the army. They declared that they would no longer participate in any surveillance activities against Palestinians. They felt they had been used as tools of military rule in the occupied territories and that the surveillance that was required of them made "no distinction between Palestinians who are, and are not, involved in violence." The information they collected, they said, "harms innocent people" and "is used for political persecution." Their letter of protest called for "all soldiers serving in the Intelligence Corps, present and future, along with all the citizens of Israel, to speak out against these injustices and to take action to bring them to an end: We believe that Israel's future depends on it." Somewhat surprisingly, although some in the liberal Left applauded the soldiers, more voices on both the right *and left* decried the revelations. General Moti Almoz, the country's chief military spokesman, told reporters that the IDF's top generals would act with the "utmost severity" and that a disciplinary response—against the dissenters—would be "sharp and clear."

It is difficult to assess the effect, if any, of these protests, but by the summer of 2016, rumors abounded of a perceptible shift in the country's political temperature, even in the halls of power. No publication did a better job of calibrating the factors contributing to the shift than the scrappy news website of Philip Weiss, an American journalist and the site's coeditor (with Adam Horowitz). Mondoweiss focuses in Talmudic detail on Israeli affairs and so vigilantly follows the activities of Israel's military and civic establishments that few if any of their policies, legal maneuvers, or diplomatic sorties escape its notice. Did the site play any role, if only a peripheral one, in Netanyahu's nightmares, I sometimes wondered? More likely Weiss's overwhelmingly critical contributions are ignored altogether in the government's hard-right, hermetically sealed high empyrean.

Events that one of Weiss's contributors chronicled to account for a sense of changes in the air began with the March 24, 2016, extrajudicial killing in Tel Rumeida of Abdel Fattah al-Sharif, which was caught on camera and went viral around the world. In the glare of international disapprobation, Israeli military leaders then made the highly unusual decision to try the soldier-medic who shot the Palestinian. Sergeant Elor Azaria was tried for and convicted of manslaughter, sentenced to eighteen months in prison, and served nine months. After being released he came home to a jubilant reception, with Israeli flags waving and signs that read "Welcome home, Elor the hero." Several cabinet ministers even called for expunging his criminal record. Mondoweiss also chronicled the April 2016 speech of the army's deputy chief of staff, Yair Golan, which included the statement that Israel was reminiscent of Nazi Germany "in its intolerance to non-Jews"; the resignation in May 2016 of the defense minister, Moshe Ya'alon, hardly a dove, after Netanyahu asked him to repudiate Golan, and he refused; Ya'alon's replacement with the unapologetically racist Avigdor Lieberman; a subsequent speech by Ya'alon in which he said the Israeli leadership exhibits "the seeds of fascism"; a speech by former prime minister Ehud Barak alleging that Netanyahu "ha[d] been taken hostage by the right and ha[s] no intention of securing the country's future by establishing a Palestinian state"; and ongoing rumors that one of the country's many well-known generals would come forward to challenge Netanyahu politically, especially after four different charges of corruption were leveled at him—and one did, the three-star general Benny Gantz.

Gantz ran a strong race. But despite the corruption charges devolving into multiple graft indictments, the April 2019 election returned Netanyahu to power. While these events may or may not portend significant changes on the horizon, it is hard to find any Palestinian who feels that even a radical shakeup in Israel's leadership would benefit Palestinians or make the slightest difference in their everyday lives.

Amid the increased critiques of Israel's policies, the country's tenth president, Reuven Rivlin, whose family has lived in Jerusalem since 1809 and belongs to the center-right to right-wing Likud party, was harshly criticized for merely appearing at a conference in New York City at which representatives of Breaking the Silence also appeared—even though his remarks at the conference were chiefly in praise of his country's military and security services. The prime minister has characterized the Breaking the Silence accusations as "slanderous," and the group has been forbidden from participating in any events for soldiers and officially banned from entering state schools and army grounds. Why is this group such a threat? I've read that its members don't support boycott, divestment, and sanctions, and they haven't urged trying IDF officers for war crimes—they believe politicians are responsible for most of the Occupation's ills. They don't condone Palestinian violence, and some of them, their protests notwithstanding, continue to report to reserve duty and don't urge anyone not to serve. It's impossible not to conclude that their sole unforgivable offense is reporting to their compatriots what they did as soldiers—and that they are despised simply for telling the truth.

CHAPTER 13

VARIETIES OF
RELIGIOUS EXPERIENCE

The comfortable small house Niveen and Mahmoud live in is in the Palestinian neighborhood of Shuafat. Not the part of Shuafat where the overcrowded refugee camp of never-ending sorrows is, but farther to the west. Many young professionals and older, established ones live there, as do a sprinkling of foreigners. It's not a cheap neighborhood. Shuafat is considered part of the Jerusalem Municipality, but the extensive municipal landscaping so prevalent in the rest of the city is here nonexistent. The approach road to their house off the main drag is heavily potholed and rough, the garbage piles are neglected, and the general aspect of the surrounding area is bleak. When I visited Niveen some months after they moved in, I mentioned all that, but she shrugged it off. Her son Muhammed was at that point still a baby; Sara had not yet come along. She and Mahmoud were happy there.

As much as she loved her family, it was wonderful to have a place of her own, and with her family's babysitting help she was managing to keep up with her work schedule and not feel too overwhelmed by the demands of motherhood. Mahmoud helped out with the house, the shopping, and general chores—a quantum leap in her culture. Workout machines filled most of one corner of the house, and colorful plastic toys were scattered around. Niveen had invited me for lunch, which was carefully scheduled for Muhammed's nap time, and he had obliged by falling asleep just before I arrived. Niveen was in her sweats.

Though I was the only guest, the table was already loaded with meze and condiments when I arrived. She invited me to sit down, and brought out a fish, a Leviathan, that had been baking in the oven, and by rearranging all the little plates already there, she somehow managed to secure it a place on the table.

I laughed. "You're expecting a crowd?" Niveen smiled. She was obviously enjoying her role in her new domain. We spoke for a while about the challenges of working and raising a child, about how much she missed her father, and about Mahmoud's worries—and hers—about the possible future withdrawal of financial support for international NGOs like the one he worked for. In time, in fact, a USAID program that supported its work ended because it was defunded. About halfway through the meal, she mentioned that she had become more religious. Her move in that direction, she said, had come about chiefly from reflecting on how close to death she had come three times, and three times been spared. She now believed that a greater force had been looking out for her.

The first experience had been on that curfew evening at the Qalandia checkpoint, when she'd felt she could easily have been shot. The second time, she had been in the West Bank, returning from a class at Birzeit University during the second Intifada, and had just stepped out of a taxi when a soldier shot her—she has no idea why. She was in pain but not bleeding. She had not been hit by bullets. "It looked like small stones were stuck in my chest." Was it buckshot? At the time she thought it might have been a disintegrated rubber bullet, but really she doesn't know what it was. No one approached her after it happened—neither the soldier who shot her nor any others—and eventually her chest healed, but to this day she can't figure out what prompted the soldier to attack her or what stopped him or others from following up on the shooting. "I saw some soldiers and others running, but I couldn't really make out what was happening."

Her third account of narrowly escaping catastrophe sounded like revival tent miracle testimony. She was walking downtown along the Jaffa Road, one of the oldest streets in Jerusalem, hurrying to catch a bus she regularly took to her family home. Close to the bus stop, a stranger asked her for directions. Niveen hesitated before stopping to help him, because she knew her bus might leave without her and it would be quite a while before the next one came. She stopped anyway, and before she had finished explaining the directions to the stranger, she heard a huge explosion and saw that it was the bus, *her* bus, on which someone had planted a bomb. The scene that then played out before her, which has become part of the all too common modern mental-atrocity archive, was one of bedlam—ambulances screaming, body parts strewn everywhere, twisted metal, school bags, and the charred remains of the dead, Israelis and Palestinians alike. Niveen can't remember how she got home. But as the three events replayed in her mind over the years and she wondered why she had been spared, she eventually concluded that a larger hand was involved. Her newly enlarged faith was her pious acknowledgment of deepening spiritual feelings. In general, according to a Pew survey, more Arabs than Jews in Israel say that religion is "very important" to them and are more religiously observant, so Niveen has had a lot of company in her new-found belief.

Other Palestinians I spoke with had had similar close calls but were more apt to attribute their escapes to luck. A successful young Palestinian architect I met described the ongoing fear she felt driving her children to and from school, an option she chose because she was afraid to let them ride the school bus. Only at the end of each ride, she said, did she relax her white-knuckle grip on the steering wheel. Israelis were the target of the bombs during the intifada, but no one seemed to notice or care that Palestinians were often part of the crowds that were the object of the attacks. "Sometimes," she added, "I'll be driving *behind* a school bus in my car with the children and begin sweating. 'What if that bus explodes and we are only inches away, trapped in traffic?'"

——◆——

Khawallah Masalha, Niveen's second-oldest sister, was also religious and longed to make the hajj to Mecca. Every Muslim is supposed to make it at least once in his or her lifetime, and her husband Khaled, though he is not religious, a few years ago said, "OK, we'll do it." Saudi Arabia does not permit Sunni women to make the hajj unless accompanied by a male relative—documentation required—or unless they are part of a prearranged, women-only tour group. "I did it for her, but I was surprised by the way it affected me," Khaled told me after they returned. It was a big commitment in time and money—all told the journey had cost close to $30,000—and with various sub-trips they were away for twenty-five days. The hajj itself required many days of ritual observance. Happily Khaled's law practice was going quite well. Most of the time he now worked in an office away from the apartment in the neighborhood of Beit Hanina, and he no longer had to keep his nursing job, which had sometimes required him to drive directly from his night shift to appear in court in the morning. They flew to Saudi Arabia, but in Mecca there were no cars, buses, or trains. The hotel they stayed in was a little over a half-mile from the Kaaba, the famous black cube at the center of the Great Mosque of Mecca, around which pilgrims are required to walk seven times counter-clockwise and that they attempt to kiss, crowds permitting. Mecca is a small town, and between two and three million pilgrims arrived the year Khawallah and Khaled came there, many of them learning from handbooks and guides about the rituals they were required to follow. After circling the Kaaba, Khawallah, Khaled, and their niece, who ac-companied them, walked back and forth between the hills of Safa and Marwa, drank from the Well of Zamzam, spent a night on the plain of Muzdalifa, performed a symbolic stoning of the devil by throw-ing stones at three pillars, participated in a ritual animal sacrifice, and celebrated the three-day festival of Eid al-Adha. It was exhausting, Khaled said, but: "I don't know, it was incredibly moving. Part of the time we were at the hotel, but for four nights we slept in tents as part of a huge tent city. There were no mattresses, and I don't think I slept more than ten hours altogether. You know, there were Muslims there from all over the world, and the feeling of it was like nothing I've ever experienced. In Medina, where we were too, inside the mosque built by Muhammed, I started to cry, and, when I looked around, every-one was crying." Everywhere, he went on, "there were huge waves of people, thousands upon thousands, going from one place to another, and people were good to each other, the way they should be, helping the old people to get through the crush, clearing spaces when some-one was overcome by the heat or fell ill and had to leave." Khawallah expected to be moved by the experience, and she was, but Khaled said

he was totally unprepared to be as strongly affected as he was. Fortu-
nately, crowd control that year went smoothly, unlike the hajj of 2015,
when more than two thousand pilgrims were either crushed or suf-
focated to death in a chaotic stampede that some attributed to violent
tension between Saudi pilgrims and those from their rival country,
Iran. No one appears to know what started it, though the following
year pilgrims from Iran were forbidden from coming.

The men at the hajj wear a special white garment that is supposed
to eliminate class and status differences, but even for those who didn't
fly to Mecca, as the Masalhas did, the fees for the hajj automatically
eliminate many of the faithful. (The Saudi government charges $533
for the visa alone.) And as it turned out, the hajj trip itself didn't end
the couple's expenses.

When they returned to Jerusalem, buoyed by their experience,
they gave a "hajj dinner"—not a religious requirement but something
they both wanted to do, Khaled told me, "as an expression of our pleasure." They held it on French Hill, at Khawallah's family's house. Four
hundred (!) people were invited, and most showed up, though fortu-
nately not all at once but in shifts throughout the day. A chef came at
six in the morning, and the party ended at ten at night.

Lying in their tent alongside three million people under the stars
had been an experience unlike any other in Khaled's and Khawallah's
lives. They felt both totally exhausted and simultaneously almost pre-
ternaturally energized the entire time they'd been there, and when it
was all over, though Khaled told anyone who asked that it had been a
transformative experience, he was sure he would never want to repeat
it. But as time went by, and he thought about the intense solemnity of
his fellow pilgrims, the sense of strong communality that bound the
mass of people, and his own enlivened spirit throughout the trip, he
changed his mind. "If they allowed me, I'd go again this year. Really. It
was a feeling from the heart—I can't explain it."

It is hard for me to imagine liking, much less wanting to return
to, any event, however spiritually meaningful, at which the crush of
people is as extreme as it is in Mecca. But perhaps at least part of
Khaled's reaction to the experience could be attributed to the wonder,
in an era when so many Arab countries are in lethal confrontation

with one another, of his Muslim coreligionists acting as one—not squabbling, not plotting against or undermining each other, not failing to respond to one another's vulnerabilities, but acting in peaceful concert. That was the embodiment of a dream. In everyday life Khaled, who is such a moderate man, and the Abuleils, who continue to grow as one discrete, symbiotic organism, might yearn for this. But they have no expectation of enjoying it anytime soon.

Travels with Fuad V

▶ From time to time, after a long day, Fuad and I drove to the Palestinian Christian West Bank town of Beit Jala, about eight miles south of Jerusalem and a stone's throw from Bethlehem, to "the chicken man," as we both had come to refer to our destination. These outings were rare, since most of the time both of us were busy working. Sometimes my husband joined us, and sometimes it was just Fuad and me. Fuad had taken his family there many times too. As soon as we were seated, the sons of the Ka'abar family, who run the small restaurant, placed before us delicious grilled chicken along with five or six generously filled plates of meze. And inevitably one of us remarked on the undisputed superiority of the Ka'abars' chicken to all others.

The "chicken man" himself, the elder Ka'abar, raises his own birds, and his customers travel great distances to eat at his pocket-size establishment, which is perched on a steep hill in an enclave of town with few parking places. The grill itself, which sits just outside the restaurant, is large and looks like it was assembled from auto parts.

Sometimes, after we've eaten, we drive into Bethlehem to peer in silence at the depressing graffiti-covered wall that encircles the city and looms in a particularly ugly way over homes and businesses. Some of the graffiti was contributed by the British artist Banksy, including an image of a girl being carried over the wall by balloons. More recently, in July 2017, the Australian street artist Lushsux painted the image of Donald Trump touching the wall (clearly based on the widely circulated photo of the US president at the Western Wall the previous May) with a thought bubble next to his head: "I'm going to build you a brother . . ."

A lively woman I met a few years back, the Palestinian American art curator Salwa Mikdadi, had been stuck in Bethlehem overnight the week before we met. The military had declared one of its intermittent curfews, and the friend she was visiting, who had serious heart problems and badly needed some medicine she'd run out of, was prevented from passing through the wall exit to get to her pharmacy. The friend had survived the experience, but the sheer stupidity of the incident still made Mikdadi's blood boil. Mikdadi divided her time between Berkeley, California, and Jerusalem, and I suspected that her en garde chafing, so different from the spirit of silent endurance I often encountered in Jerusalem, probably arose from her American side. Mikdadi told me she was heartened by some young people she talked with who had fresh ideas about changing the political situation, but in general everything looked "practically hopeless. . . . How can you make a nation out of this? . . . It's like a big refugee camp. . . . The West Bank should not be called the West Bank. It's a refugee camp. The largest Palestinian refugee camp."

————•————

When I discovered the extraordinary poems of Taha Muhammad Ali, I began asking Fuad, whenever we found ourselves in Bethlehem, to indulge me by driving slowly down the street on which, I believed, the poet ran a souvenir shop, though I didn't know which one. In fact his souvenir shop was in Nazareth, but I didn't learn that for many years. From photographs I'd seen of Ali's long, expressive face, I did know exactly what he looked like, and one day, I hoped and believed, I would spot him. What I'd do next if that happened I had no idea, but it hadn't by 2011, when the poet died, passing well beyond stalking range. Of all the words poured over the wounds of the conflict, his seem the truest and the most enduring. The day I heard of his death I took refuge in his plainspoken, powerful death poem, "Twigs," which ends:

> After we die
> and the weary heart
> has lowered its final eyelid
> on all that we've done,

and on all that we've longed for,
and all that we've dreamt of,
all we've desired
or felt,
hate will be
the first thing
to putrefy
within us.

ACKNOWLEDGMENTS

In this book's long gestation period, a small army of people contributed immeasurably to its progress. Ruth HaCohen and Niveen Abuleil were beyond generous, finding time for me in their incredibly busy lives, and so were their husbands, Yaron Ezrahi and Mahmoud Abu Rumeileh. To my deepest sorrow and shock, Yaron died shortly after I submitted the book's manuscript. For his unique voice and his protestations, elaborations, and corroborations I owe a debt that is not payable. I am grateful, too, to the entire Abuleil family, particularly Zaineb, Sana, Khawallah and Khaled Masalha, Nisreen, and Ruqaya, and to the Ezrahis and Pinczowers—Ofra, Talya, Ariel, Tehila, Yotam, Nechama, Rami, and Yehuda. Ruth's remarkable mother, Esther, now deceased, provided rich insights into the experience of a Holocaust-surviving émigré, as did Hannah Urbach, who celebrated her hundredth birthday in the summer of 2018. Abdallah Abuleil, also now deceased, patiently revisited painful memories of his early days in Lifta and exponentially deepened my sense of that time. Nazmi Jubeh offered a broader perspective on the toll taken by the conflict. In my project's early days, I received invaluable guidance from Joyce Ajlouny, Albert Aghazrian and his wife, Madeleine, Eyal Benvenisti, Salim Tamari, Menny Mautner, Dan Bietan, Rajai and Fadwa Dejani, Samar Daoud, Rami Elhanan, Ruth Firer, Daphna Golan-Agnon, Dorothy Harman, Shlomo Hasson, Amal Jamal, Elias Khoury, Michael Karayanni, Dave Kretzmer, Deena and Yousef Khoury, Uri Dromi, Ilene Prusher, Danny Rubenstein, Khalil Shikaki, and Yael, Aviva, and Gil Sher.

I am grateful, too, for the friendship of Magda Zaher, who from the start felt like a sister, and to the wisdom and thousand-and-one kindnesses extended to me by Fuad Abu Awwad. David and Connie Green provided unflagging support and delicious meals, and David never ceased to be willing to wrestle with the knottiest of problems. Sami Abu-Dyyeh enlarged my understanding of the travails of running a business in East Jerusalem; his hotel lobby provided a welcome meeting place that I returned to again and again. Robi Damelen and Ali Abu Awwad led me to the amazing people and work of the Parents Circle. Ali Kleibo generously introduced me to his wide circle of friends and fed me at the end of many over-exciting days, and Lihi Gatt was a delightful companion and much-needed source of reality checks. Sna'it Gissis helped me find my way to Ruth HaCohen, and Peter Cole and Adina Hoffman provided great company and the comforting comradeship of fellow writers. I owe a mountainous debt to Menachem Klein—no one was more instrumental in helping guide me through the intricacies of Israel's political and social labyrinths and no one quicker to answer my blizzards of emails.

Thanks to Thomas Struth for his patience herding everyone together and generous gift of the two families' beautiful portraits, to Connie and Bill for their friendship and trees, to Hilda and Teddy and Rosie and Debbie for years of warm hospitality, and to Ayelet Pritzker and Rami Zifroni for inviting us to camp in their home. For research and fact checking I am indebted to Aura Davies and Suleiman Maswadeh, and especially Cynthia Polutanovich for her conscientious digging, and Jasmine Shaadi Vojdani, who labored tirelessly and heroically through a decade's worth of complicated reporting.

I am lucky to have Georges Borchardt, whose civility and literary values are unflagging, as an agent and friend, and Amy Caldwell, whose clear eye and intelligence made the book better, for my editor. Thanks, too, to the Beacon team—Marcy Barnes, Susan Lumenello, Pamela MacColl, Isabella Sanchez, Caitlin Meyer, and Molly Velázquez-Brown—for so ably shepherding the book into the world.

To my family, Nick, Amy, Sydney, Samantha, David, Mary, Thomas, Claudia, Ben, Julie, Elias, Madeline, Philip, and Alice, thank you for the joy you bring me and for keeping me always aware of how lucky we are to enjoy the blessings of peace.

Finally, I thank my beloved husband, Martin Washburn, editor, collaborator, stir-fry chef, and patient endurer of a decade of obsession, for his sustaining love.

BIBLIOGRAPHY

Ali, Taha Muhammad. *So What: New and Selected Poems, 1971–2005*. Trans. Peter Cole, Yahya Hijazi, and Gabriel Levin. Port Townsend, WA: Copper Canyon Press, 2006.

Almog, Oz. *The Sabra: The Creation of the New Jew*. Trans. Haim Watzman. Berkeley: University of California Press, 2000.

Backmann, René. *A Wall in Palestine*. Trans. A. Kaiser. New York: Picador, 2010.

Barghouti, Mourid. *I Saw Ramallah*. Trans. Ahdaf Soueif. New York: Anchor Books, 2003. This translation first published 2001 by the American University in Cairo Press (Cairo).

Beilin, Yossi. *Israel: A Concise Political History*. London: Butler & Tanner, 1992.

———. *The Path to Geneva: The Quest for a Permanent Agreement, 1996–2004*. Canada: RDV Books/Akashic Books, 2004.

Ben-Ami, Shlomo. *Scars of War, Wounds of Peace: The Israeli-Arab Tragedy*. New York: Oxford University Press, 2007.

Ben-Gurion, David. *Letters to Paula*. Trans. Aubrey Hodes. London: Vallentine Mitchell, 1971.

———. *Memoirs*. Cleveland: World Publishing, 1970.

———. *The Peel Report and the Jewish State*. London: Palestine Labour Studies Group, 1938.

Benvenisti, Meron. *Son of the Cypresses: Memories, Reflections, and Regrets from a Political Life*. Trans. Maxine Kaufman-Lacusta. Berkeley: University of California Press, 2007.

Black, Ian. *Enemies and Neighbors: Arabs and Jews in Palestine and Israel, 1917–2017*. New York: Grove Atlantic, 2017.

Boyarin, Jonathan. *Palestine and Jewish History: Criticism at the Borders of Ethnography*. Minneapolis: University of Minnesota Press, 1996.

Burke, Edmund, III, and Ira Lapidus, eds. *Islam, Politics, and Social Movements*. Berkeley: University of California Press, 1988.

Buruma, Ian, and Avishai Margalit. *Occidentalism: The West in the Eyes of Its Enemies.* New York: Penguin Press, 2004.

Busailah, Reja-e. *In the Land of My Birth: A Palestinian Boyhood.* Washington, DC: Institute for Palestine Studies, 2017.

Cahill, Thomas. *The Gifts of the Jews: How a Tribe of Desert Nomads Changed the Way Everyone Thinks and Feels.* New York: Nan A. Talese/Anchor Books, 1998.

Carey, Roane, and Jonathan Shainin, eds. *The Other Israel: Voices of Refusal and Dissent.* New York: New Press, 2002.

Carter, Jimmy. *Palestine: Peace Not Apartheid.* New York: Simon & Schuster, 2006.

Chehab, Zaki. *Inside Hamas: The Untold Story of the Militant Islamic Movement.* New York: Nation Books, 2007.

Cheshin, Amir, Bill Hutman, and Avi Melamed. *Separate and Unequal: The Inside Story of Israeli Rule in East Jerusalem.* Cambridge, MA: Harvard University Press, 1999.

Chomsky, Noam. *The Fateful Triangle: The United States, Israel, and the Palestinians.* Boston: South End Press, 1983.

Ciezadlo, Annia. *Day of Honey: A Memoir of Food, Love, and War.* New York: Free Press, 2011.

Cockburn, Alexander, and Jeffrey St. Clair, eds. *The Politics of Anti-Semitism.* Petrolia, CA: CounterPunch and AK Press, 2003.

Cole, Peter. *The Dream of the Poem: Hebrew Poetry from Muslim and Christian Spain, 950–1492.* Princeton, NJ: Princeton University Press, 2007.

Cortas, Wadad Makdisi. *A World I Loved: The Story of an Arab Woman.* New York: Nation Books, 2009.

Cypel, Sylvain. *Walled: Israeli Society at an Impasse.* New York: Other Press, 2006.

Daniel, Jean. *The Jewish Prison: A Rebellious Meditation on the State of Judaism.* Trans. Charlotte Mandell. Hoboken, NJ: Melville House, 2005.

David, Anthony. *An Improbable Friendship: The Secret Friendship Between Yasser Arafat's Mother-in-Law and the Wife of Israel's Top General.* North Sydney, Australia: William Heinemann, 2015.

Dunsky, Marda. *Pens and Swords: How the American Mainstream Media Report the Israeli-Palestinian Conflict.* New York: Columbia University Press, 2008.

Edelman, Martin. *Courts, Politics, and Culture in Israel.* Charlottesville: University Press of Virginia, 1994.

Elon, Amos. *The Israelis: Founders and Sons*. Lexington, MA: Plunkett Lake Press, 2014.

———. *The Pity of It All: A Portrait of the German-Jewish Epoch, 1743–1933*. New York: Picador, 2002.

Enderlin, Charles. *Shattered Dreams: The Failure of the Peace Process in the Middle East, 1995–2002*. Trans. Susan Fairfield. New York: Other Press, 2003.

Evans, Malcolm D. *Blackstone's International Law Documents*. 6th ed. Oxford, UK: Oxford University Press, 2003.

Ezrahi, Yaron. *The Descent of Icarus: Science and the Transformation of Contemporary Democracy*. Cambridge, MA: Harvard University Press, 1990.

———. *Imagined Democracies: Necessary Political Fictions*. Cambridge, UK: Cambridge University Press, 2012.

———. *Rubber Bullets: Power and Conscience in Modern Israel*. New York: Farrar, Straus and Giroux, 1997.

Falk, Richard. *Palestine: The Legitimacy of Hope*. Charlottesville, VA: Just World Publishing, 2014.

Fischbach, Michael R. *Records of Dispossession: Palestinian Refugee Property and the Arab-Israeli Conflict*. New York: Columbia University Press, 2003.

Fraser, T. G. *Chaim Weizmann: The Zionist Dream*. London: Haus Publishing, 2009.

Friedman, Thomas L. *From Beirut to Jerusalem*. New York: Anchor Books, 1989.

Friedmann, Georges. *The End of the Jewish People?* Trans. Eric Mosbacher. New York: Anchor Books, 1968.

Fromkin, David. *A Peace to End All Peace: Creating the Modern Middle East, 1914–1922*. New York: Henry Holt, 1989.

Ginsburg, Shai. *Rhetoric and Nation: The Formation of Hebrew National Culture, 1880–1990*. Syracuse, NY: Syracuse University Press, 2014.

Goldberg, Jeffrey. *Prisoners: A Muslim and a Jew Across the Middle East Divide*. New York: Alfred A. Knopf, 2006.

Goldhill, Simon. *Jerusalem: City of Longing*. Cambridge, MA: Belknap Press of Harvard University Press, 2008.

Gonen, Amiram. *From Yeshiva to Work: The American Experience and Lessons for Israel*. Jerusalem: Floersheimer Institute for Policy Studies, 2001.

Gonen, Amiram, and Rasem Khameyseh. *Joint Arab and Jewish*

Regional Development Centers in Israel. Jerusalem: Floersheimer Institute for Policy Studies, 1993.

———. *The Arabs in Israel in the Wake of Peace.* Jerusalem: Floersheimer Institute for Policy Studies, 1993.

Gorenberg, Gershom. *The Accidental Empire: Israel and the Birth of the Settlements, 1967–1977.* New York: Henry Holt, 2006.

Gorny, Yosef. *Zionism and the Arabs, 1882–1948: A Study of Ideology.* Oxford, UK: Clarendon Press, 1987.

Grossman, David. *Death as a Way of Life: Israel Ten Years After Oslo.* Ed. Efrat Lev. Trans. Haim Watzman. New York: Farrar, Straus and Giroux, 2003.

———. *Sleeping on a Wire: Conversations with Palestinians in Israel.* Trans. Haim Watzman. New York: Farrar, Straus and Giroux, 2003. Originally published 1993.

———. *The Yellow Wind.* Trans. Haim Watzman. New York: Picador, 1988.

Gutmann, Stephanie. *The Other War: Israelis, Palestinians and the Struggle for Media Supremacy.* San Francisco: Encounter Books, 2005.

Ha'am, Ahad (Asher Ginzberg). *Nationalism and the Jewish Ethic: Basic Writings of Ahad Ha'am.* Ed. Hans Kohn. New York: Schocken Books, 1962.

———. *Selected Essays by Ahad Ha'am.* Trans. and ed. Leon Simon. Cleveland: World Publishing, 1962.

HaCohen, Ruth. *The Music Libel Against the Jews.* New Haven, CT: Yale University Press, 2011.

Hagopian, Elaine C. *Civil Rights in Peril: The Targeting of Arabs and Muslims.* Chicago: Haymarket Books and Pluto Press, 2004.

Hajjar, Lisa. *Courting Conflict: The Israeli Military Court System in the West Bank and Gaza.* Berkeley: University of California Press, 2005.

Halevi, Yossi Klein. *The Jerusalem Problem: The Struggle for Permanent Status.* Trans. Haim Watzman. Gainesville: University Press of Florida, 2003.

———. *Letters to My Palestinian Neighbor.* New York: HarperCollins, 2018.

———. *Memoirs of a Jewish Extremist: An American Story.* Boston: Little, Brown, 1995.

Halkin, Hillel. *Across the Sabbath River: In Search of a Lost Tribe of Israel.* Boston: Houghton Mifflin, 2002.

Harris, Ron, Alexandre (Sandy) Kedar, Pnina Lahav, and Assaf

Likhovski, eds. *The History of Law in a Multi-Cultural Society: Israel 1917–1967*. Aldershot, UK: Ashgate, 2002.

Hass, Amira. *Reporting from Ramallah: An Israeli Journalist in an Occupied Land*. Ed. and trans. Rachel Leah Jones. Los Angeles: Semiotext(e), 2003.

Hasson, Shlomo. *The Struggle for Hegemony in Jerusalem: Secular and Ultra-Orthodox Urban Politics*. Jerusalem: Floersheimer Institute for Policy Studies, 2002.

Hedges, Chris. *War Is a Force That Gives Us Meaning*. New York: Anchor Books, 2003.

Herr, Michael. *Dispatches*. New York: Vintage Books, 1991. First published 1968.

Hertzberg, Arthur. *The Fate of Zionism: A Secular Future for Israel and Palestine*. San Francisco: HarperSanFrancisco, 2003.

———. *A Jew in America: My Life and a People's Struggle for Identity*. San Francisco: HarperSanFrancisco, 2002.

Herzl, Theodor. *The Jewish State*. New York: Dover Publications, 1988. First published 1896.

———. *The Old New Land (Altneuland)*. New York: CreateSpace Independent Publishing Platform, 2015. First published 1902.

Hiro, Dilip. *The Essential Middle East: A Comprehensive Guide*. New York: Carroll & Graf, 2003.

Hoffman, Adina. *House of Windows: Portraits from a Jerusalem Neighborhood*. New York: Broadway Books, 2000.

———. *My Happiness Bears No Relation to Happiness: A Poet's Life in the Palestinian Century*. New Haven, CT: Yale University Press, 2009.

Jacobson, Howard. *The Finkler Question*. London: Bloomsbury, 2010.

Jamal, Amal. *The Palestinian National Movement: Politics of Contention, 1967–2005*. Bloomington: Indiana University Press, 2005.

Jawad, Saleh Abdel. "The Arab and Palestinian Narratives of the 1948 War." Chap. 4 in *Israeli and Palestinian Narratives of Conflict: History's Double Helix*. Ed. Robert I. Rotberg. Bloomington: Indiana University Press, 2006.

Jawhariyyeh, Wasif. *The Storyteller of Jerusalem: The Life and Times of Wasif Jawhariyyeh*. Trans. Nada Elzeer. Ed. Salim Tamari and Issam Nasser. Northampton, MA: Olive Branch Press, 2013.

Judt, Tony. *The Memory Chalet*. New York: Penguin Press, 2010.

Kanaaneh, Hatim. *A Doctor in Galilee: The Life and Struggle of a Palestinian in Israel*. London: Pluto Press, 2008.

Karmi, Ghada. *In Search of Fatima: A Palestinian Story*. London: Verso, 2002.

———. *Return: A Palestinian Memoir*. London: Verso, 2015.

Khalidi, Rashid. *The Iron Cage: The Story of the Palestinian Struggle for Statehood*. Boston: Beacon Press, 2006.

———. *Palestinian Identity: The Construction of Modern National Consciousnesses*. New York: Columbia University Press, 1997.

———. *Resurrecting Empire: Western Footprints and America's Perilous Path in the Middle East*. Boston: Beacon Press, 2004.

Khalidi, Rashid, Lisa Anderson, Muhammad Muslih, and Reeva S. Simon, eds. *The Origins of Arab Nationalism*. New York: Columbia University Press, 1991.

Khalidi, Walid. *All That Remains: The Palestinian Villages Occupied and Depopulated by Israel in 1948*. Beirut: Institute for Palestine Studies, 1992.

Khamaisi, Rassem. *New Palestinian Towns Alongside Existing Old Ones*. Jerusalem: Floersheimer Institute for Policy Studies, 1997.

Khoury, Elias. *Gate of the Sun*. Trans. Humphrey Davies. Brooklyn, NY: Archipelago Books, 2005.

Kimmerling, Baruch. *The Invention and Decline of Israeliness: State, Society, and the Military*. Berkeley: University of California Press, 2001.

Kimmerling, Baruch, and Joel S. Migdal. *The Palestinian People: A History*. Cambridge, MA: Harvard University Press, 2003.

Klein, Menachem. *Jerusalem: The Contested City*. Trans. Haim Watzman. New York: New York University Press, 2001.

———. *Lives in Common: Arabs and Jews in Jerusalem, Jaffa and Hebron*. Trans. Haim Watzman. Oxford, UK: Oxford University Press, 2014.

———. *A Possible Peace Between Israel and Palestine: An Insider's Account of the Geneva Initiative*. Translation by Haim Watzman. New York: Columbia University Press, 2007.

Kuriansky, Judy, ed. *Terror in the Holy Land: Inside the Anguish of the Israeli-Palestinian Conflict*. Westport, CT: Praeger, 2006.

Kushner, Tony, and Alisa Solomon, eds. *Wrestling with Zion: Progressive Jewish-American Responses to the Israeli-Palestinian Conflict*. New York: Grove Press, 2003.

Laqueur, Walter. *A History of Zionism: From the French Revolution to the Establishment of the State of Israel*. New York: Schocken Books, 2003. First published 1972.

Lavie, Smadar, and Ted Swedenburg, eds. *Displacement, Diaspora, and Geographies of Identity*. Durham, NC: Duke University Press, 1996.

Lawrence, T. E. *Seven Pillars of Wisdom: A Triumph*. Garden City, NY: Doubleday, 1966. First published 1926.

Lazar, Hadara. *Out of Palestine: The Making of Modern Israel*. New York: Atlas, 2011.

Leon, Dan, ed. *Who's Left in Israel? Radical Political Alternatives for the Future of Israel*. Brighton, UK: Sussex Academic Press, 2004.

Lewis, Bernard. *What Went Wrong? Western Impact and Middle Eastern Response*. New York: Oxford University Press, 2002.

Lustick, Ian. *Arabs in the Jewish State: Israel's Control of a National Minority*. Austin: University of Texas Press, 1980.

Manji, Irshad. *The Trouble with Islam: A Muslim's Call for Reform in Her Faith*. New York: St. Martin's Press, 2003.

Maraniss, David. *They Marched into Sunlight: War and Peace, Vietnam and America, October 1967*. New York: Simon & Schuster, 2003.

Massad, Joseph A. *The Persistence of the Palestinian Question: Essays on Zionism and the Palestinians*. New York: Routledge, 2006.

Matthews, Weldon C. *Confronting an Empire, Constructing a Nation: Arab Nationalists and Popular Politics in Mandate Palestine*. London: I.B. Tauris, 1988.

Miller, Aaron David. *The Much Too Promised Land: America's Elusive Search for Arab-Israeli Peace*. New York: Bantam Books, 2008.

Miller, Jennifer. *Inheriting the Holy Land: An American's Search for Hope in the Middle East*. New York: Ballantine Books, 2005.

Mishal, Shaul, and Avraham Sela. *The Palestinian Hamas: Vision, Violence, and Coexistence*. New York: Columbia University Press, 2000.

Montefiore, Simon Sebag. *Jerusalem: The Biography*. New York: Vintage Books, 2012.

Morris, Benny. *The Birth of the Palestinian Refugee Problem Revisited*. Cambridge, UK: Cambridge University Press, 2004.

———. *1948: A History of the First Arab-Israeli War*. New Haven, CT: Yale University Press, 2008.

———. *Righteous Victims: A History of the Zionist-Arab Conflict, 1881–2001*. New York: Vintage, 2001.

Nashashibi, Nasser Eddin. *Jerusalem's Other Voice: Ragheb Nashashibi and Moderation in Palestinian Politics, 1920–1948*. Exeter, UK: Ithaca Press, 1990.

Nasr, Vali. *Forces of Fortune: The Rise of the New Muslim Middle*

Class and What It Will Mean for Our World. New York: Free Press, 2009.

Nasrin, Taslima. *Revenge: A Fable.* Trans. Honor Moore, with Taslima Nasrin. New York: Feminist Press, 2010.

Norris, Jacob. *Land of Progress: Palestine in the Age of Colonial Development, 1905–1948.* Oxford, UK: Oxford University Press, 2013.

Nusseibeh, Sari. *The Story of Reason in Islam: Cultural Memory in the Present.* Stanford, CA: Stanford University Press, 2016.

Nusseibeh, Sari, and Anthony David. *Once upon a Country: A Palestinian Life.* New York: Farrar, Straus and Giroux, 2007.

Orange, Wendy. *Coming Home to Jerusalem: A Personal Journey.* New York: Simon & Schuster, 2000.

Oren, Michael B. *Power, Faith, and Fantasy: America in the Middle East, 1776 to the Present.* New York: W. W. Norton, 2007.

———. *Six Days of War: June 1967 and the Making of the Modern Middle East.* New York: Ballantine Books, 2003.

Oz, Amos. *In the Land of Israel.* Trans. Maurie Goldberg-Bartura. New York: Vintage Books, 1984.

———. *A Tale of Love and Darkness.* Trans. Nicholas de Lange. Orlando, FL: Harcourt, 2004.

Pawel, Ernst. *The Labyrinth of Exile: A Life of Theodor Herzl.* New York: Farrar, Straus and Giroux. 1989.

Pearlman, Wendy. *Occupied Voices: Stories of Everyday Life from the Second Intifada.* New York: Thunder's Mouth Press/Nation Books, 2003.

Peled-Elhanan, Nurit. *Palestine in Israeli School Books: Ideology and Propaganda in Education.* London: I. B. Tauris, 2012.

Peretz, Don. *Intifada: The Palestinian Uprising.* Boulder, CO: Westview Press, 1990.

Picard, Jacques, Jacques Revel, Michael P. Steinberg, and Idith Zertal, eds. *Makers of Jewish Modernity: Thinkers, Artists, Leaders, and the World They Made.* Princeton, NJ: Princeton University Press, 2016.

Qleibo, Ali H. *Before the Mountains Disappear: An Ethnographic Chronicle of the Modern Palestinians.* Jerusalem: Kloreus Publications, 1992.

———. *Jerusalem in the Heart.* Jerusalem: Kloreus Publications, 2000.

Rabinovich, Abraham. *The Yom Kippur War: The Epic Encounter That Transformed the Middle East.* New York: Schocken Books, 2004.

Rabinowitz, Dan, and Khawla Abu-Baker. *Coffins on Our Shoulders:*

The Experience of the Palestinian Citizens of Israel. Berkeley: University of California Press, 2005.

Rees, Matt. *Cain's Field: Faith, Fratricide, and Fear in the Middle East.* New York: Free Press, 2004.

Rodrigue, Aron. *Jews and Muslims: Images of Sephardi and Eastern Jewries in Modern Times.* Seattle: University of Washington Press, 2003.

Rose, Jacqueline. *The Question of Zion.* Princeton, NJ: Princeton University Press, 2005.

Rosenthal, Donna. *The Israelis: Ordinary People in an Extraordinary Land.* New York: Free Press, 2003.

Rotberg, Robert I., ed. *Israeli and Palestinian Narratives of Conflict: History's Double Helix.* Bloomington: Indiana University Press, 2006.

Said, Edward W. *The End of the Peace Process: Oslo and After.* New York: Vintage Books, 2001.

———. Foreword to *Peace Under Fire: Israel/Palestine and the International Solidarity Movement.* Ed. Josie Sandercock, Radhika Sainath, Marissa McLaughlin, Hussein Khalili, Nicholas Blincoe, Huwaida Arraf, and Ghassan Andoni. London: Verso, 2004.

———. *Freud and the Non-European.* London: Verso, 2003.

———. *Orientalism.* New York: Vintage Books, 1979.

———. *The Politics of Dispossession: The Struggle for Palestinian Self-Determination, 1963–1993.* New York: Pantheon Books, 1994.

———. *The Question of Palestine.* New York: Vintage Books, 1992.

Said, Edward W., and Christopher Hitchens, eds. *Blaming the Victims: Spurious Scholarship and the Palestinian Question.* London: Verso, 2001. First published 1988.

Salinas, Moises F. *Planting Hatred, Sowing Pain: The Psychology of the Israeli-Palestinian Conflict.* Westport, CT: Praeger, 2007.

Sand, Schlomo. *The Invention of the Jewish People.* Trans. Yael Lotan. London: Verso, 2009.

Sandercock, Josie, Radhika Sainath, Marissa McLaughlin, Hussein Khalili, Nicholas Blincoe, Huwaida Arraf, and Ghassan Andoni, eds. *Peace Under Fire: Israel/Palestine and the International Solidarity Movement.* London: Verso, 2004.

Schalit, Joel. *Jerusalem Calling: A Homeless Conscience in a Post-Everything World.* New York: Akashic Books, 2003.

Schneer, Jonathan. *The Balfour Declaration: The Origins of the Arab-Israeli Conflict.* New York: Random House, 2010.

Schölch, Alexander. *Palestine in Transformation, 1856–1882: Studies in Social, Economic, and Political Development.* Trans. William C. Young and Michael C. Gerrity. Washington, DC: Institute for Palestine Studies, 1993.

Segev, Tom. *1967: Israel, the War, and the Year That Transformed the Middle East.* New York: Henry Holt, 2007.

————. *One Palestine, Complete: Jews and Arabs Under the British Mandate.* Trans. Haim Watzman. New York: Henry Holt, 2000.

Selfa, Lance, ed. *The Struggle for Palestine.* Chicago: Haymarket Books, 2002.

Shapira, Anita, ed. *Israeli Identity in Transition.* Westport, CT: Praeger, 2004.

————. *Land and Power: The Zionist Resort to Force, 1881–1948.* Trans. William Templer. New York: Oxford University Press, 1992.

Shavit, Ari. *My Promised Land.* New York: Spiegel & Grau, 2013.

Shehadeh, Raja. *Palestinian Walks: Forays into Vanishing Landscapes.* New York: Scribner, 2007.

Shilhav, Yosseph. *Ultra-Orthodoxy in Urban Governance.* Jerusalem: Floersheimer Institute for Policy Studies, 1998.

Shlaim, Avi. *The Iron Wall: Israel and the Arab World.* New York: W. W. Norton, 2001.

————. *Israel and Palestine: Reprisals, Revisions, and Refutations.* London: Verso, 2009.

Shulman, David. *Dark Hope: Working for Peace in Israel and Palestine.* Chicago: University of Chicago Press, 2007.

Simon, Leon. *Ahad Ha-am, Asher Ginzberg: A Biography.* Philadelphia: Jewish Publication Society of America, 1960.

Smith, Charles D. *Palestine and the Arab-Israeli Conflict: A History with Documents.* 7th ed. Boston: Bedford/St. Martin's, 2010.

Smith, Michael. *Foley: The Spy Who Saved 10,000 Jews.* London: Hodder & Stoughton, 1999.

Spark, Muriel. *The Mandelbaum Gate.* New York: Welcome Rain, 2001. First published 1965 by Macmillan (London).

Stein, Rebecca L., and Ted Swedenburg, eds. *Palestine, Israel, and the Politics of Popular Culture.* Durham, NC: Duke University Press, 2005.

Storrs, Ronald. *The Memoirs of Sir Ronald Storrs.* New York: G. P. Putnam's Sons, 1937.

Strum, Philippa. *The Women Are Marching: The Second Sex and the Palestinian Revolution.* Brooklyn, NY: Lawrence Hill Books, 1992.

Swedenburg, Ted. *Memories of Revolt: The 1936–1939 Rebellion and the Palestinian National Past.* Fayetteville: University of Arkansas Press, 2003.

Tamari, Salim, ed. *Jerusalem 1948: The Arab Neighbourhoods and Their Fate in the War*. Jerusalem: Institute of Jerusalem Studies, 1999.

———. *Mountain Against the Sea: Essays on Palestinian Society and Culture*. Berkeley: University of California Press, 2009.

Thackeray, William Makepeace. *Notes of a Journey from Cornhill to Grand Cairo*. London: Chapman and Hall, 1846.

Tolan, Sandy. *The Lemon Tree: An Arab, a Jew, and the Heart of the Middle East*. New York: Bloomsbury, 2006.

Traverso, Enzo. *The End of Jewish Modernity*. Trans. David Fernbach. London: Pluto Press, 2016.

Twain, Mark. *The Innocents Abroad*. London: Oxford University Press, 1996. First published 1869 by American Publishing.

Wesley, David A. *State Practices and Zionist Images: Shaping Economic Development in Arab Towns in Israel*. Brooklyn, NY: Berghahn Books, 2009.

Westrate, Bruce. *The Arab Bureau: British Policy in the Middle East, 1916–1920*. University Park: Penn State University Press, 1992.

Williams, Emma. *It's Easier to Reach Heaven Than the End of the Street: A Jerusalem Memoir*. London: Bloomsbury, 2006.

Yehoshua, A. B. *The Liberated Bride*. Trans. Hillel Halkin. Orlando, FL: Harcourt, 2003.

Yizhar, S. *Khirbet Khizeh*. Trans. Nicholas de Lange and Yaacob Dweck. Jerusalem: Ibis Editions, 2008.

Zertal, Idith, and Akiva Eldar. *Lords of the Land: The War over Israel's Settlements in the Occupied Territories, 1967–2007*. Trans. Vivian Eden. New York: Nation Books, 2005.

Zipperstein, Steven J. *Elusive Prophet: Ahad Ha'am and the Origins of Zionism*. Los Angeles: University of California Press, 1993.

INDEX

Tlass, Mustafa, 147–48
torture, 161, 168–72, 174–75
Totah, Muhammed, 102, 103, 104, 105
Transparency Bill, 154
travel: and checkpoints, 77–81, 82–85;
    international, 88–92; restrictions
    on, 78–81
two-state solution, 104, 158, 182–84

Unit 8200, 197
United Nations (UN): Partition Plan
    of, 19–21, 46, 70, 71; Relief and
    Works Agency of, 163
United States, immigration
    policies of, 43

vandalism in French Hill, 13, 17
victimhood, 66, 114
Village Files, 24, 25
violence, Occupation-related, 83,
    85–89, 94, 143–44
vulnerability, national, 109–10

walls, 78–81, 98
War of Independence (1948), 18–19, 49
Weiss, Philip, 198
Weizman, Chaim, 46, 50

Weizman, Ezer, 140
West Bank: capture of, 112, 117;
    checkpoints in, 78–81; refugees in,
    207; settlements in, 116
Western ideas imposed on Middle
    Eastern world, 182–84
Western Wall, 113, 115
White Paper of 1939, 46–47, 48

Ya'alon, Moshe, 196, 198
Yadin, Yigael, 28
Yishuv, 23, 25
Yom Kippur War (1973), 116, 147–48,
    187–90, 193
youth movement groups, 61, 63,
    107–8, 120–22

Zikhron Ya'akov, 65
Zionism: Cultural, 58–60; and
    democracy, 145–46; and land
    acquisition, 127; and Lydda,
    28–29; vs. "native" Jews, 123, 131; and
    Palestinian women's movement,
    166; utopian, 138, 144; various
    models of, 57–63; youth groups
    and, 116
Zoabi, Hanin, 159–60